IMAGES
of America

UNION COUNTY

On the Cover: The Clifford Seminary. Operating from 1881 until around 1920, the Clifford Seminary housed and educated female students from South Carolina, North Carolina, Georgia, and Florida. After its closure, part of the building was utilized by Union High School until the 1950s. (Courtesy of the Union County Historical Society.)

IMAGES
of America

UNION COUNTY

Peter J. Triggiani with Amber Jackson

ARCADIA
PUBLISHING

ISBN 978-1-4671-1428-8

Published by Arcadia Publishing
Charleston, South Carolina

Printed in the United States of America

Library of Congress Control Number: 2015938266

For all general information, please contact Arcadia Publishing:
Telephone 843-853-2070
Fax 843-853-0044
E-mail sales@arcadiapublishing.com
For customer service and orders:
Toll-Free 1-888-313-2665

Visit us on the Internet at www.arcadiapublishing.com

To the memory of Col. William J. Whitener, service over self

Contents

Acknowledgments		6
Introduction		7
1.	Wars, Local Patriots, and Personalities	9
2.	Early Union Community Life	25
3.	Local Parades and Celebrations	49
4.	Places of Worship	59
5.	Union's Railroads	73
6.	Antebellum and Main Street Architecture	87
7.	Union's Cotton and Textile Mills and Communities	103
8.	Music, Fire, Law, and Education	115

ACKNOWLEDGMENTS

The authors would like to acknowledge those who assisted in the preparation of this book. First and foremost, we thank the executive director of the Union County Museum, Ola Jean Kelly, for her vision and assistance in the development of this book. With her aid, the history of many obscure photographs has been unlocked.

The Union County Historical Society, its board of directors, and assorted members have been the keepers of the historical archives and the photographs in this work for many years. Their dedicated work, in conjunction with the Union County Museum, has helped preserve, collect, and document the history of Union. These people have been invaluable resources for this work, and we acknowledge our great debt for their efforts. A great expression of gratitude is extended to Dr. Allan D. Charles for his continued guidance and lifelong commitment to promoting Union County's history.

The authors would also like to concede in the difficulty in regards to selecting the images for this book. Although there were a myriad of important historical images that were worthy of this volume, only the absolute highest quality original photographs could be used.

The authors would also like to extend their thanks and appreciation to Jesse Darland of Arcadia Publishing. For standing firm on Arcadia's photographic requirements, Jesse assisted in delivering a higher level of excellence in regards to the quality of images found within the pages of this book.

Finally, we would like to thank the contributions of those many individuals who have loaned or donated photographs for this collection. These include the following individuals and organizations: William Earl Sprouse, Chris Prince, Steve Blackwell, Union's Progress Club, Ted Trantham, Sharon Thompson, Amy Garner, and many others.

Unless otherwise noted, all images contained within this book are from the archives of the Union County Historical Society and its museum.

INTRODUCTION

Union County is the historical gem of Upstate South Carolina; few, if any, other counties in the region can boast as much history. Prior to the arrival of European immigrants, this area was initially inhabited by Paleo or Mississippian Indians approximately 10,000 to 15,000 years ago. The skills of these peoples likely were responsible for the construction of Indian burial mounds located around the Broad River. Various early stone relics created by Native Americans have been unearthed within Union County, particularly around these mounds and in the proximity of the Broad River and other such bodies of water. Later, Cherokee and Catawba tribes dwelled within this vicinity. After a war fought around 1620 between these two nations, the terms for a peace treaty mandated that the Cherokee and Catawba occupy separate parts of the region. The Cherokee agreed to reside west of the Broad River in the vicinity of what would become Union County and the Catawba to the east of the river. Consequently, the Native American name for Broad River was Eswa Huppeday (Eswaspuddenah), which translates as "line river." Before and during the primary influx of European migrants, there was abundant game in Union County. The area absolutely teemed with antelope, deer, buffalo, wolves, beavers, and bears, not to mention numerous species of feral cats.

Union's humble history began with European settlers populating newly acquired land bequeathed to them by royal land grants in the mid-to-late 1700s. These new colonists began cultivating Union's rich soil and sowing the seeds of a fledgling community. Union—both city and county—was christened after a 1760s log-construction meetinghouse known simply as the Union Church and built for usage by all local Christian congregations. Diversity in Union was measured primarily by religious denominations; notable populations of these were Presbyterians, Episcopalians, and Quakers. As Union grew alongside its diverse settlers, history has recorded the many challenges that tested its people's resolve. Within the span of 100 years, the citizens of Union struggled through three major periods of sociopolitical turmoil: the American Revolutionary War, the Civil War, and lastly the Reconstruction period, in which Congress passed forced acts of legislation that enabled radicals to take control of South Carolina policy. South Carolina had more Revolutionary War battles than any other of the 13 original colonies, with numerous skirmishes and three major engagements that took place in and around Union County: Blackstock's Farm, Musgrove Mill, and Fish Dam. Fought primarily by local militia rather than the Continental army's regimented forces, Patriots opposed and conquered British troops. The most notable example of Patriot victory in the aforementioned assaults is that of Blackstock's, in which a militia ambush put over 100 British Redcoats out of action while suffering only three local American casualties. These battlefields remain as historic sites and state parks.

The question of the day transformed into the question of the decade during the 1850s; numerous local politicians, including General Wallace and soon-to-be South Carolina governor William H. Gist, spoke out in favor of Southern independence. Although no Civil War battles were fought in Union County, roots of the war are found here. Secessionist governor Gist's plantation is located on the outskirts of Union County; his personal secretary, Benjamin F. Arthur, also lived in Union and was nominated to the position of clerk of the Secession Convention in December 1860. Arthur's desk, on which the Declaration of Secession was penned, survived the war and is housed in the Union County Museum. Later in the war, Confederate president Jefferson Davis spent two days in Union while fleeing Yankee personnel. In the last days of the Civil War, Governor Magrath, last Confederate governor of South Carolina, fled Columbia prior to General Sherman's advance and retreated to Union. He temporarily based himself at the Dawkins House, used its library as his office, and carried on state affairs in this refuge, consequently making Union a provisional South Carolina capital. His neighbor Benjamin F. Arthur, Edward John Arthur, and Governor Magrath burned documents in the Dawkins House library's fireplace. These classified documents would have condemned many Southerners to death had they fallen into Northern hands. After the downfall of the Confederacy, nine counties in South Carolina were declared to be in a state of rebellion; Union was one of these. This time became known as Reconstruction and was viewed by many South Carolinians as a time of oppressive leadership engineered by Federal authority. Residents of Union, deprived of their wealth due to the fall of the Confederacy, slipped into a state of financial decline.

In the early 1900s, Union became home to the world's largest cotton mill. Other mills emerged and opened the area to mill village communities, whose culture was rich in both family and spiritual life. Thomas Cary Duncan founded both the Union and Buffalo Mills, as well as the Union & Glenn Springs Railroad and multiple power plants. This investment in local industry propelled Union into the 20th century seemingly overnight. The massive number of employees required by these new mills forced them to seek labor from as far away as North Carolina. Union's population swelled accordingly to accommodate the thousands of people contracted by the large manufacturing facilities. As a growing county seat, Union featured a bustling Main Street that played host to opera houses, railroads, hotels, banks, theaters, and numerous private businesses.

To accommodate the growing industry of Union County, the first short-line railroad was laid in Union during 1846. Its sole purpose was to transport iron ore away from mines in the northernmost part of the county. Subsequent railroads were laid in the vicinity of Union County, including the following transportation systems: the early Spartanburg & Union Railroad, the Buffalo & Glenn Springs Railroad (later changed to the Buffalo Union-Carolina Railroad, or BUC), a dedicated Glenn Springs Railroad (which serviced the Glenn Springs Resort), the Southern Rail line, and the Seaboard Railway.

The Union County Historical Society has opened its vast archives to present Images of America: *Union County*. Represented are rarely seen images from the Civil War, local personalities, early celebrations, places of worship, railroads, Antebellum and main street architecture, mill village culture, and various incarnations of the arts. As a testament to Union, the authors of this book present the greatest asset Union has to offer—its history.

One

Wars, Local Patriots, and Personalities

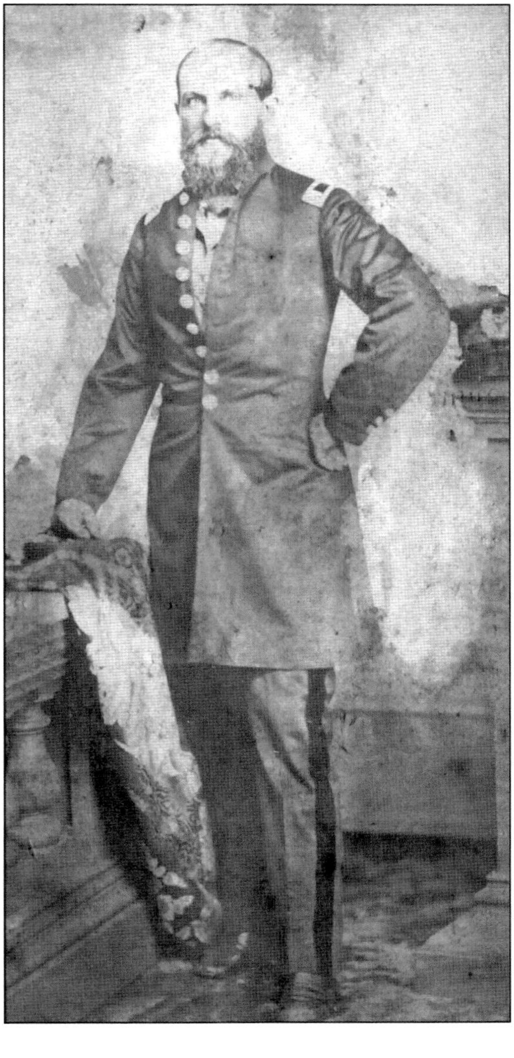

Dr. Andrew Wallace Thomson. Born in 1828, Dr. Wallace was a Confederate general whose works benefited many soldiers. Dr. Wallace's hygiene techniques were instrumental in saving numerous injured troops from death by infection. His position in the CSA army was Confederate surgeon for the 18th Regiment, South Carolina Volunteers. When it was discovered Dr. Thomson's regiment had a higher survival rate than other regiments, other surgeons were ordered to mimic his surgery protocol. After the war, Dr. Thomson continued his practice and was known as the "leading physician in this portion of the state." When Union opened its first hospital in 1911, it was agreed that the facility should be named for the famous Confederate surgeon and beloved local physician. Wallace Thomson Hospital is still in operation.

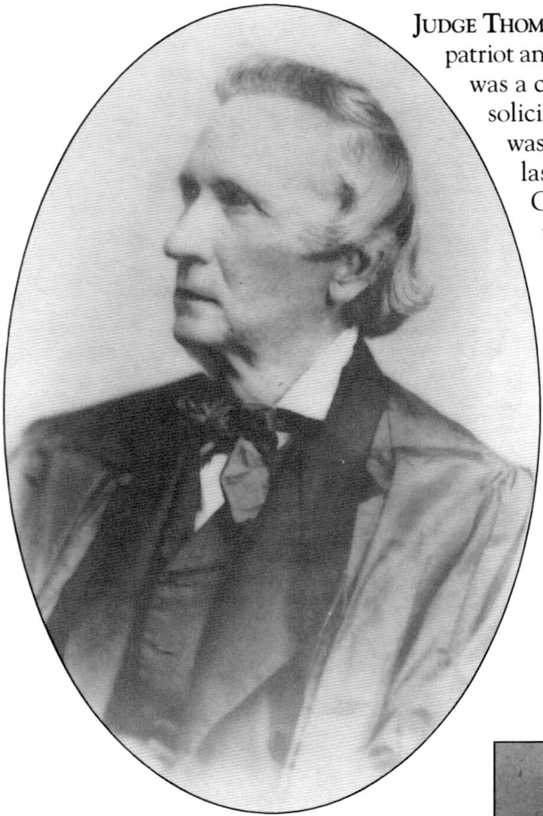

JUDGE THOMAS NUCKOLLS DAWKINS. The great-grandson of patriot and martyr John Nuckolls of Whig Hill, Dawkins was a circuit court judge from 1865 to 1869 and the solicitor from 1849 to 1865. His home, the Shrubs, was used by Gov. Andrew Gordon Magrath as the last provisional South Carolina capitol of the Confederacy at the end of the War between the States.

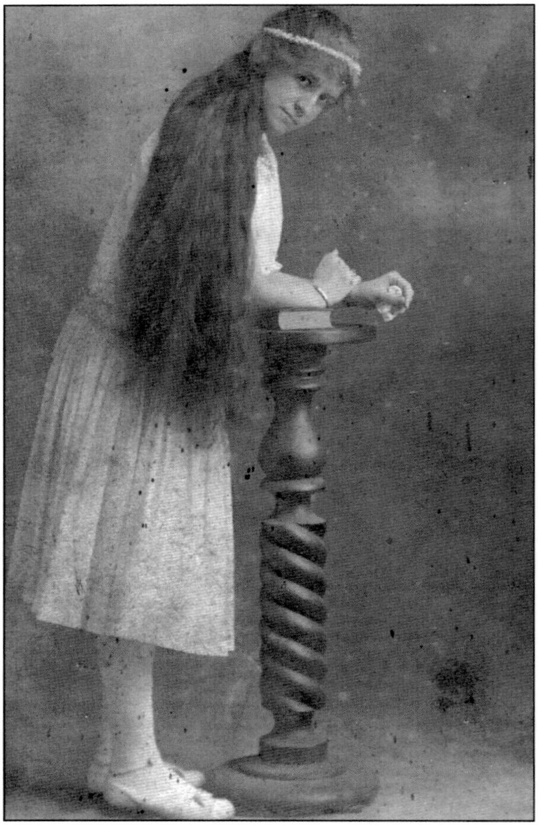

MARGARET "PERCY" PURCELL. For many years, the Purcell family was the only Catholic family in Union, and they were instrumental in building St. Augustine Catholic Church. This postcard was made by P.B. Barnes, a prolific local photographer. (Courtesy of James Canupp.)

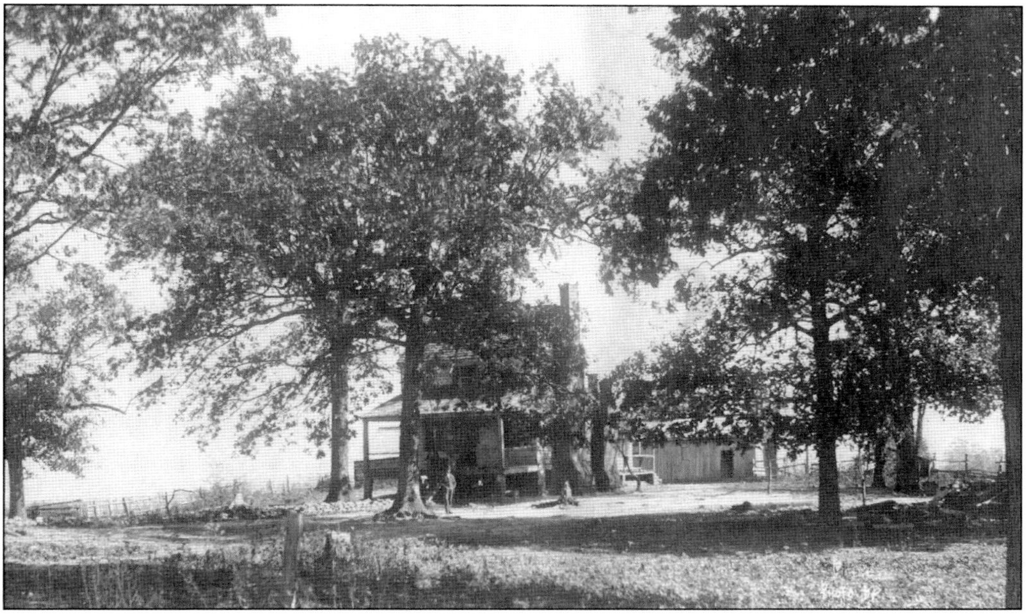

Mrs. J.R.R. Giles Place. Mrs. J.R.R. Giles entertained Confederate president Jefferson Davis and his entourage in this home overnight during his flight south in April 1865. Later, the house was known as the country home of Mrs. J. Douglas.

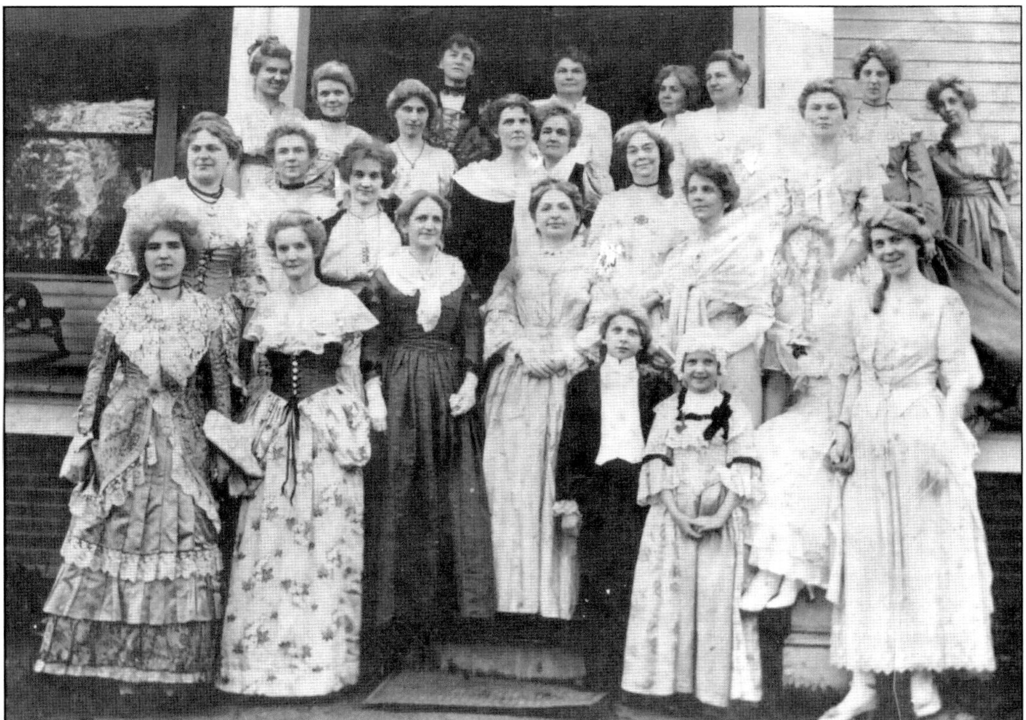

Daughter of the American Revolution (DAR). Members and guests of the Fairforest DAR pose at a Washington's Birthday tea party that was held at Mrs. John A. Fant's home on East Main Street. The photograph was taken on December 22, 1917. Consequently, the DAR also had their state convention in Union in 1917.

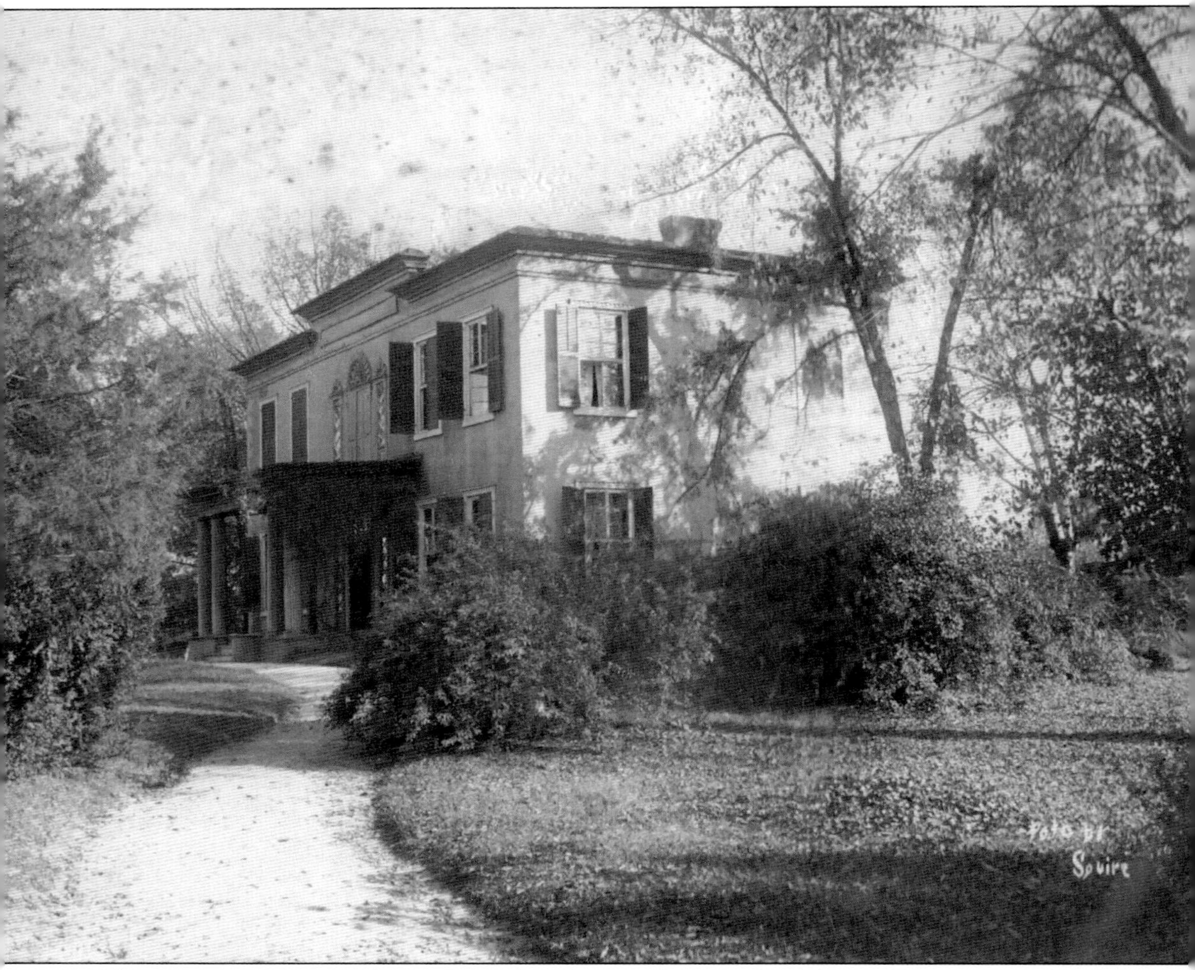

THE WALLACE HOUSE. This is the earliest known photograph of the Wallace House, taken by Squire's Photography. Note the second-story decorated balcony and doors and the decorative pediment extending over the roofline (neither exists in the current configuration of the house). Confederate president Jefferson Davis lunched here during his flight south in 1865.

Rose Hill before Restoration. Pictured here in the early 1940s is a dilapidated Rose Hill Plantation prior to restoration. It is surprising a home in such a state of disrepair was able to make a splendid revitalization.

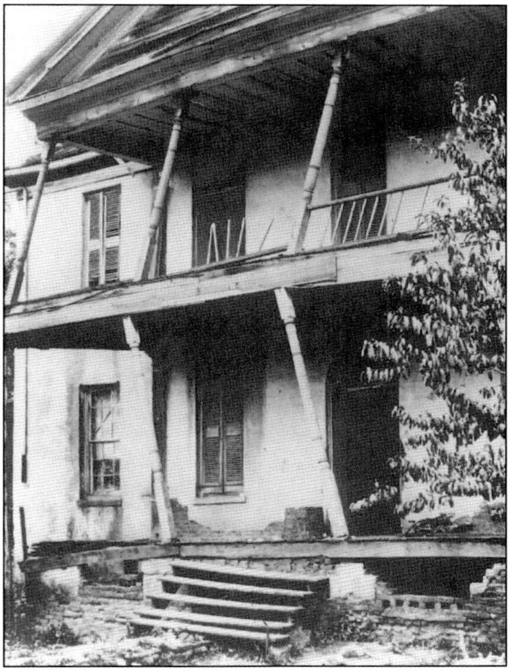

Rose Hill after Restoration. The Rose Hill Mansion is pictured here after restoration on December 20, 1960. Marking the centennial anniversary of the signing of the Article of Secession, Rose Hill was sanctioned as a state park.

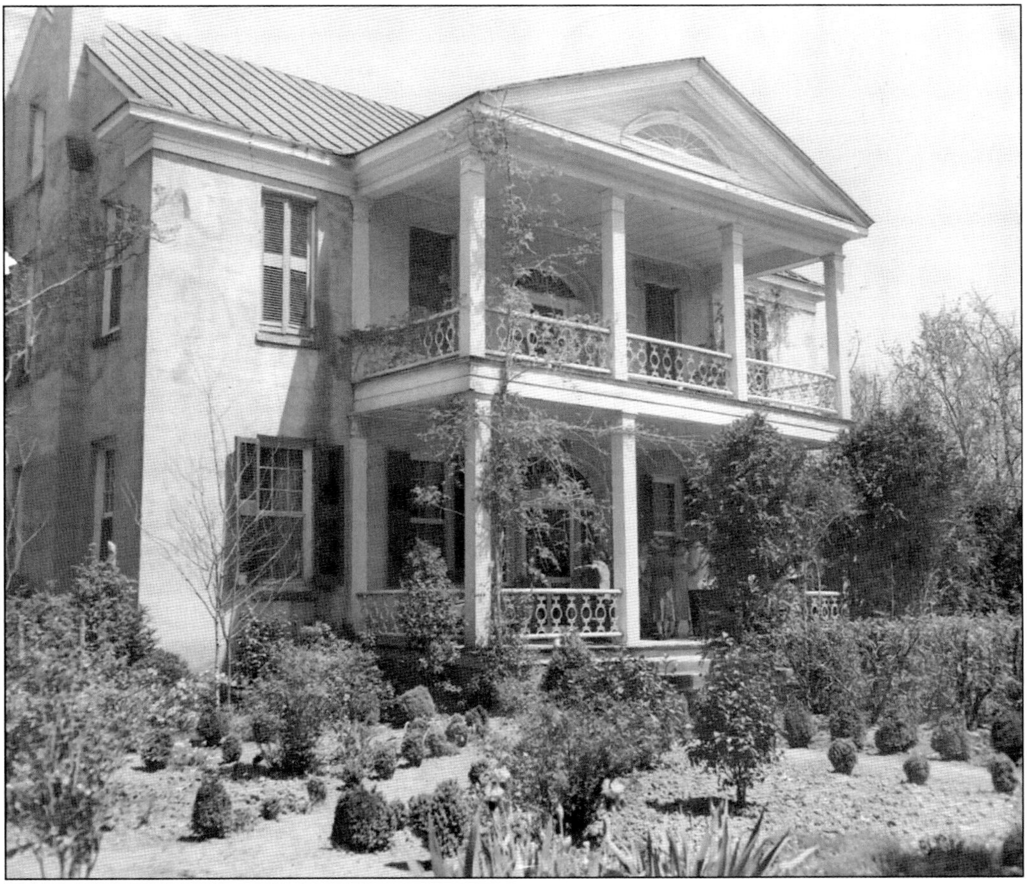

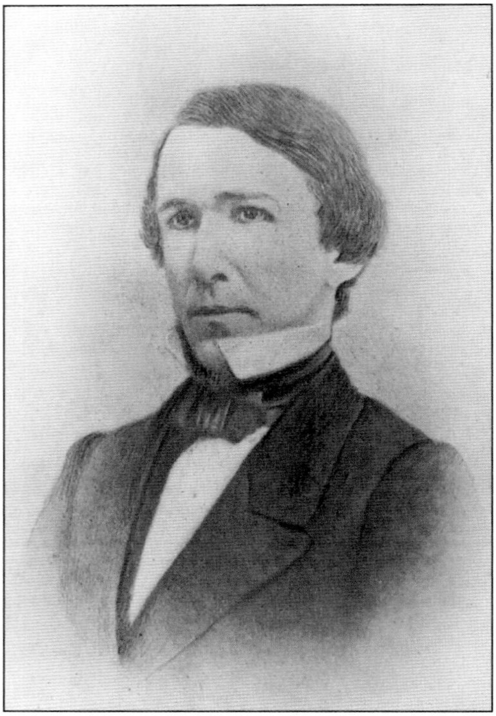

Benjamin Franklin Arthur. A barrister and associate of Governor Gist, B.F. Arthur drafted the South Carolina's Article of Secession and served as the secretary of the Secession Convention. Not physically fit for combat, he also worked as a civilian consultant for the army. He died at the age of 44 in 1870. Arthur's writing desk was known as the secession table, as the Article of Secession was drafted upon it on December 17, 1860. It is on display at the Union County Museum.

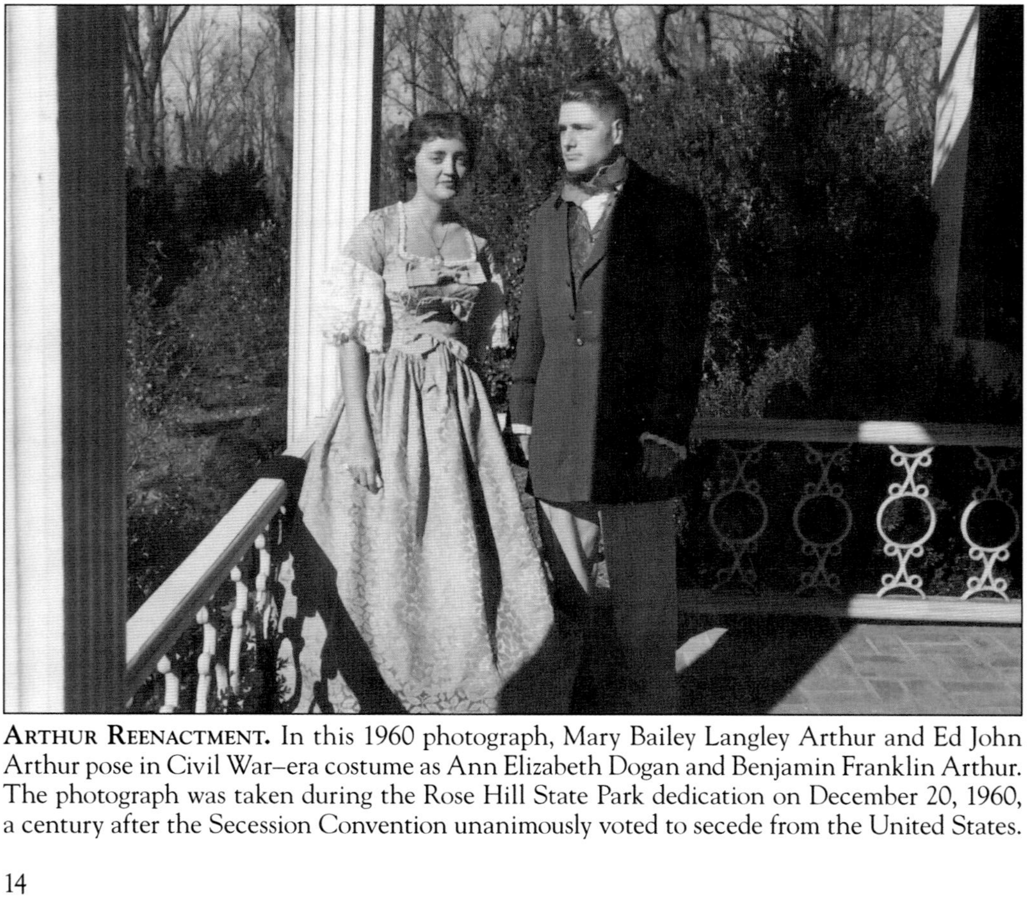

Arthur Reenactment. In this 1960 photograph, Mary Bailey Langley Arthur and Ed John Arthur pose in Civil War–era costume as Ann Elizabeth Dogan and Benjamin Franklin Arthur. The photograph was taken during the Rose Hill State Park dedication on December 20, 1960, a century after the Secession Convention unanimously voted to secede from the United States.

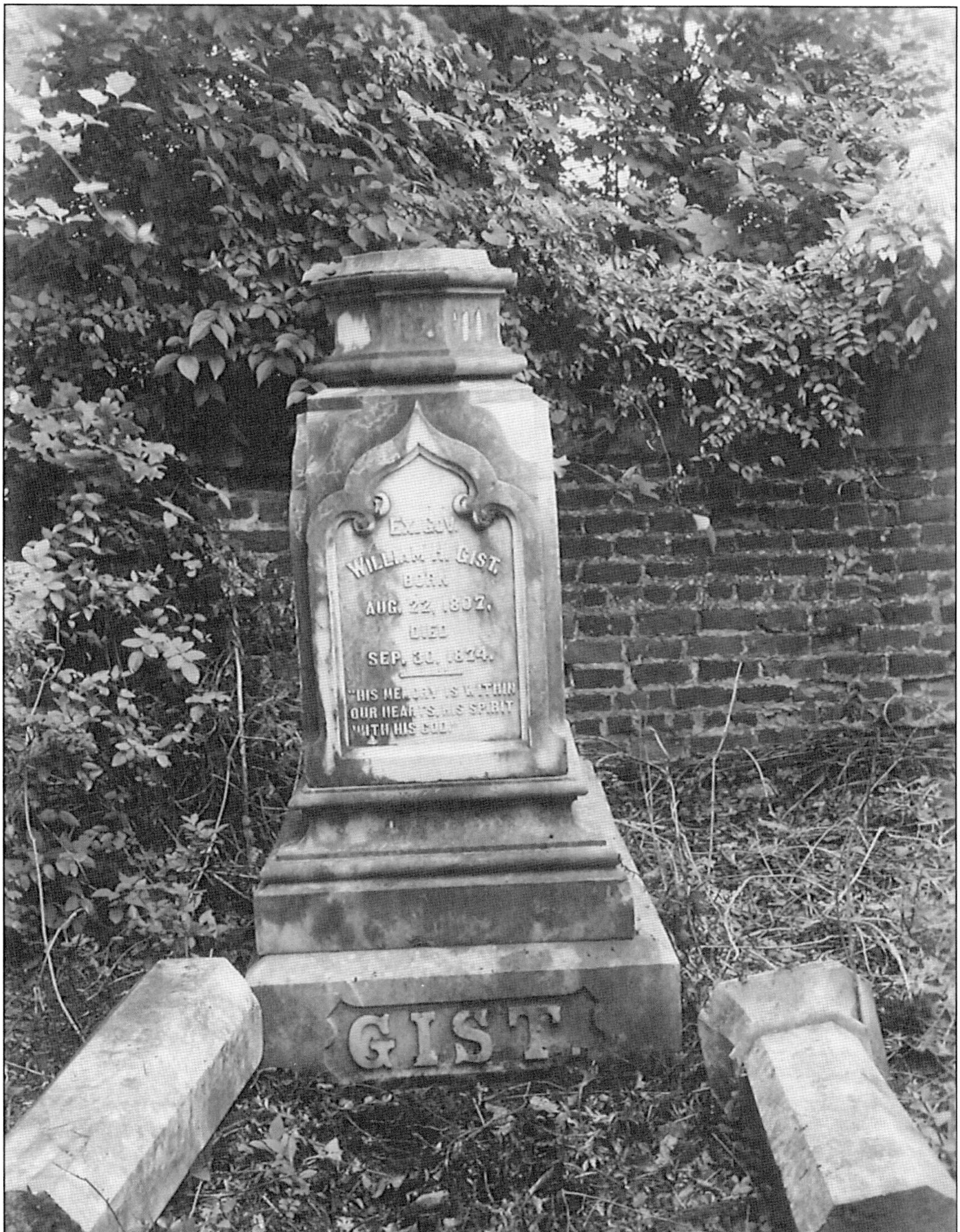

Gist Grave Marker. Gov. William Henry Gist's (1807–1874) grave marker and the adjoining graveyard are in a relative state of disrepair. The Gist graveyard is in close proximity to Rose Hill Plantation.

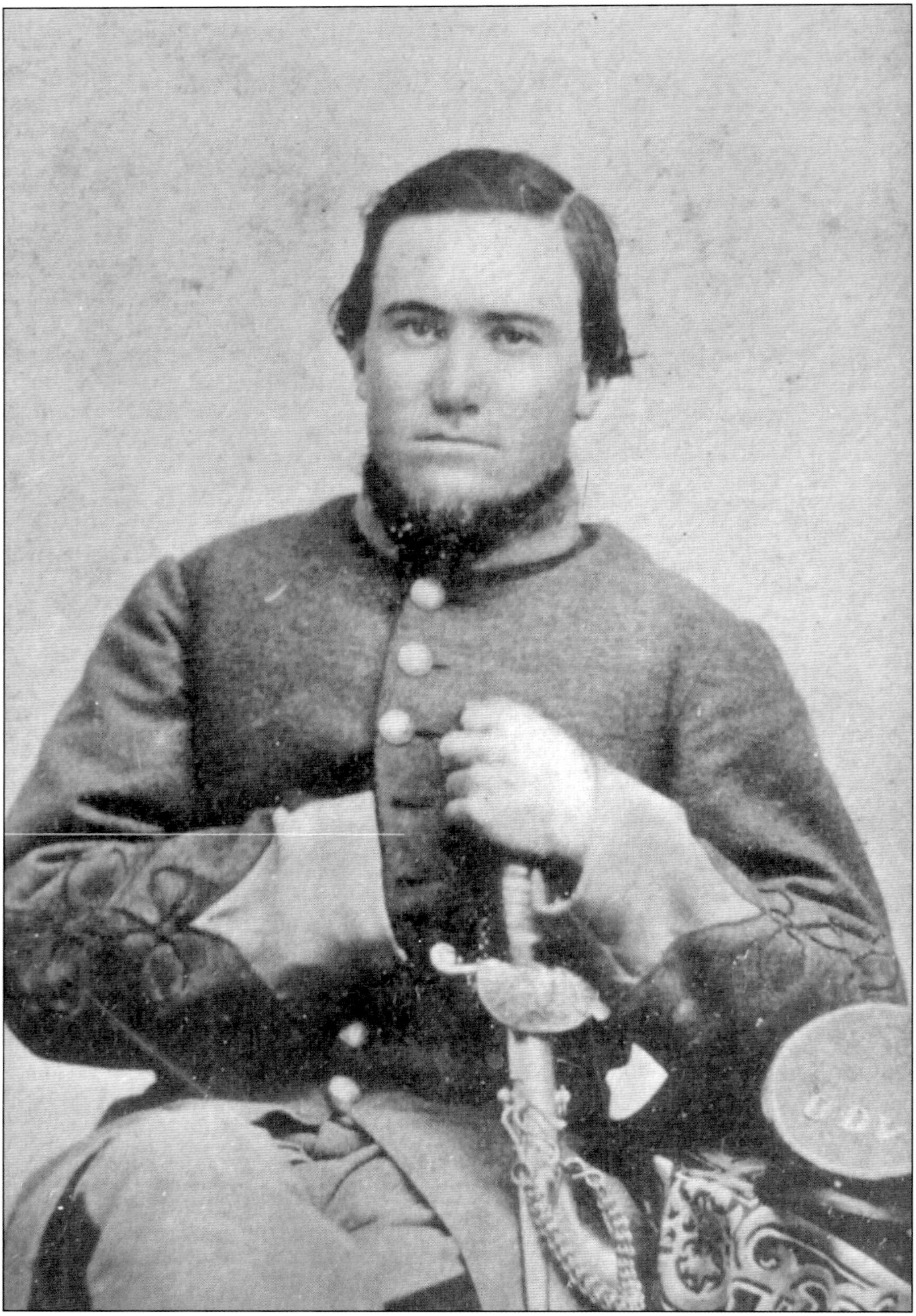

CAPT. JOHN E. HAMES. Captain Hames was part of Company B, 18th Infantry Regiment, South Carolina Volunteers, and he died at the battle of Second Manassas, Virginia, on August 30, 1862. His Union District Volunteers kepi hat, pictured here, is on display at the Union County Museum.

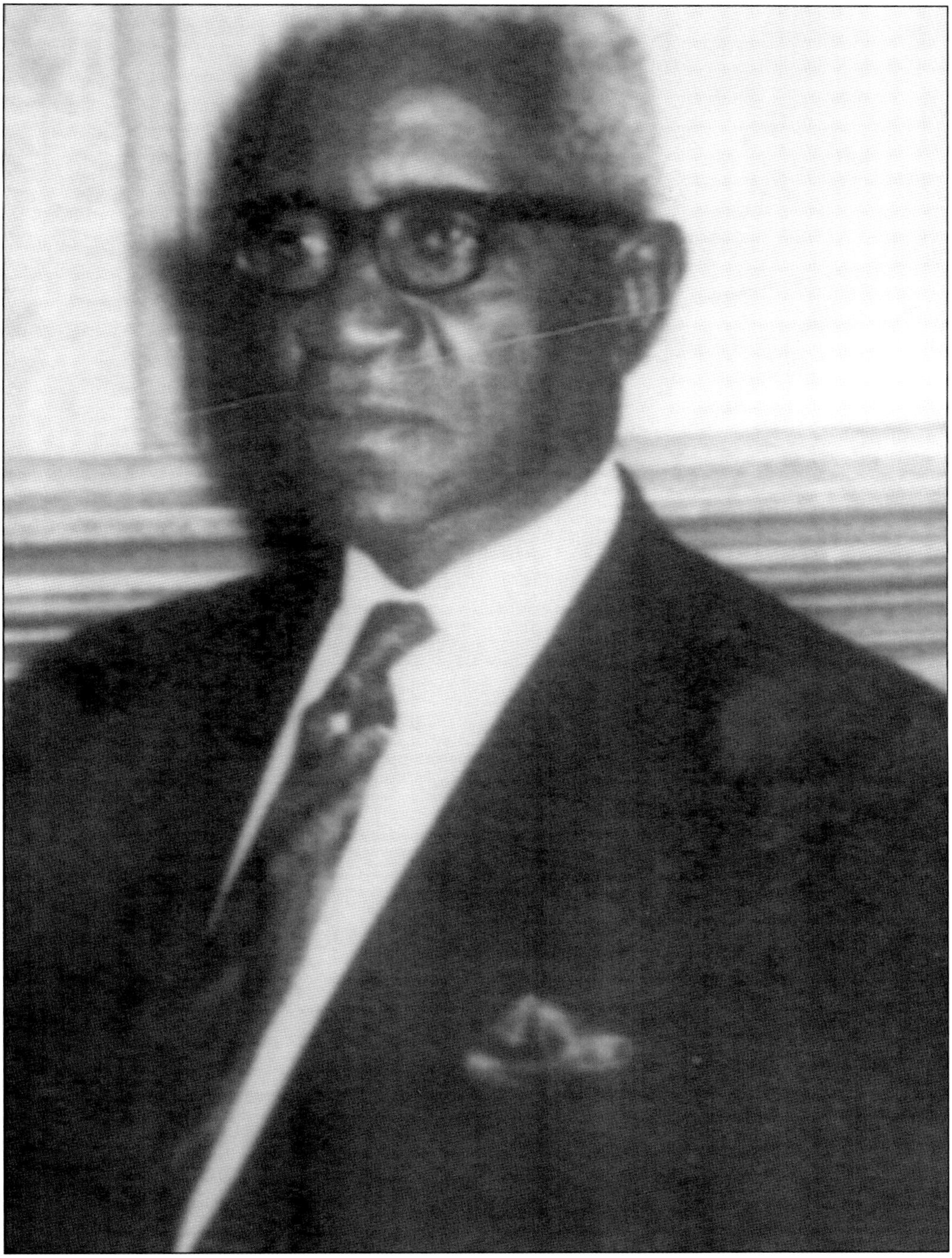

Dr. Lawrence W. Long. Dr. Long founded the Union Community Hospital in 1932. The hospital served Union's black community, and it was located directly across from the Union County Courthouse. In 1949, a new brick structure was built for his hospital. For 46 years, Dr. Long held clinics and maintained his practice in the hospital. The hospital closed its doors in 1977, but the building remains and is listed in the National Register of Historic Places.

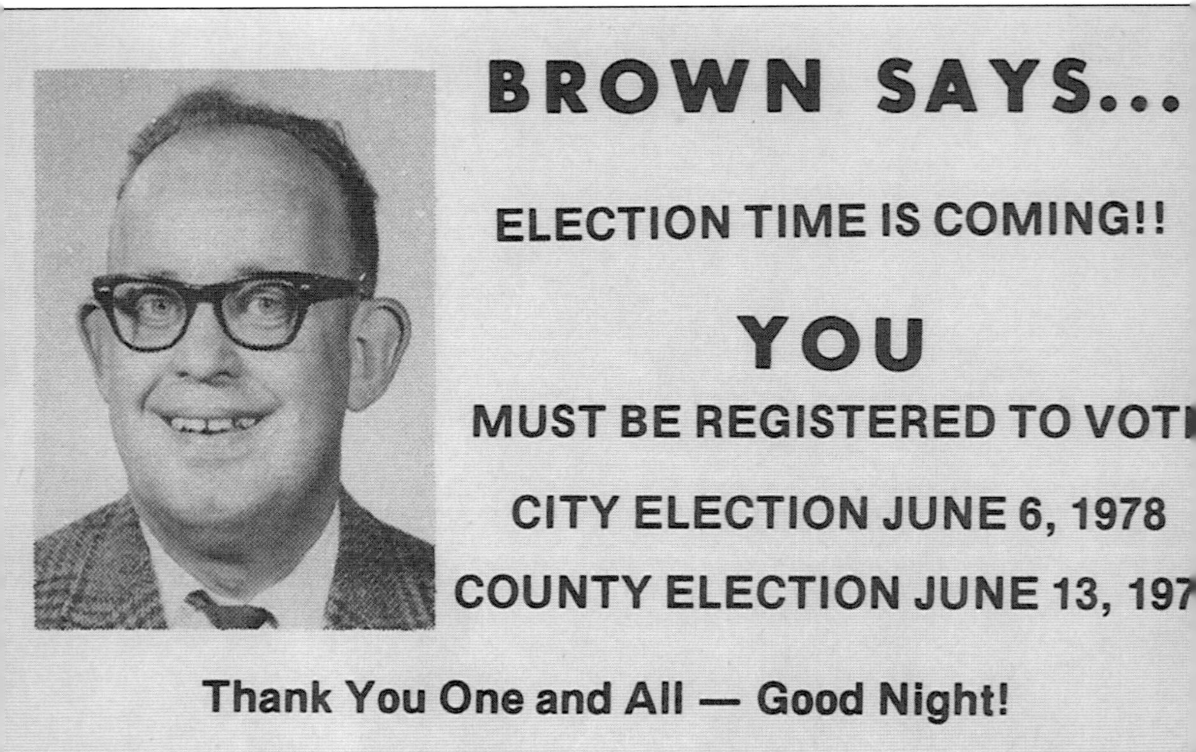

BILL "OGGIE" BROWN. Although Bill Brown may have had a disability, it did not prevent him from being a local radio announcer and an active personality in the community. It seems he was found peddling his bogus insurance policies on Main Street almost daily.

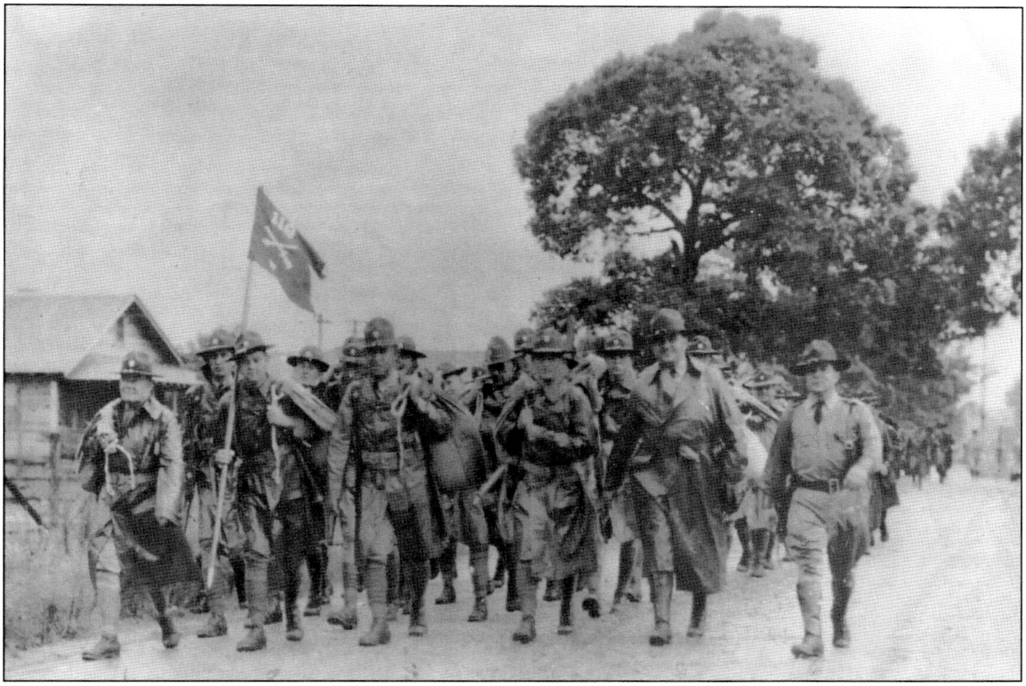

HARRY M. ARTHUR. Harry Arthur (first row, far right) leads the local 118th Infantry at Hattiesburg, Mississippi, in 1938. By the time he finished his term of service with the military, Arthur reached the rank of major general. He was well known as the president of the Arthur State Bank, a position he held from 1933 until his death in 1988.

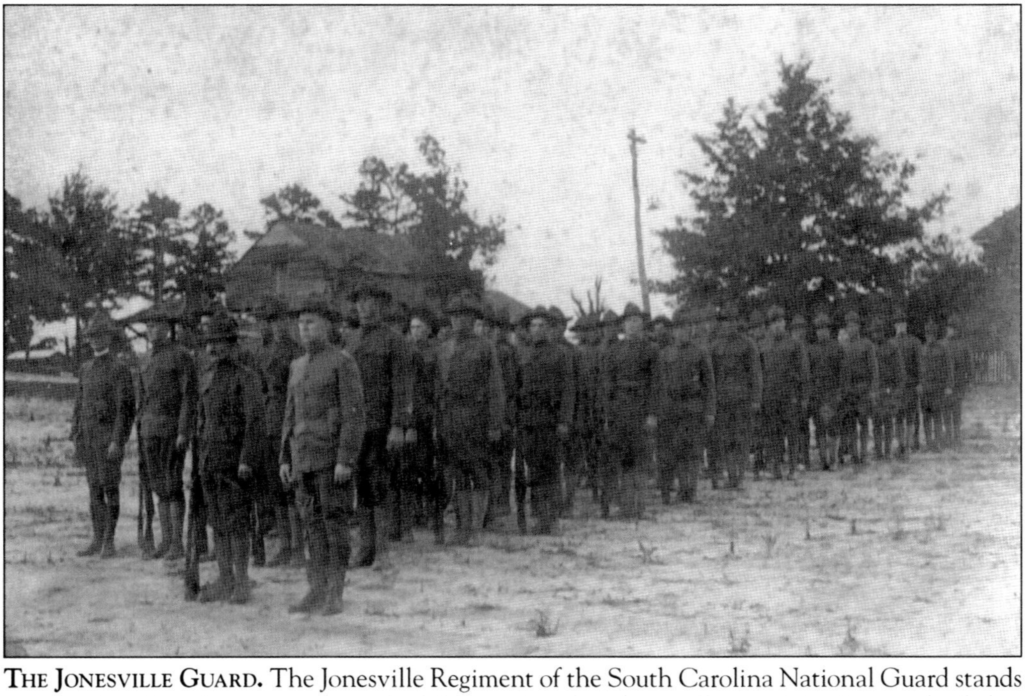

THE JONESVILLE GUARD. The Jonesville Regiment of the South Carolina National Guard stands at attention. The first person from the left, sporting the white collar, is a Mr. Hames, the father of Boyd Hames.

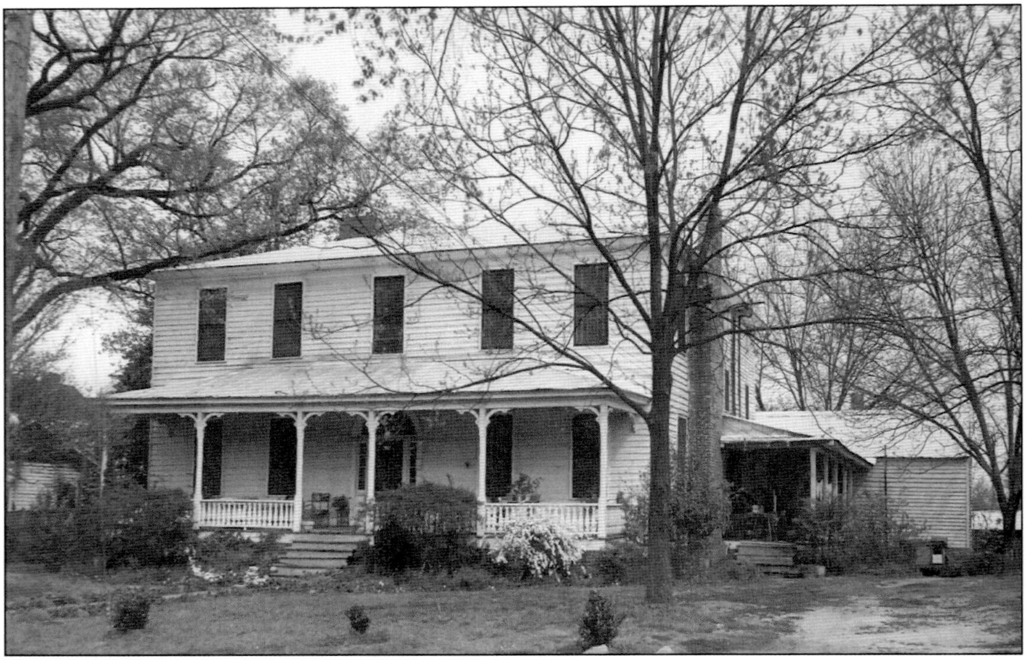

THE DAWKINS HOUSE. Located behind the Union branch of the University of South Carolina, the Dawkins House is known locally as the last provisional South Carolina capitol of the Confederacy. Governor Magrath made the library his office for a duration after he fled the burning of Columbia by General Sherman's troops.

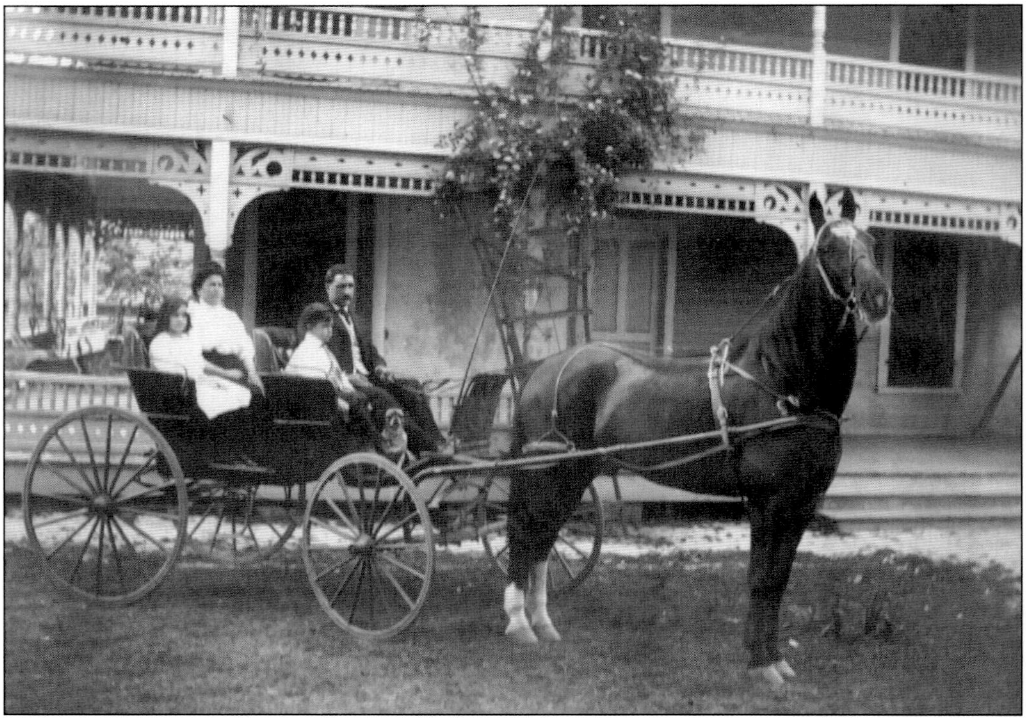

TRAVELING WITH THE TINSLEYS. The Tinsley family poses in their carriage. They owned Tinsley's Jewelers, the oldest running business in Union County.

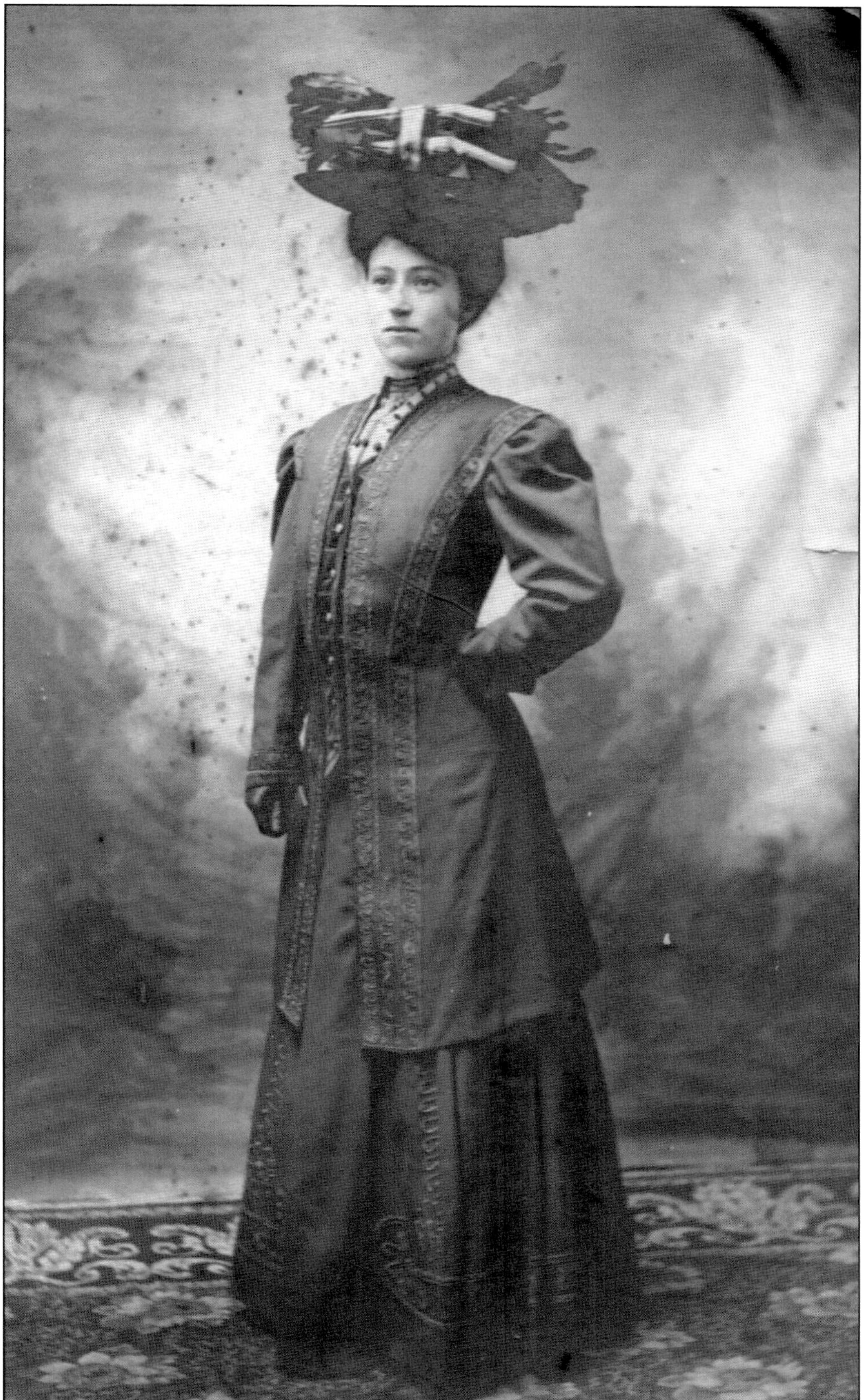

Magdaline "Maggie" Tinsley. Maggie was married to a local physician, Dr. Pryor, and the status of her style and wealth is quite apparent in this 1890s photograph. She was the daughter of Waring and Sarah Jane Tinsley, the founders of Tinsley's Jewelers.

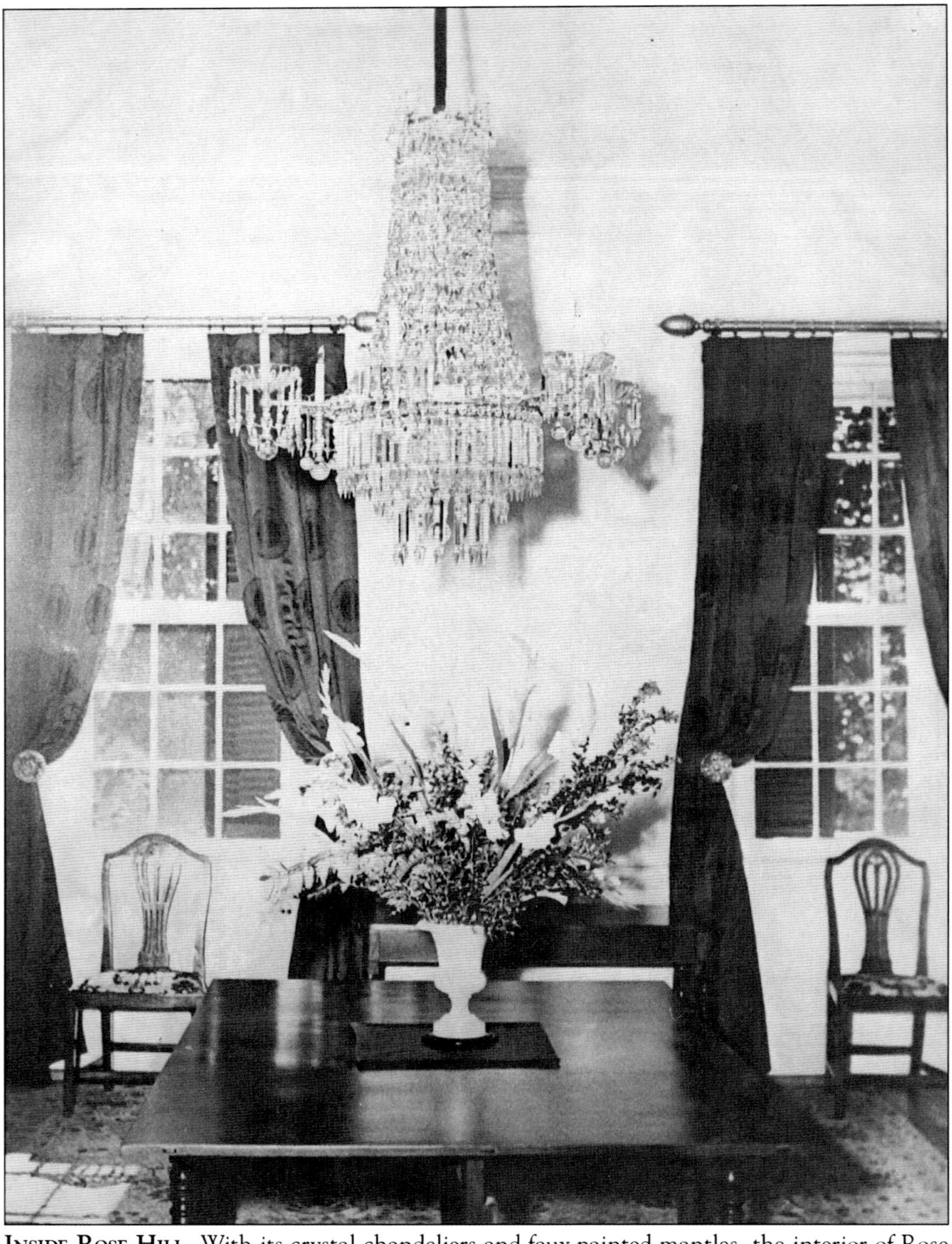

Inside Rose Hill. With its crystal chandeliers and faux-painted mantles, the interior of Rose Hill Plantation is depicted in this photograph. Rose Hill Plantation, or the Gist Mansion, was the home of Gov. William H. Gist. Now a state park, Rose Hill is open for daily tours, and the mansion retains many of its original accouterments and furniture.

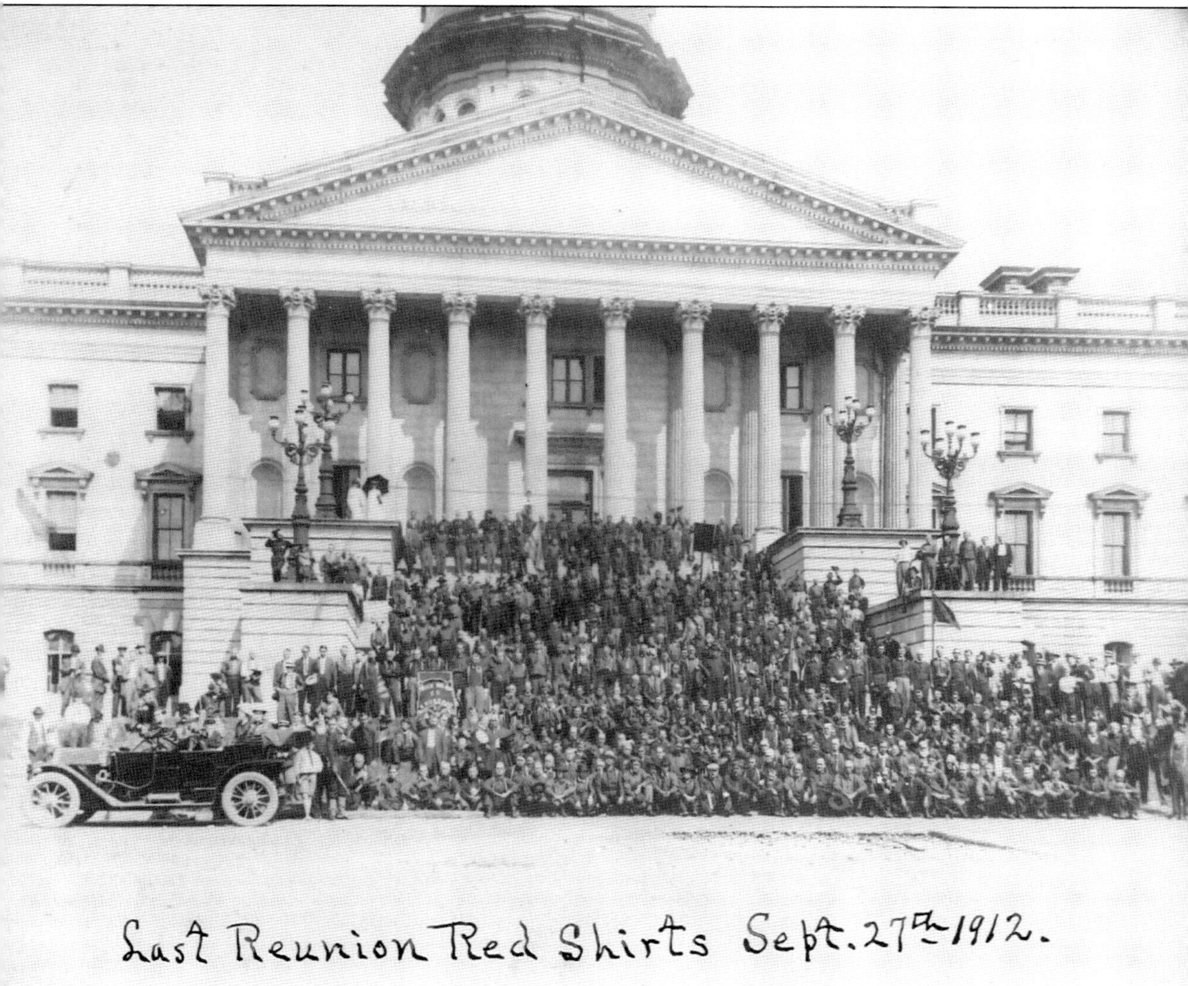

The Last Reunion of the Red Shirts. The Red Shirts were the muscle and voice of the Wade Hampton campaign at the end of Reconstruction in South Carolina. Wade Hampton won the election and brought an end to the Federal policies and occupation.

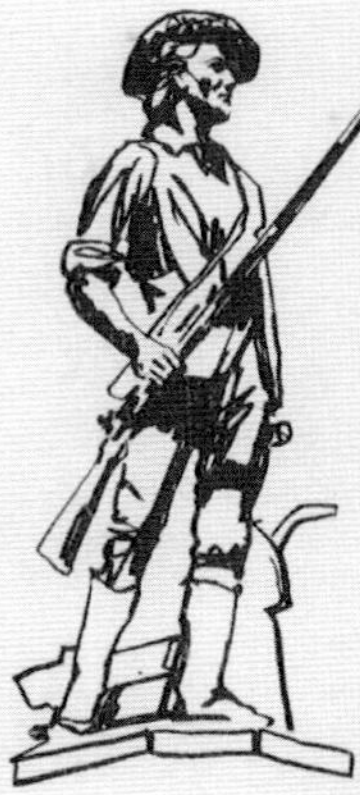

MG [RET] HARRY M. ARTHUR

Armory Dedication

SUNDAY, DECEMBER 7, 1980
2:00 P.M.

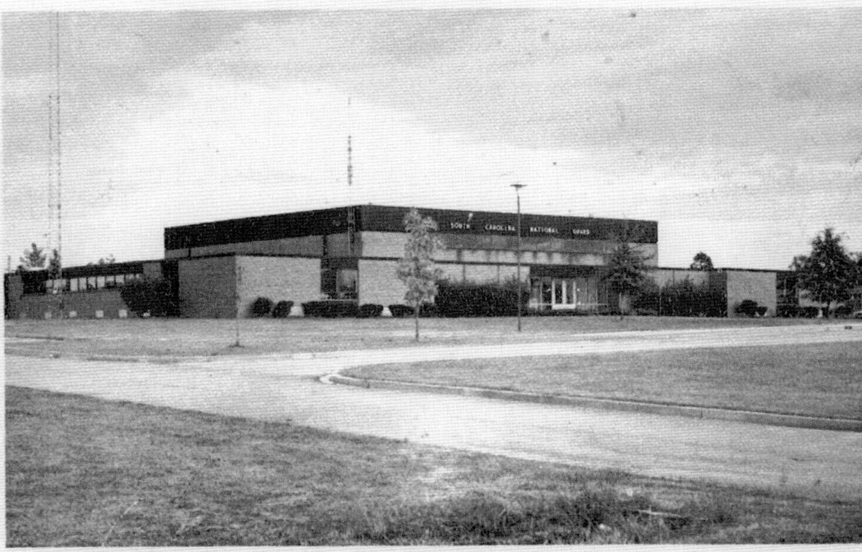

JOHNSON RIFLES
Organized 1846

HEADQUARTERS and HEADQUARTERS COMPANY
4th BATTALION [Mech] 118th INFANTRY
UNION, SOUTH CAROLINA 29379

HEADQUARTERS OF THE 118TH. Existing to this day as a National Guard regiment, the 118th began in 1846 as the Johnson Rifles, a local volunteer militia named after Gov. David Johnson. During World War I, the Johnson Rifles regiment was sent to Fort Jackson in Columbia, where it was reorganized as Company E, 118th Regiment, and it has been known as the 118th ever since.

Two

Early Union Community Life

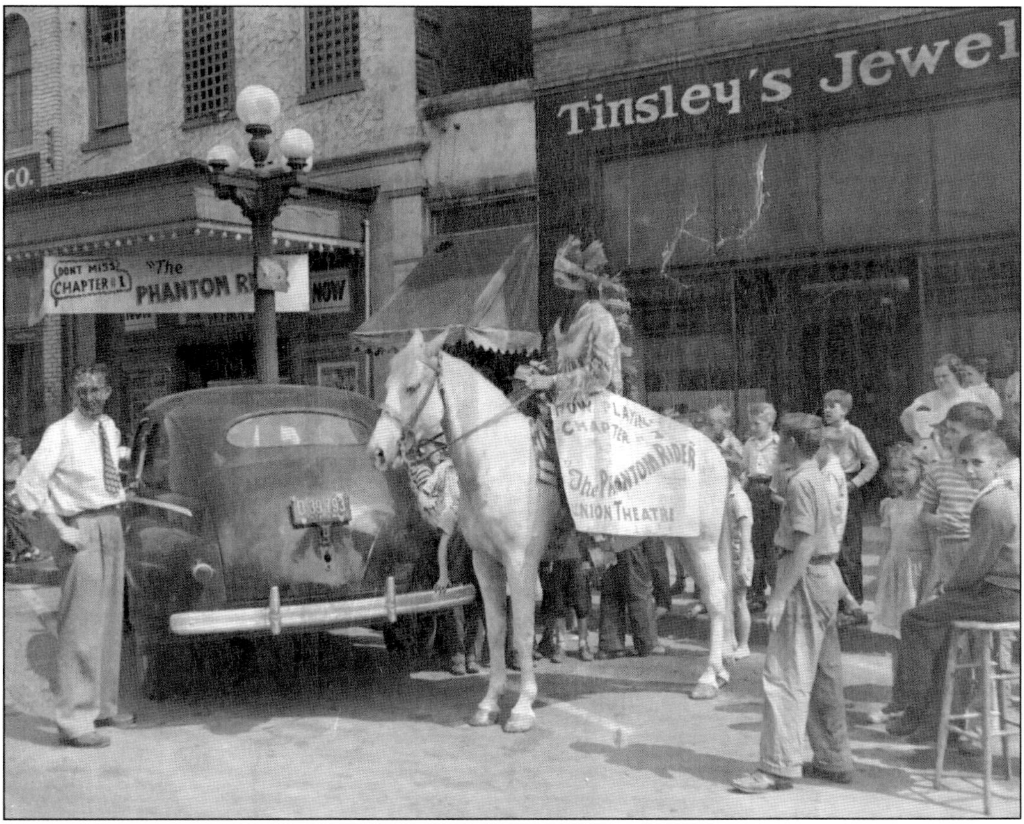

Union Theatre and Tinsley's Jewelers. The Union Theatre was originally called the Edisonia, later known as the Rialto in the 1920s and Duncan Theatre in the 1940s, after World War II. It closed in 1979 with the retirement of manager Frank James. The very last showing in the theater was George Hamilton's *Love at First Bite*. The *Phantom Rider* movie was promoted with a live actor on horseback at the theater that occupied 102 and 106 Main Street.

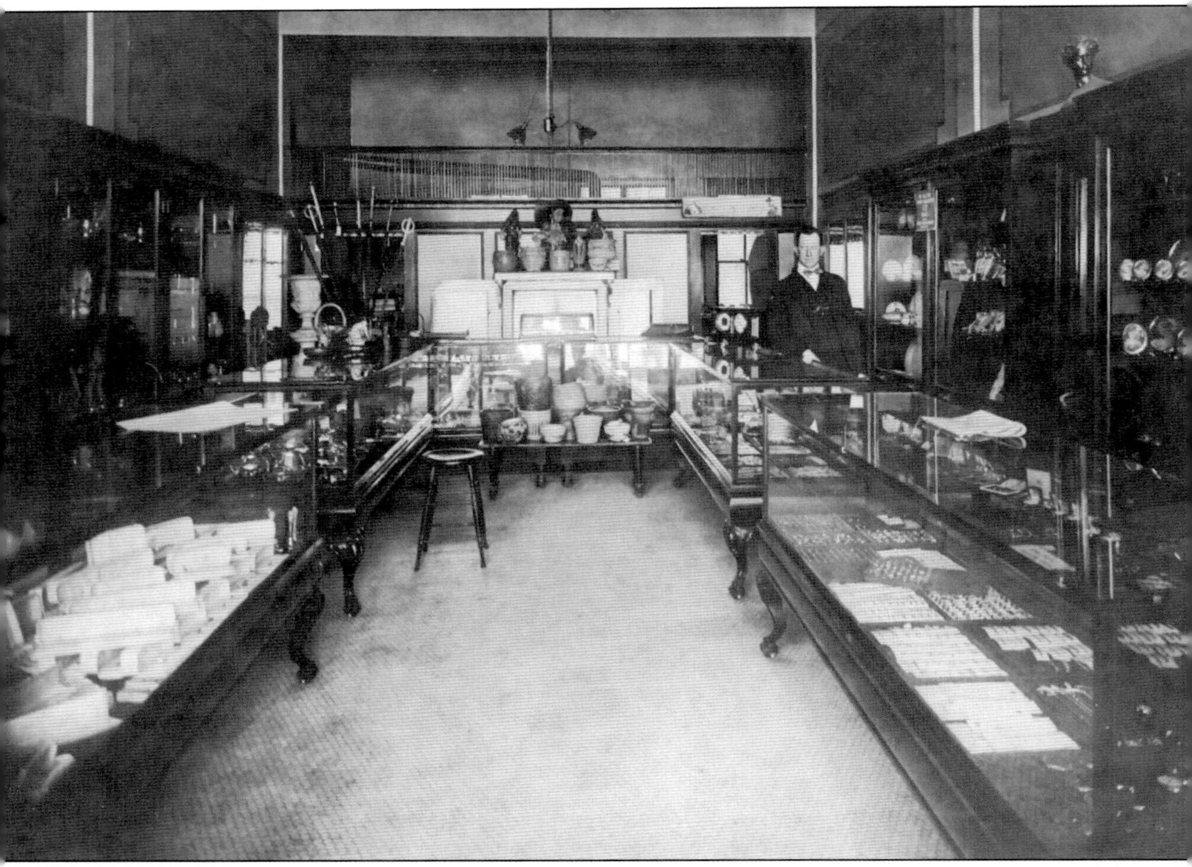

The Interior of Tinsley's Jewelers, c. 1910. Rufus Waring Tinsley opened the store in 1866, and his family ran it at various locations on Main Street until it closed around 1980. When Tinsley's closed, it was South Carolina's oldest jewelry store and Union County's longest-running business.

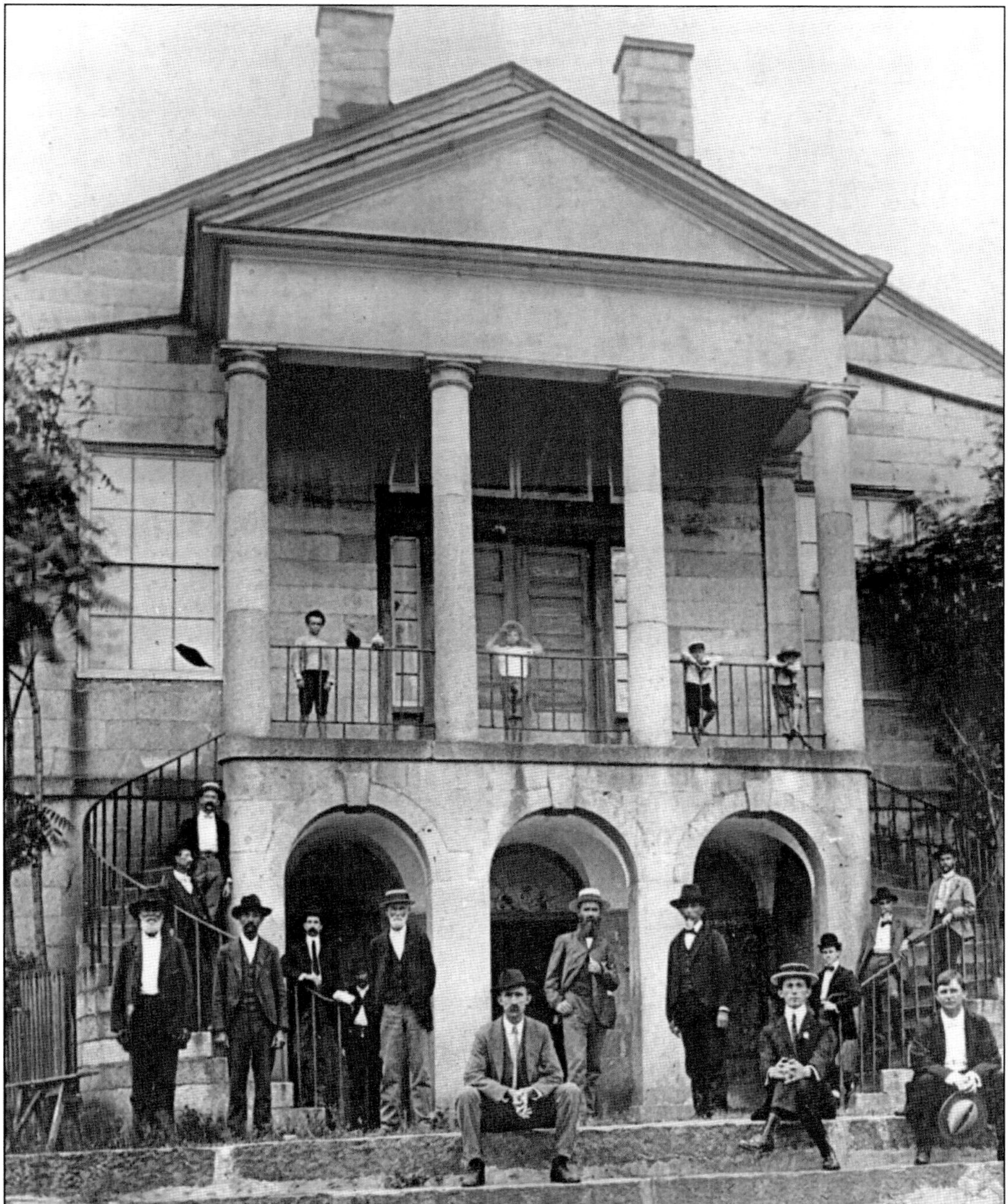

ROBERT MILLS'S COURTHOUSE, c. 1904. Built in 1823, the Union County Courthouse was designed by famous South Carolinian architect Robert Mills. The structure was actually the third courthouse developed on the plat. The first courthouse was composed of hand-hewn logs. Mills also designed the city jail, which still stands; both buildings were constructed of local granite. In addition to designing many well-known South Carolina structures, Mills also designed the Washington Monument and the US Treasury Building in Washington, DC.

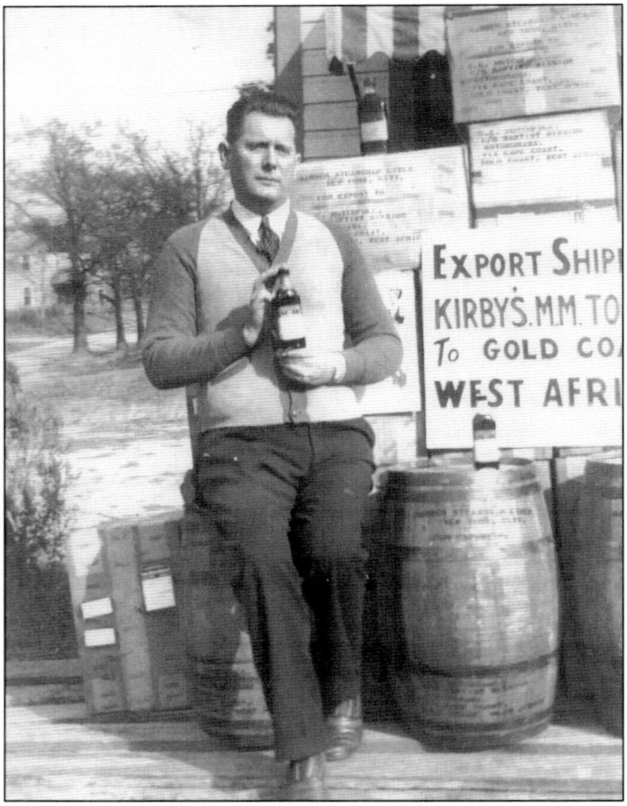

HYDRICK KIRBY. The owner of Kirby's Products, Hydrick Kirby poses with one of his creations. Kirby's business was located at 16 Fike Avenue, and he sold numerous products, including hygiene items popular with African Americans.

THE UNION CITY QUARRY, 1913. Union's quarry furnished the city and surrounding areas with granite. The quarry engine pulls three to four cars capable of carrying 2.5 yards of stone each.

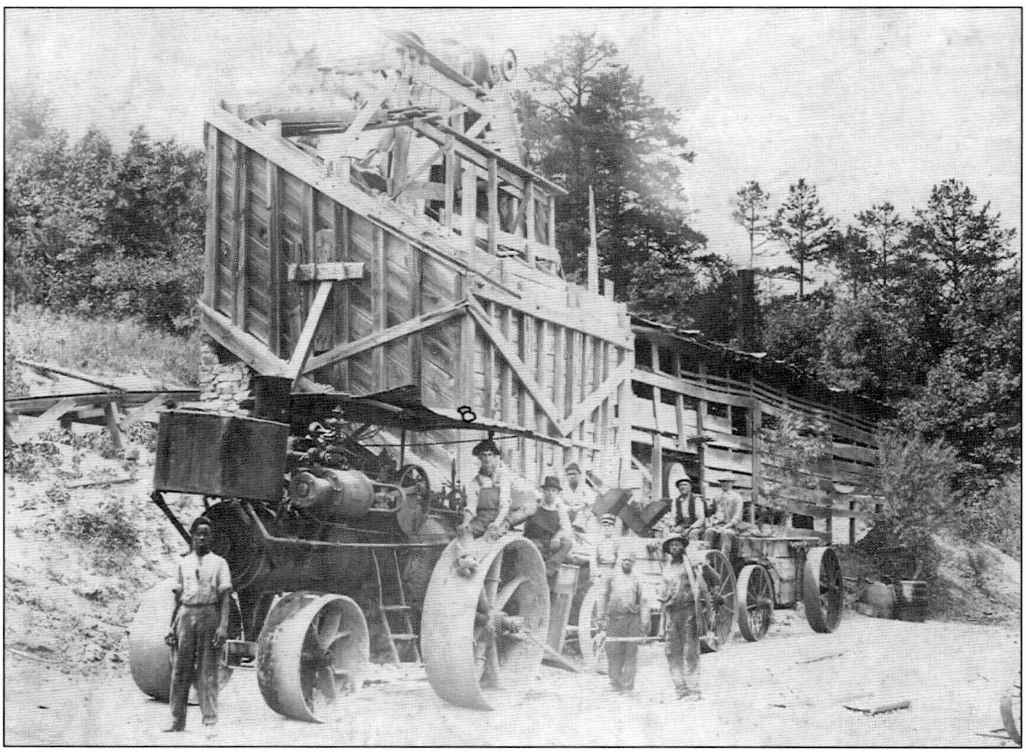

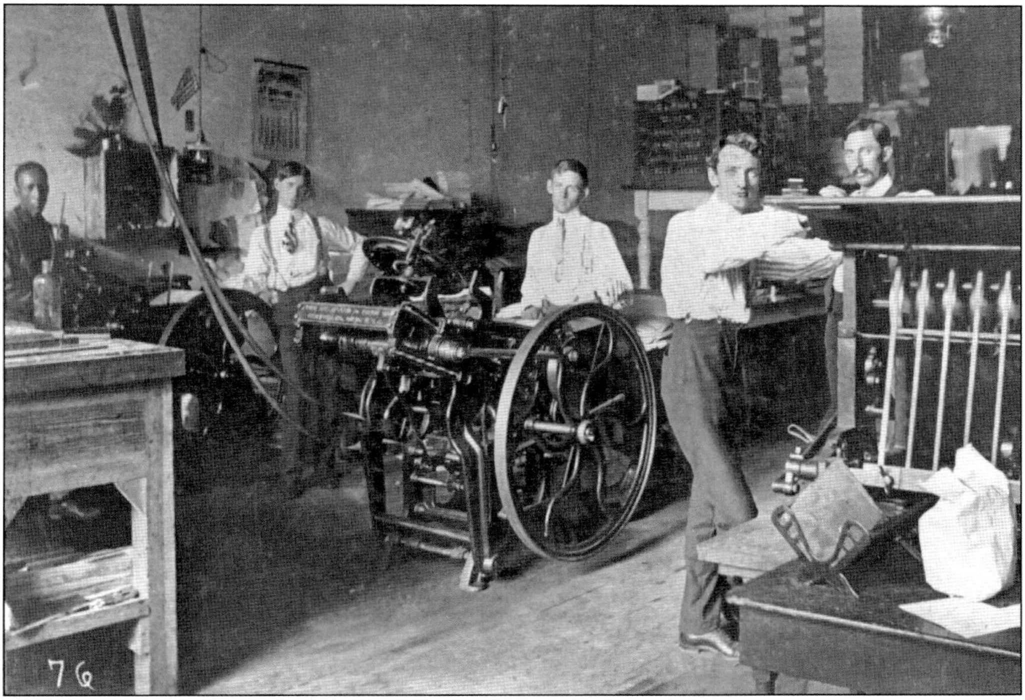

The Office of the *Progress News*. Allan Nicholson opened the *Progress News* in January 1900. The South Carolina Dispensary bottle on the table dates this photograph between 1900 and 1907. Nicholson printed and managed the paper until he sold it in 1925. The business went bankrupt and closed after six months of new ownership.

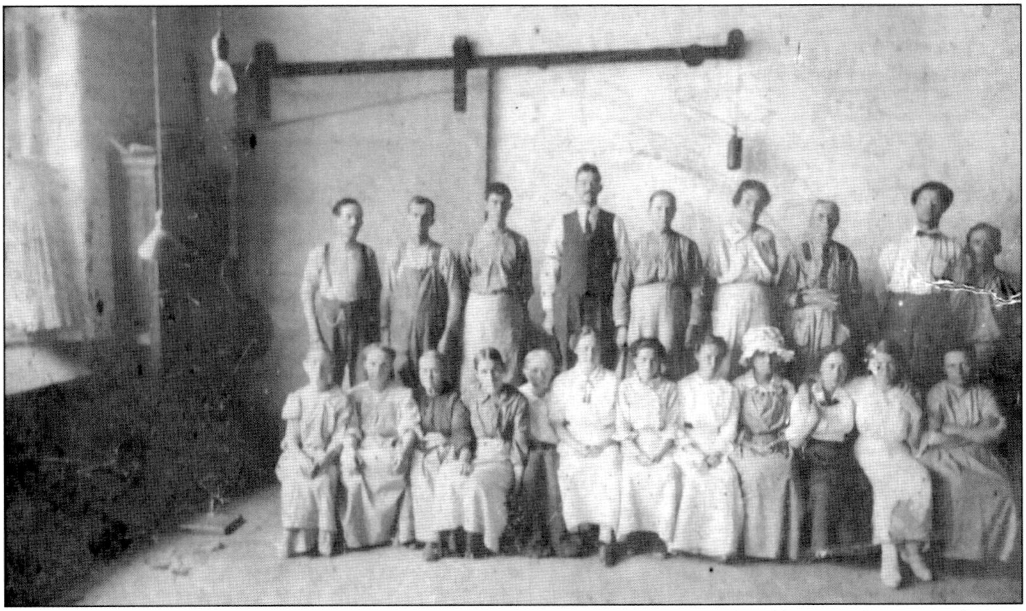

Union Mill Workers. The textile mills were the great financial backbone of Union during the early 20h century. Mill employment offered not only men work opportunities, but woman and children as well. This photograph was possibly taken at the Monarch Mill, but no location was listed.

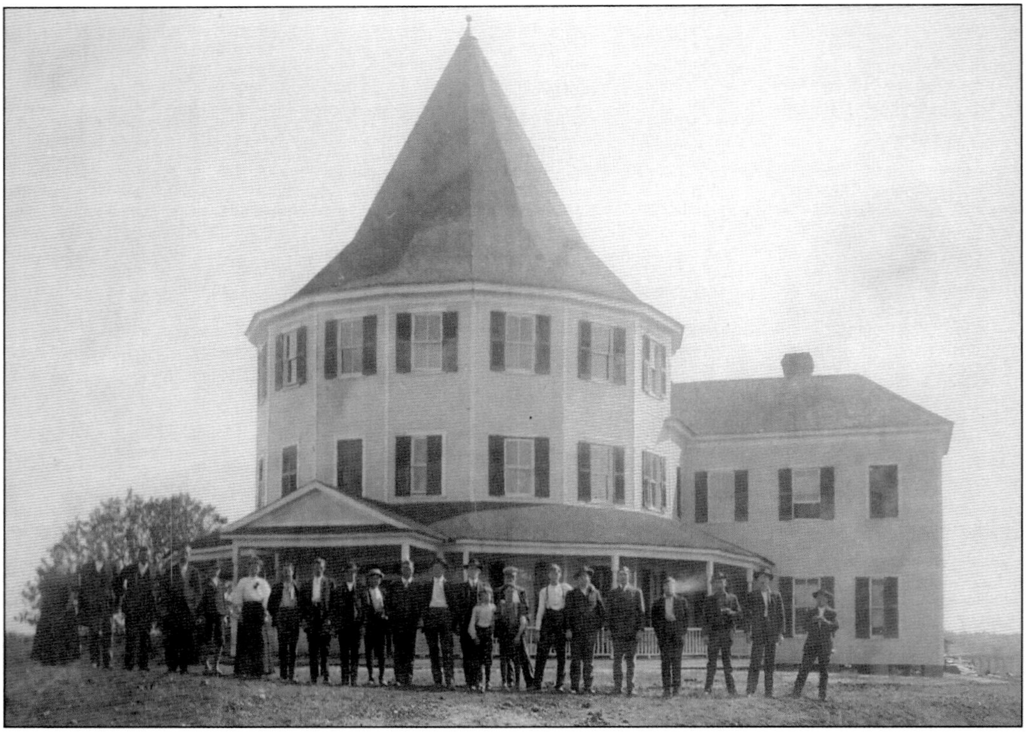

The Buffalo Hotel, c. 1908. Many schoolteachers boarded at this hotel during the school year. Unfortunately, all that remains of the hotel is this photograph, as it no longer exists.

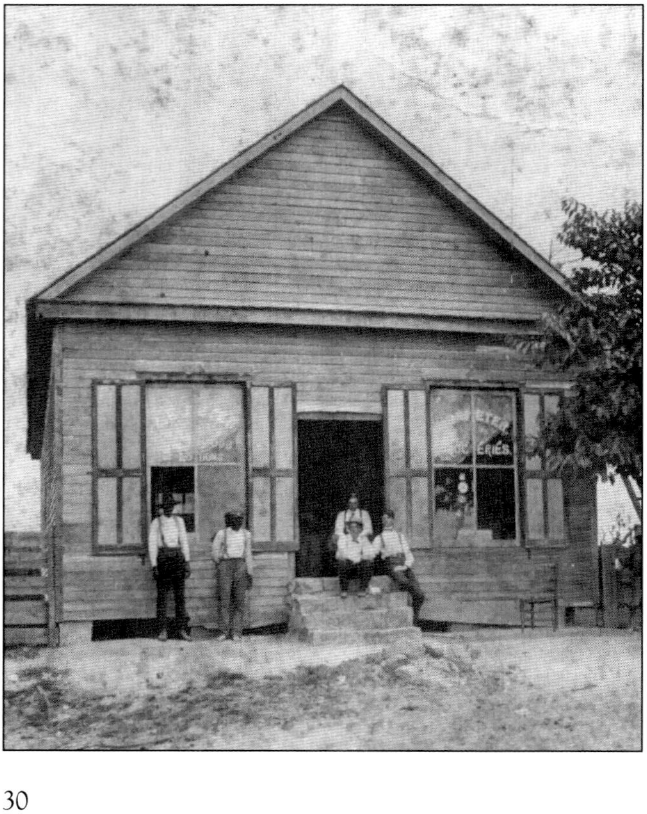

L.B. Jeter General Merchandise Store. Located in the Santuck community, this general merchandise store was opened by Little Berry Jeter Sr. in 1875, and he operated the business until his death in 1931. The business continued as a family endeavor until the store was closed in 1954. The granite supports, seen under the building in the photograph, are all that remain of his shop.

Steam-Powered Tractor. A steam-powered tractor is operated by two workers in this undated photograph. Upon retiring the horse and mule as major tools for agricultural work, steam tractors were an important implement for early farmers. Local foundries such as the one located in Gaffney, which was part of Union County until its integration into Cherokee County in 1897, were instrumental in repairing and maintaining local steam tractors and engines.

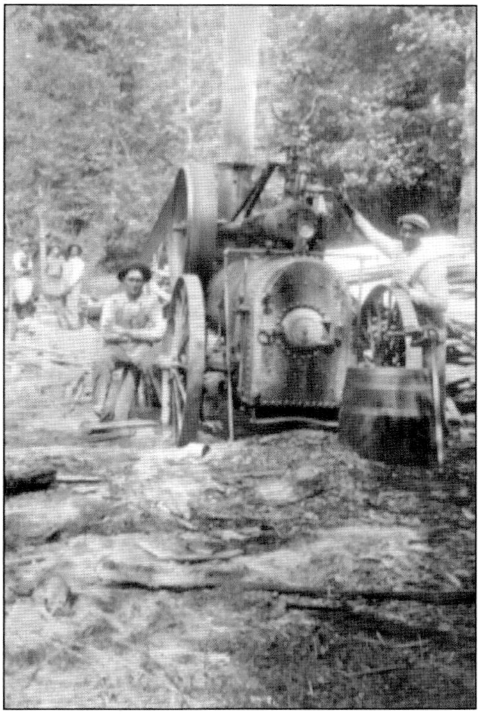

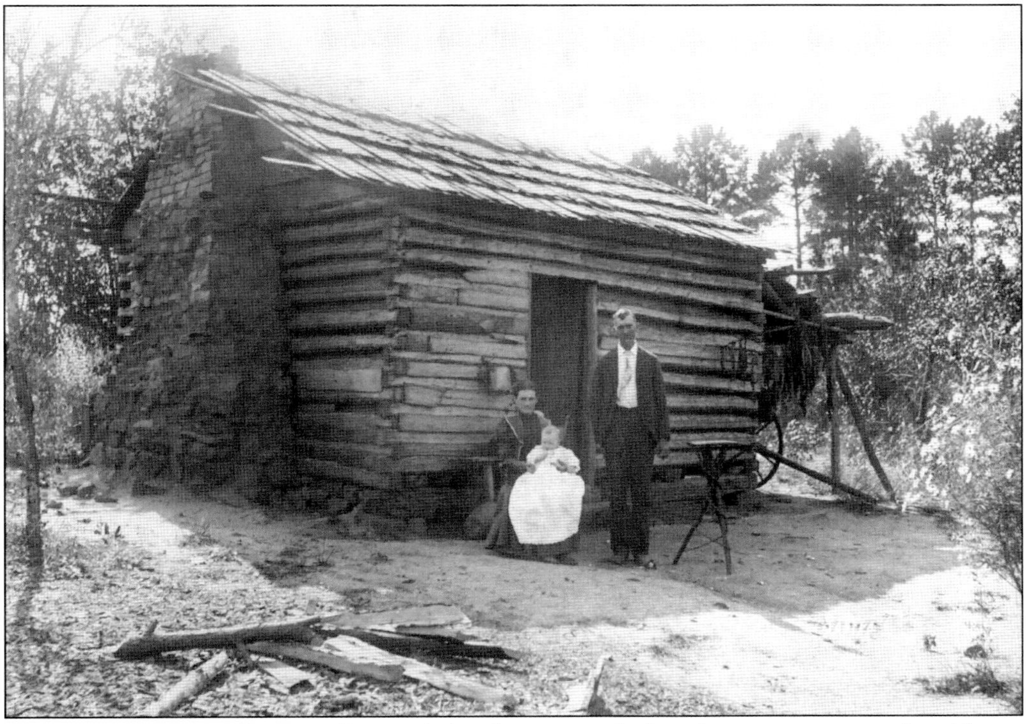

An Austere Union County Cabin. A family poses with their home, a one-story, hand-hewn log cabin. Although many intricate homes were constructed in Union, there were also numerous simpler structures. Farmers often lived without running water or electricity, and heat was provided typically from a wood-fueled fireplace or a potbellied stove.

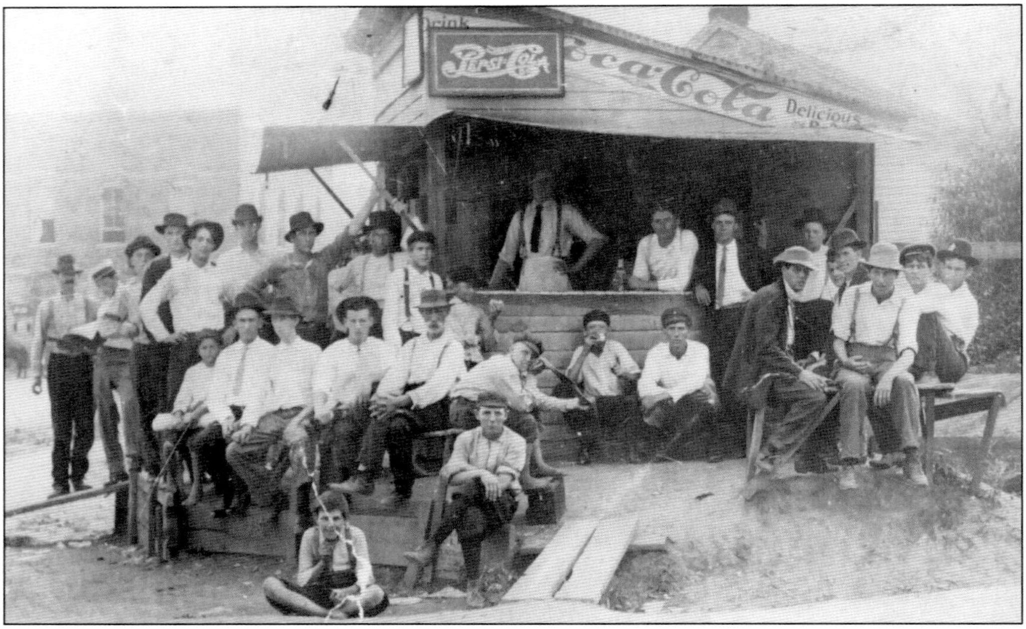

THE BUFFALO SNACK STAND. Note the early Pepsi and Coca-Cola advertisements adorning this local Buffalo Flats meeting place. Although the Coca-Cola Company had a local bottling business in Union from the early 1900s until contemporary times, Pepsi's Union Bottle Company was short lived. It is believed that the Union Pepsi Company was active just prior to the beginning of World War I, and its business operations ceased around peacetime in 1918.

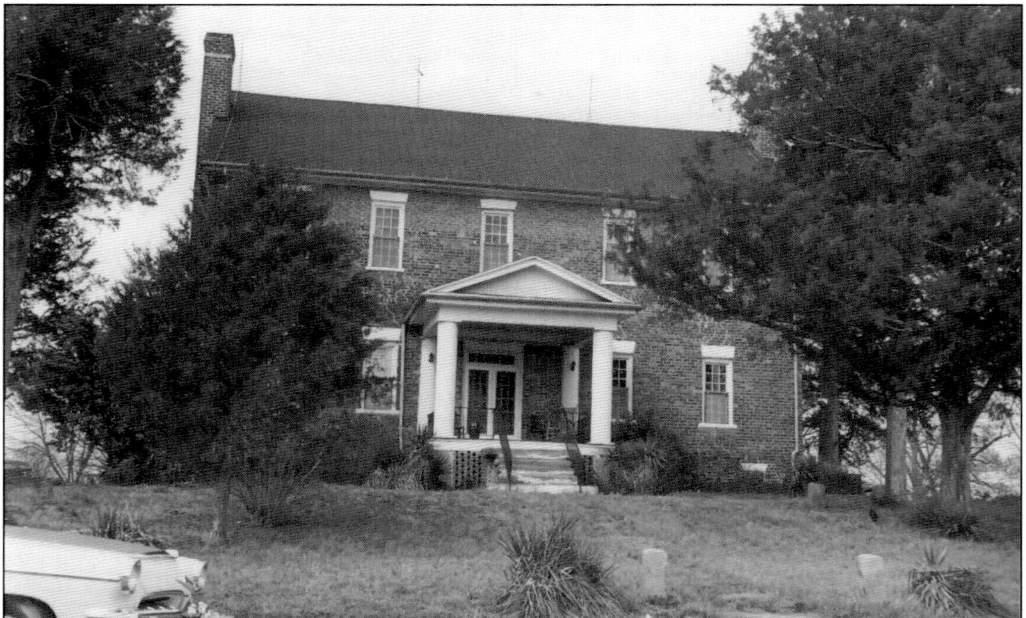

THE CROSS KEYS HOUSE. The 1886 Charleston earthquake severely damaged the Cross Keys House. The tremors were experienced in the Upstate, mostly through the collapse of numerous brick chimneys. Cross Keys is also in close proximity to a local earthquake fault, and it was near an earthquake epicenter during another quake in 1913.

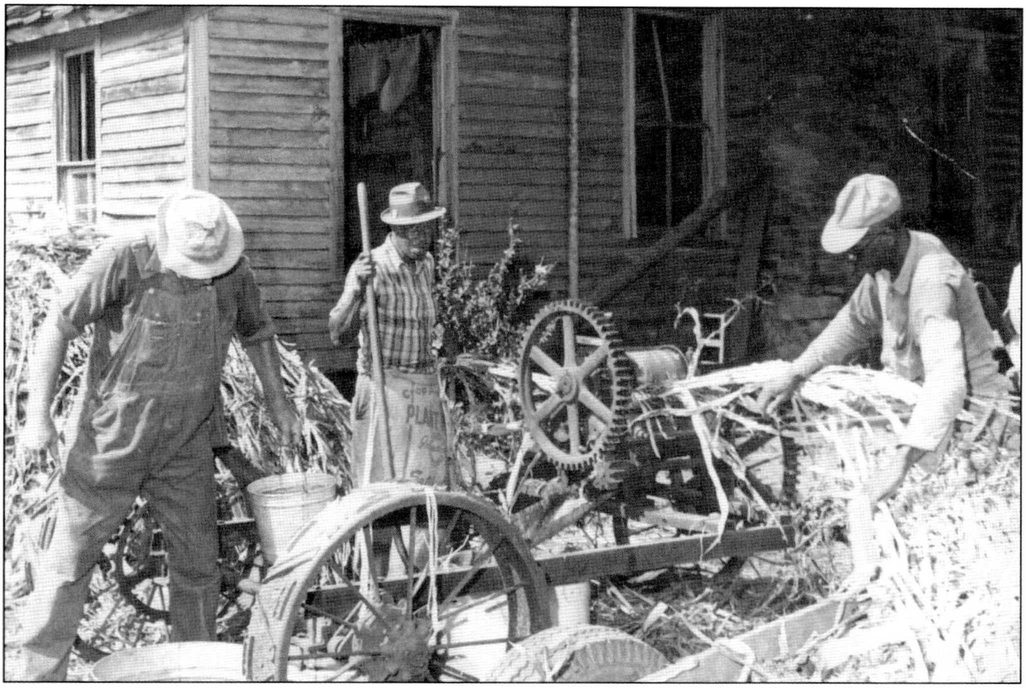

Making Molasses, c. 1975. Meador Wilburn (center, holding rake) and his men are pictured here making sorghum molasses, an early staple product produced in Union. The photograph was taken west of Lower Fairforest Baptist Church.

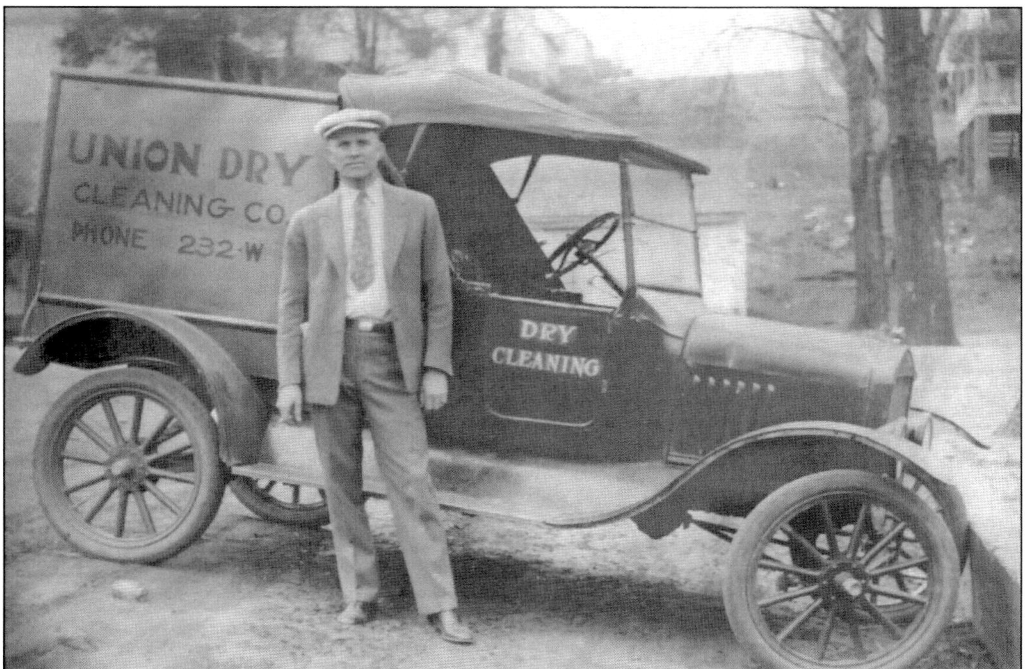

Union Dry Cleaners Truck. The Union Dry Cleaners was located at 38 East Main Street. The business maintained its own delivery truck, pictured here. The individual depicted in the photograph may be the owner of the business.

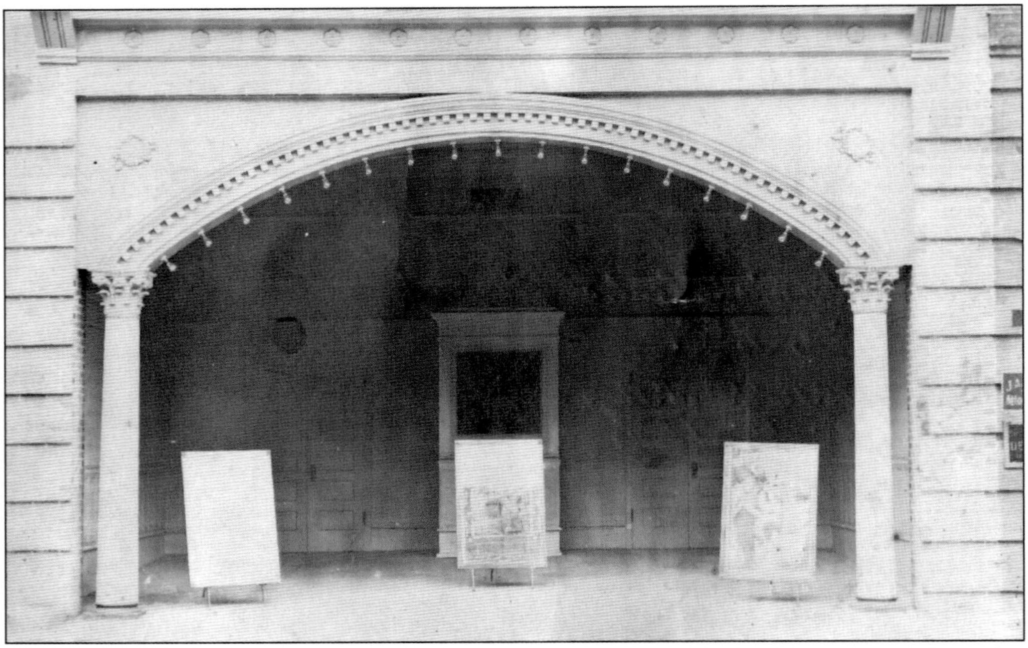

The Edisonia. The entrance to the Edisonia Theatre on Main Street was adorned with lights and a pair of Corinthian columns. Union's first theater, pictured in this postcard, opened around World War I with a "Capacity 308 Seats, Good Stage, Opera Chairs, Handsomely Equipped. C.E. Storm, Manager & Owner."

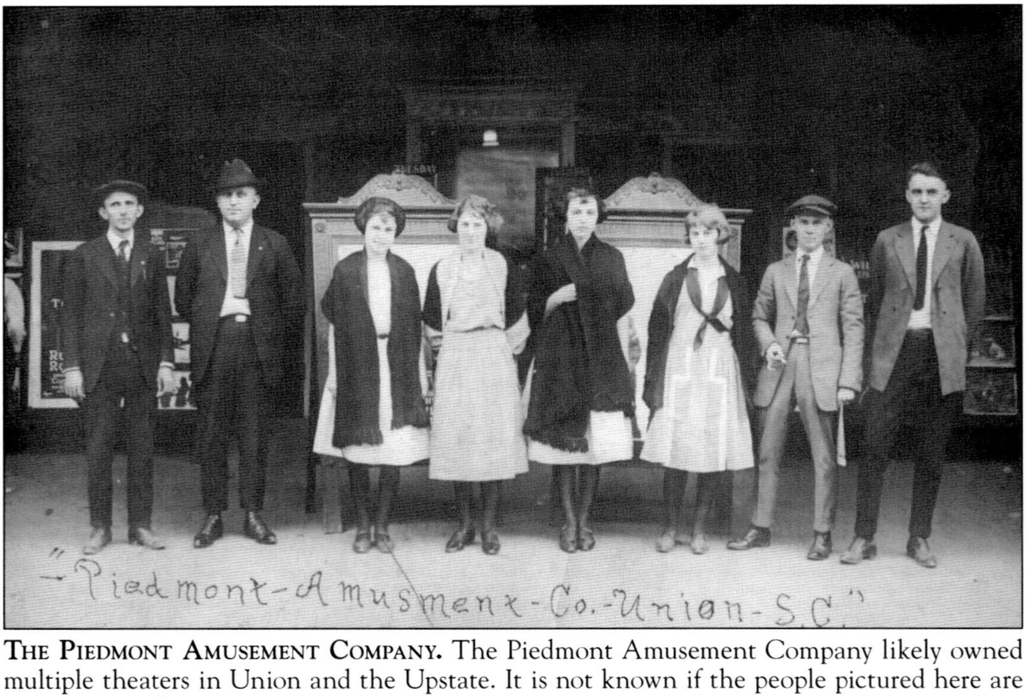

The Piedmont Amusement Company. The Piedmont Amusement Company likely owned multiple theaters in Union and the Upstate. It is not known if the people pictured here are patrons or performers.

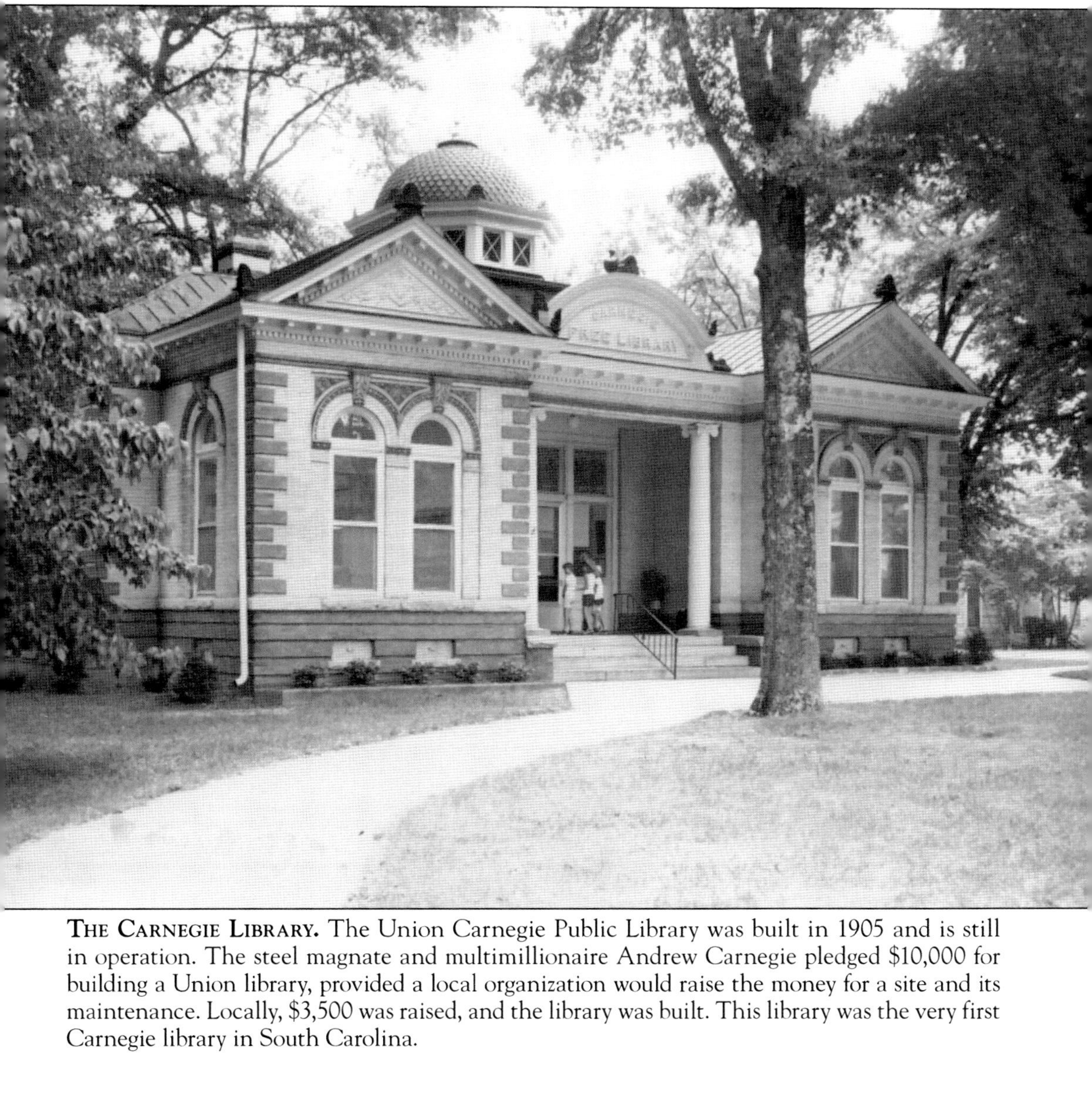

THE CARNEGIE LIBRARY. The Union Carnegie Public Library was built in 1905 and is still in operation. The steel magnate and multimillionaire Andrew Carnegie pledged $10,000 for building a Union library, provided a local organization would raise the money for a site and its maintenance. Locally, $3,500 was raised, and the library was built. This library was the very first Carnegie library in South Carolina.

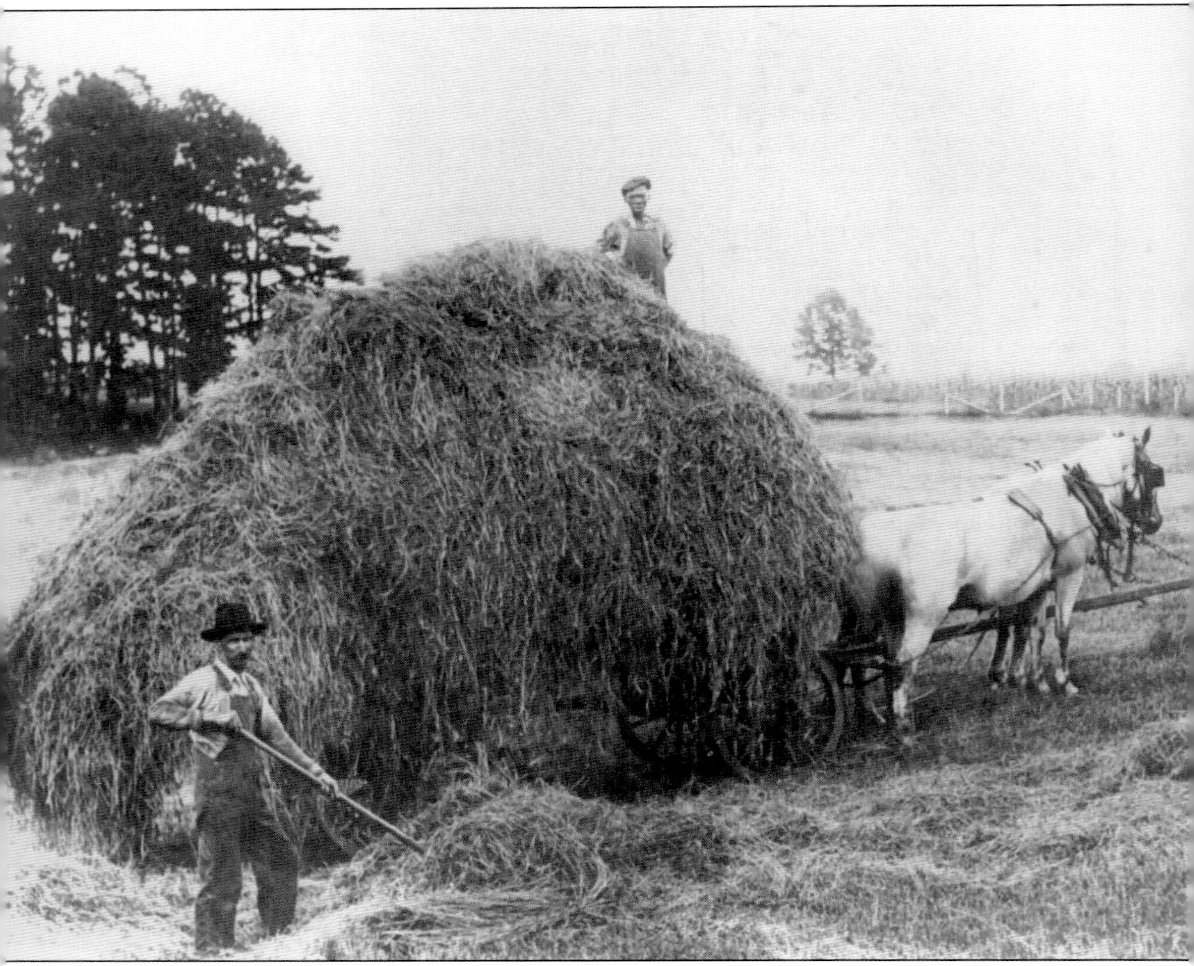

The Hay Harvest. A Union farmer and his worker, along with a horse and wagon team, harvest hay. This photograph was purportedly taken at the Fowken farm. Fowken farm was known to encompass thousands of acres near Jonesville, and it was in close proximity to the site of the original Fairforest Presbyterian Church and its cemetery.

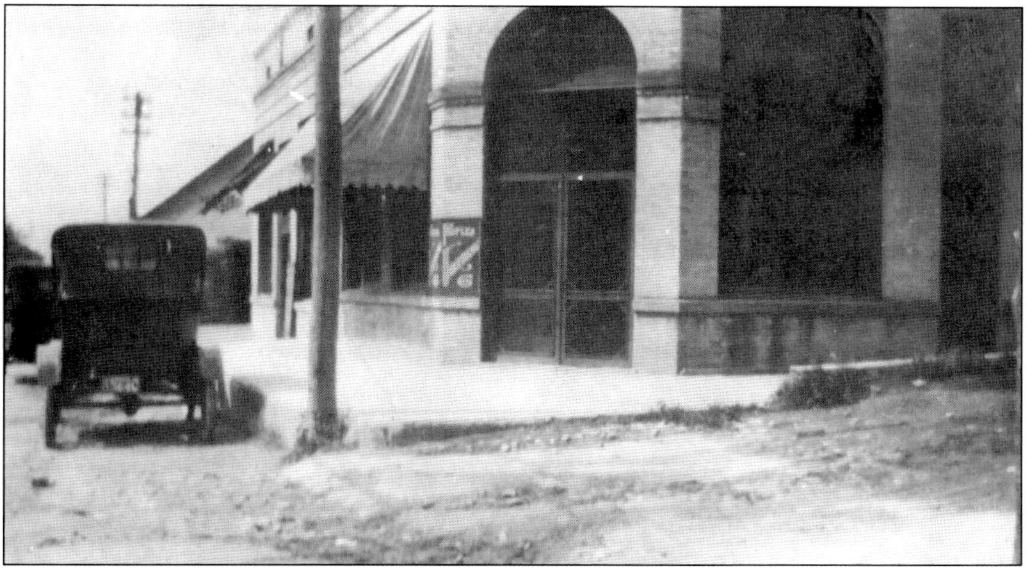

JOLLY'S MARKET. Located on Union's South Gadberry Street, Jolly's Market was a butcher shop and later a restaurant. It operated under different owners and names.

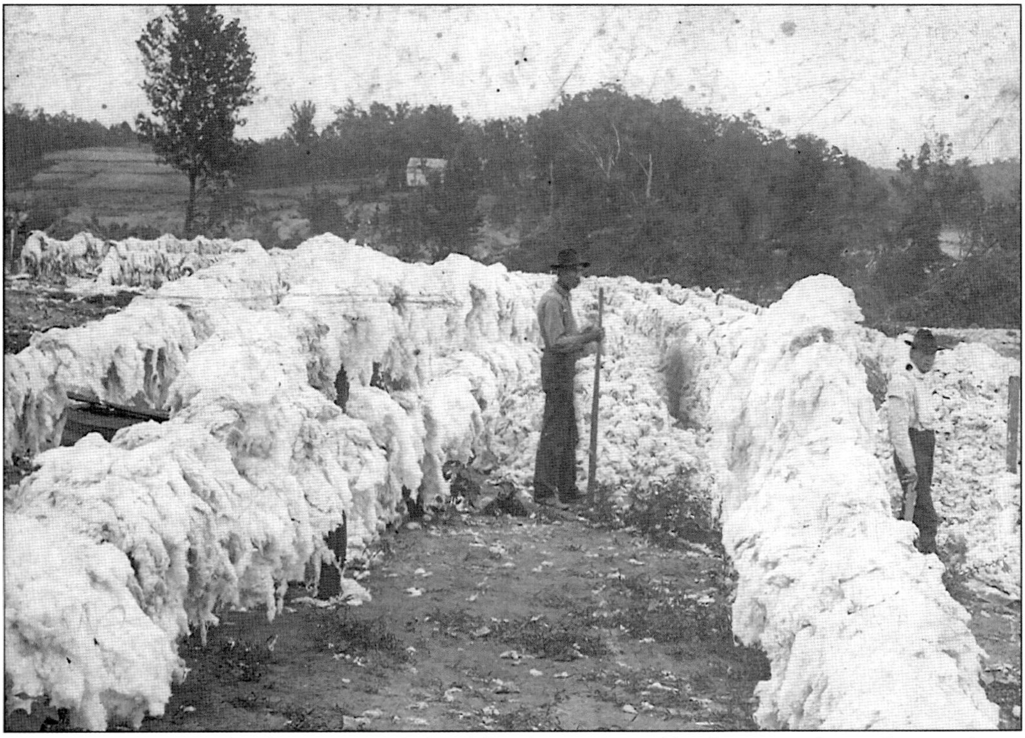

THE GREAT FLOOD. The destruction of a local flood is evidenced by the cotton littered everywhere. There have been many damaging floods originating from the Broad River and its tributaries. Floods wiped out the first Pinckneyville and ravaged local mills built close to the river.

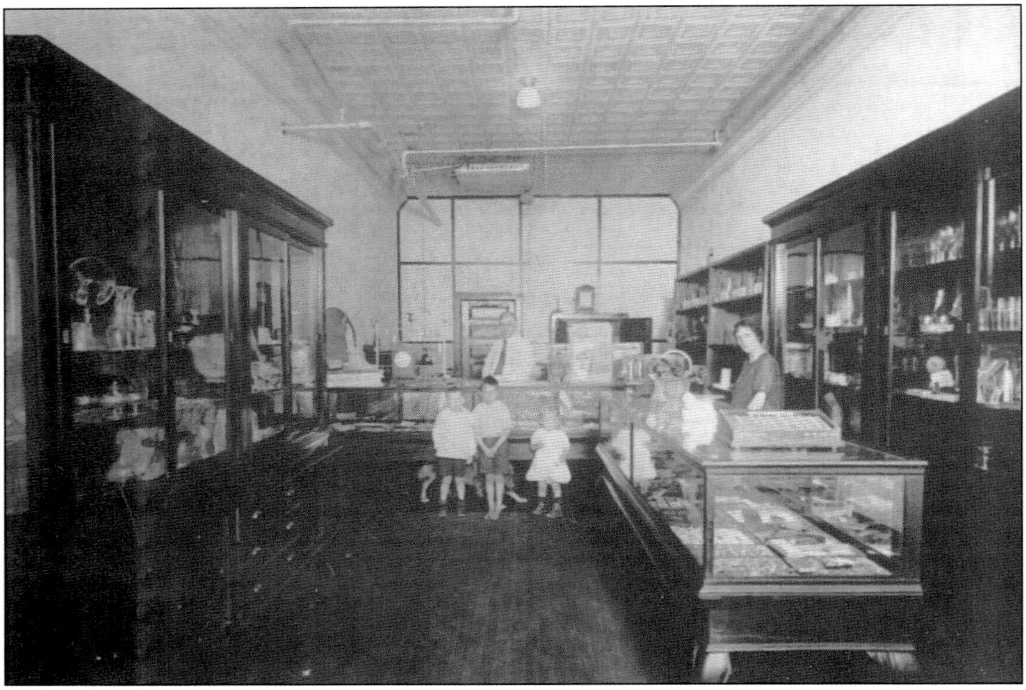

Watts Jewelry Store. The interior of Watts Jewelry Store shows all manner of exquisite goods, which were sold on Main Street. A Mrs. Watts is behind the counter, and her children pose in the center of the showroom.

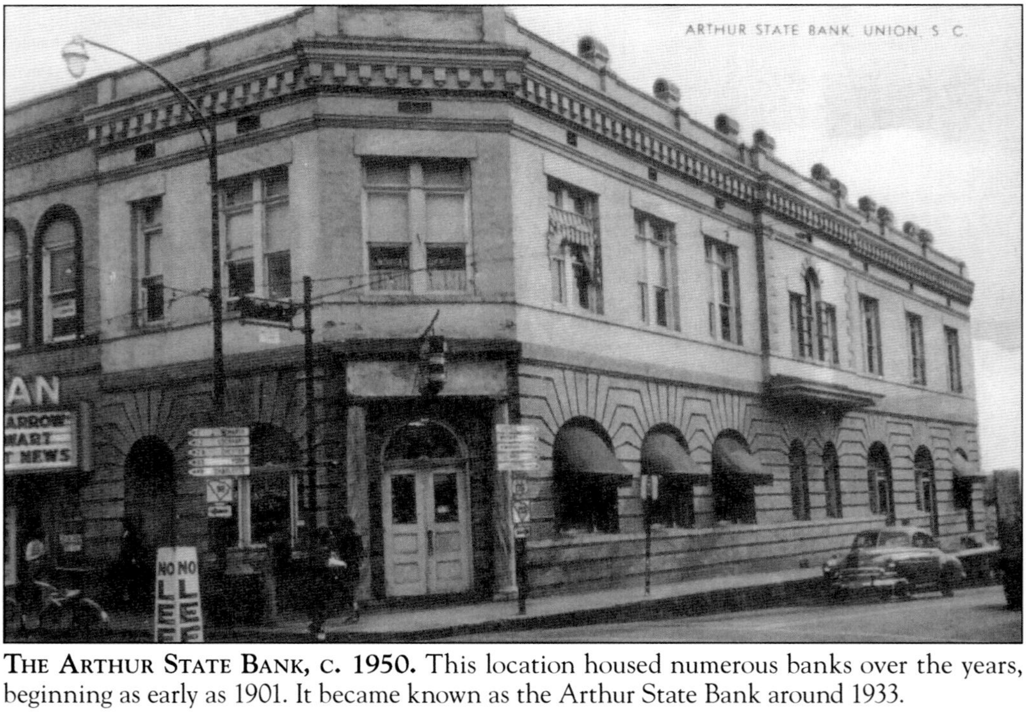

The Arthur State Bank, c. 1950. This location housed numerous banks over the years, beginning as early as 1901. It became known as the Arthur State Bank around 1933.

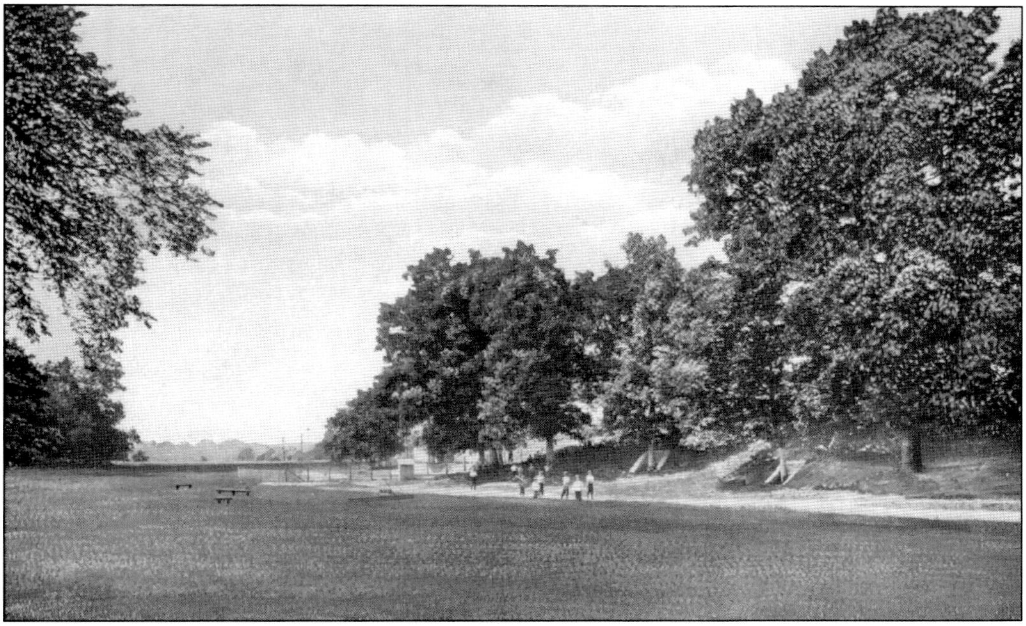

The City Park. An early postcard of City Park shows off its playground. Although it already existed as a private park, the city purchased approximately eight acres in 1913 to bring it under its jurisdiction. The Union Mill's sports teams used this park.

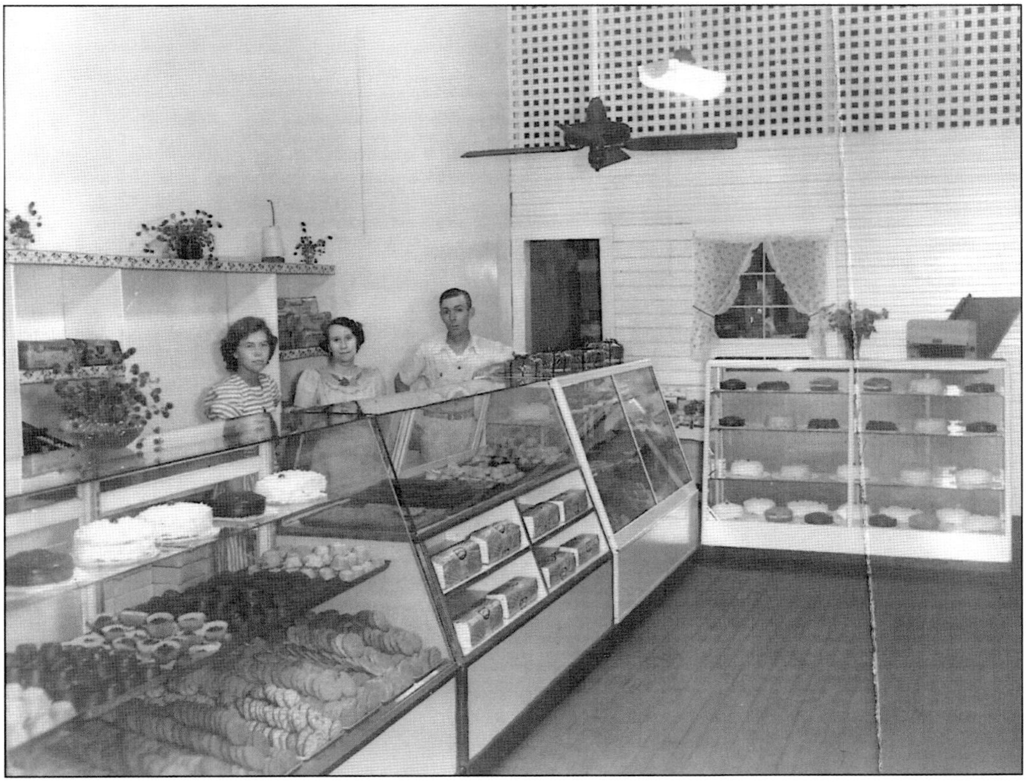

Aunt Harriet's Bakery. Aunt Harriet's Bakery is located in the 100 block of West Main Street on the south side. Aunt Harriet is pictured here between two of her employees.

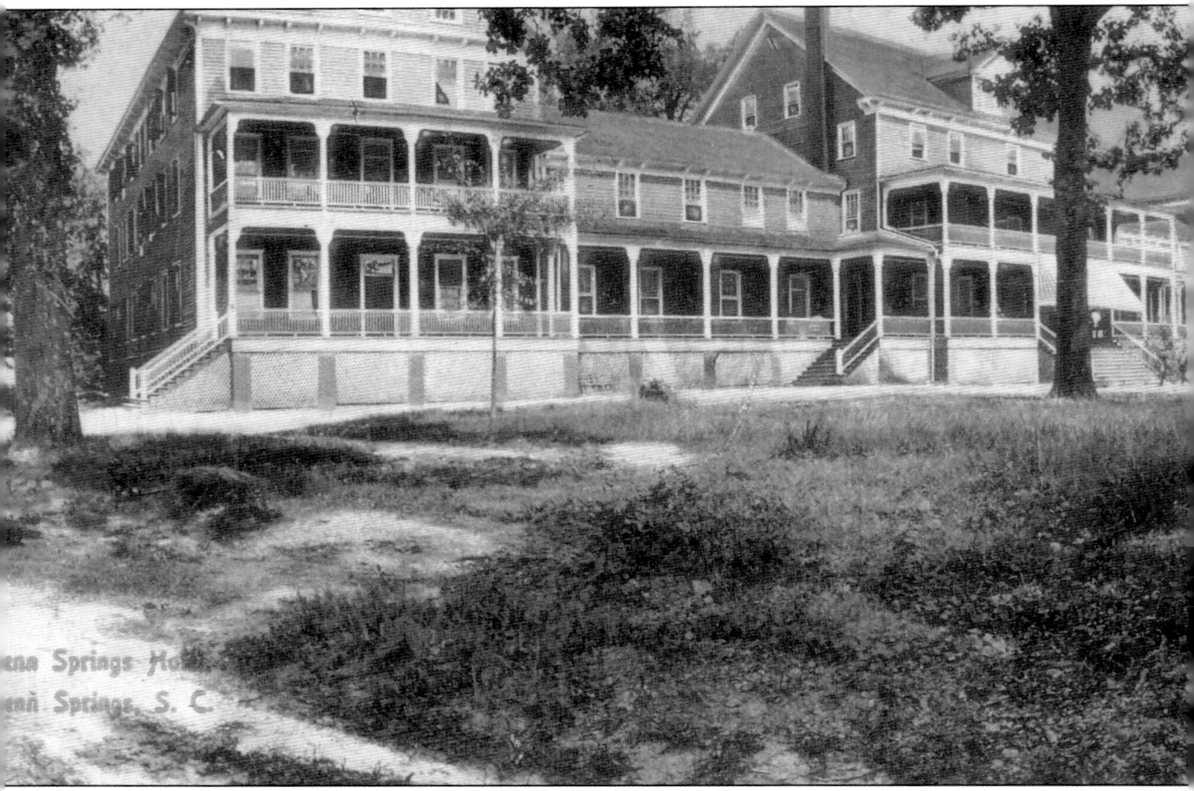

THE GLENN SPRINGS HOTEL, C. 1909. A panorama double postcard of the Glenn Springs Hotel is pictured here. Although Glenn Springs is not located in Union County, many residents sought employment there, and numerous festivities and dances were held at the hotel. The property

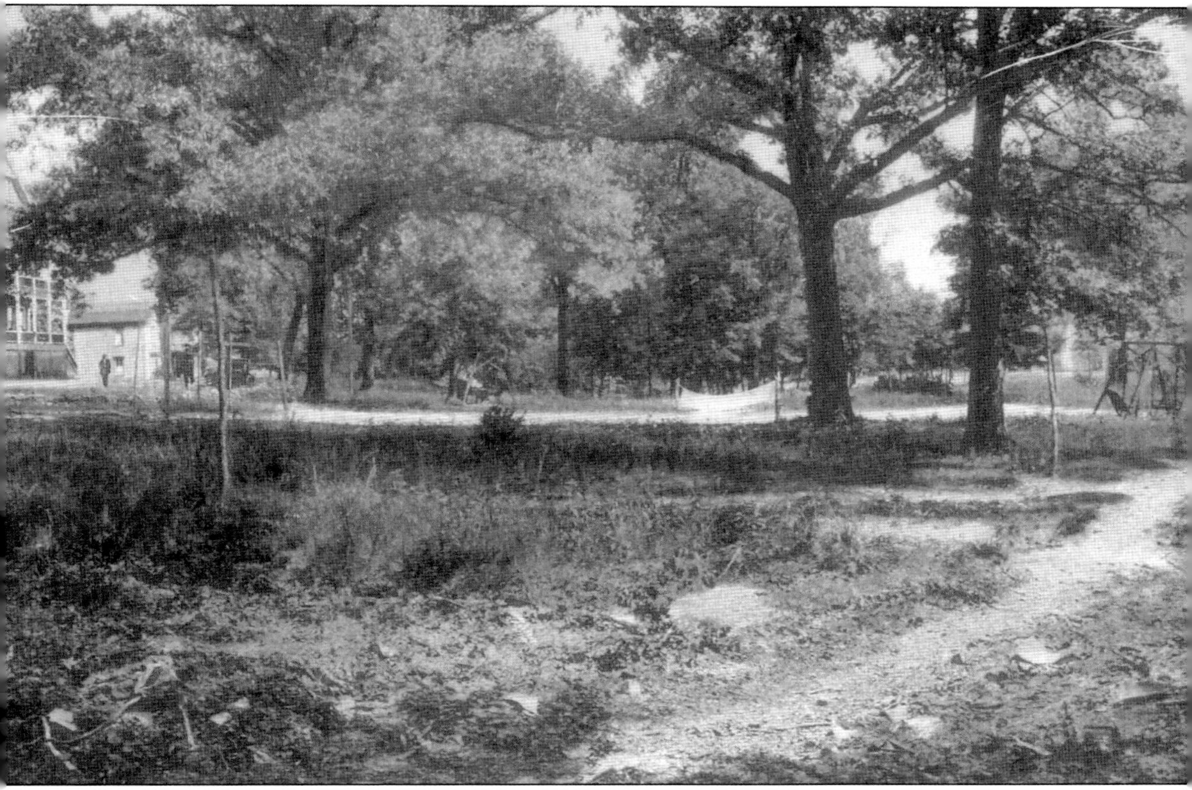

consisted of a hotel, spa, and spring water bottling company. A huge structure at 58,000 square feet, the hotel was in operation from 1836 until it burned down in 1941.

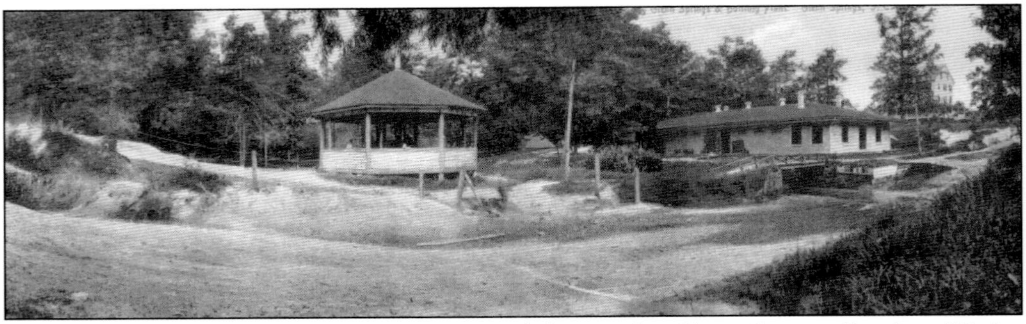

THE BOTTLING WORKS. Another rare postcard depicts the Glenn Springs Bottling Works. Glenn Springs manufactured bottles in numerous sizes, and their bottles are a popular local collectible.

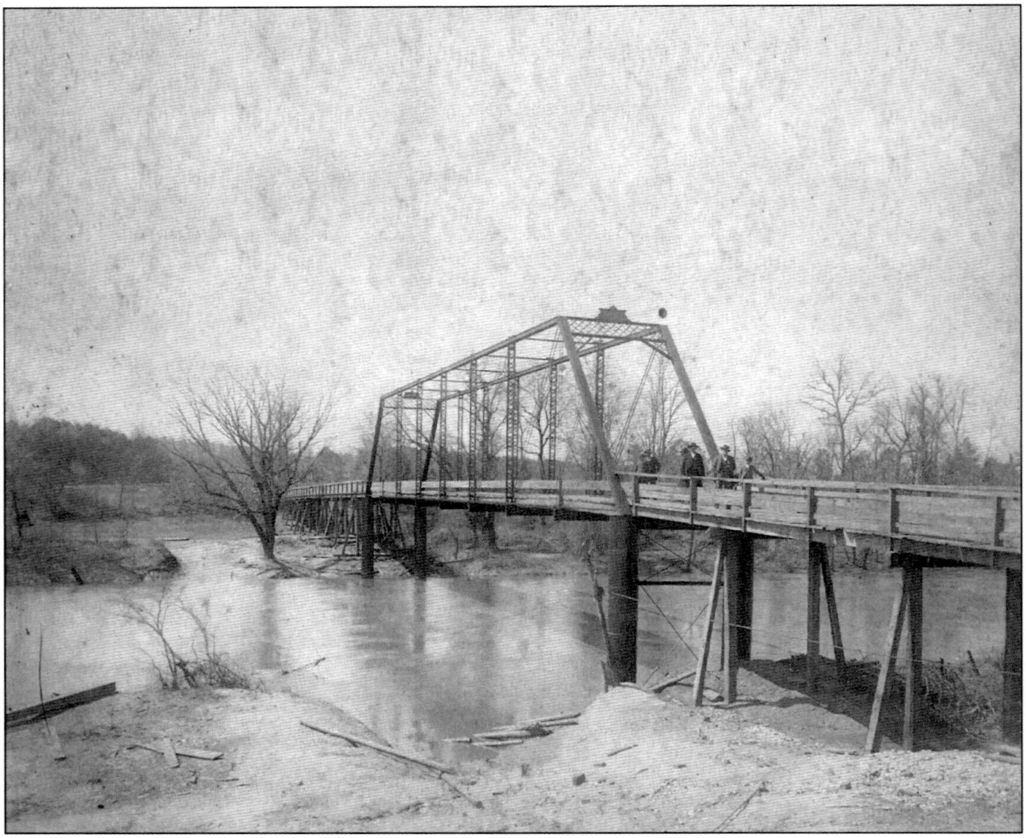

THE BEATY BRIDGE. The Beaty Bridge spanned from Union to Whitmire on Route 176. The road has changed, and a new bridge has subsequently been built to replace this 19th-century structure.

The Monarch Drugstore. Children line up, waiting for their favorite goodies from their local merchant. The Monarch Drugstore was a popular local meeting place.

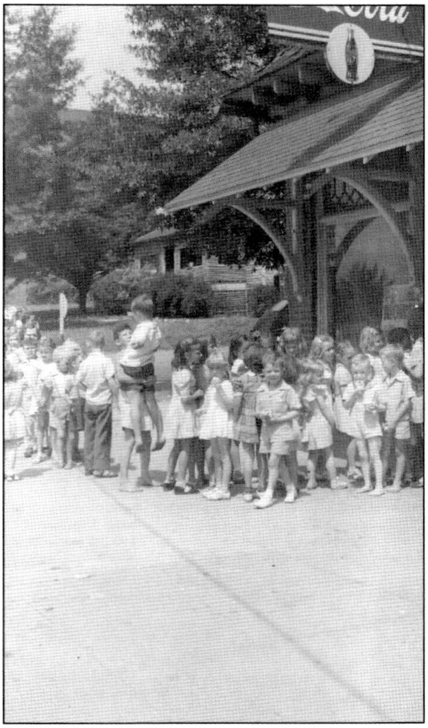

M.W. Bobo's Department Store, c. 1902. Located on Main Street, Bobo's original store was founded in Sedalia. The Bobos owned and operated a store before the outbreak of the Civil War.

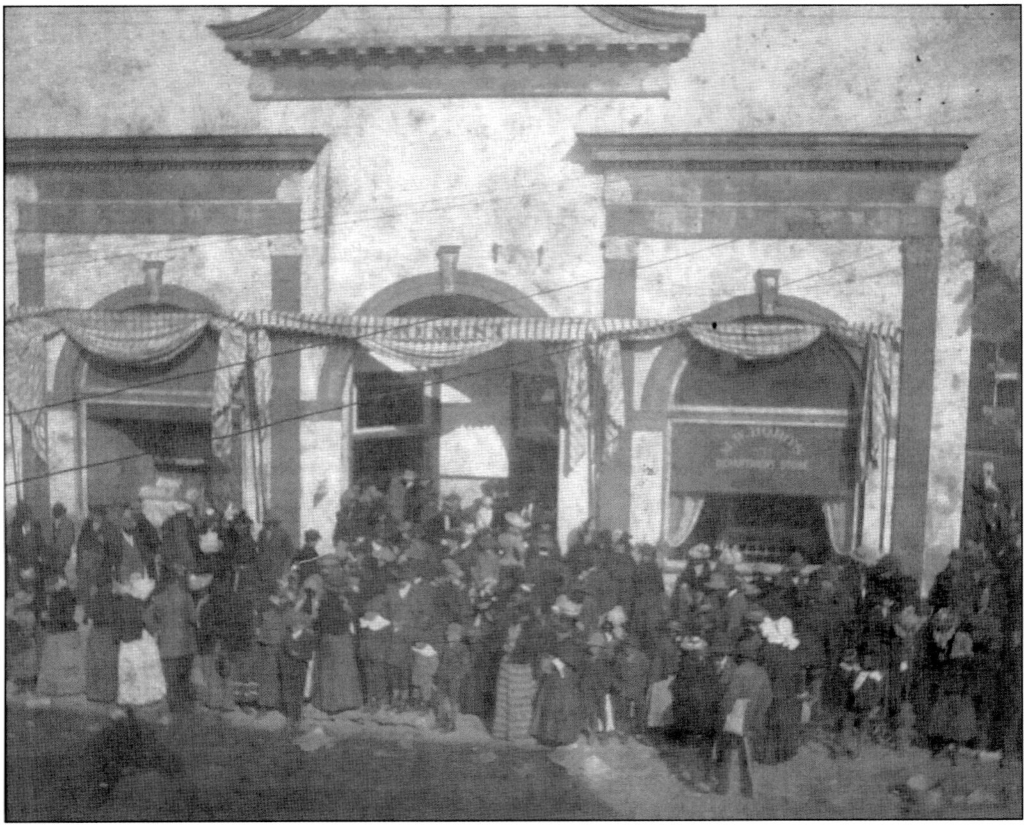

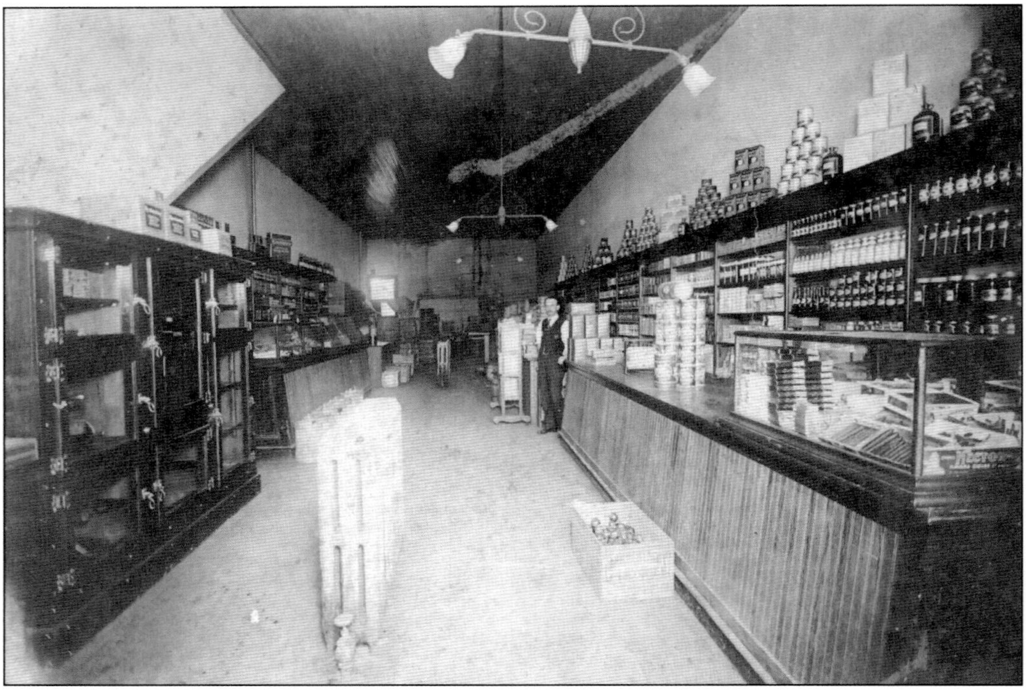

Interior of C.B. Sparks Store. Pictured here in the late 1910s, numerous sole proprietors operated their own businesses in early Union. Like many other enterprises in early Union, Sparks was a sole proprietor whose business shared his name. Dry goods and grocery stores flourished with the development of local mills, whose workers frequented them.

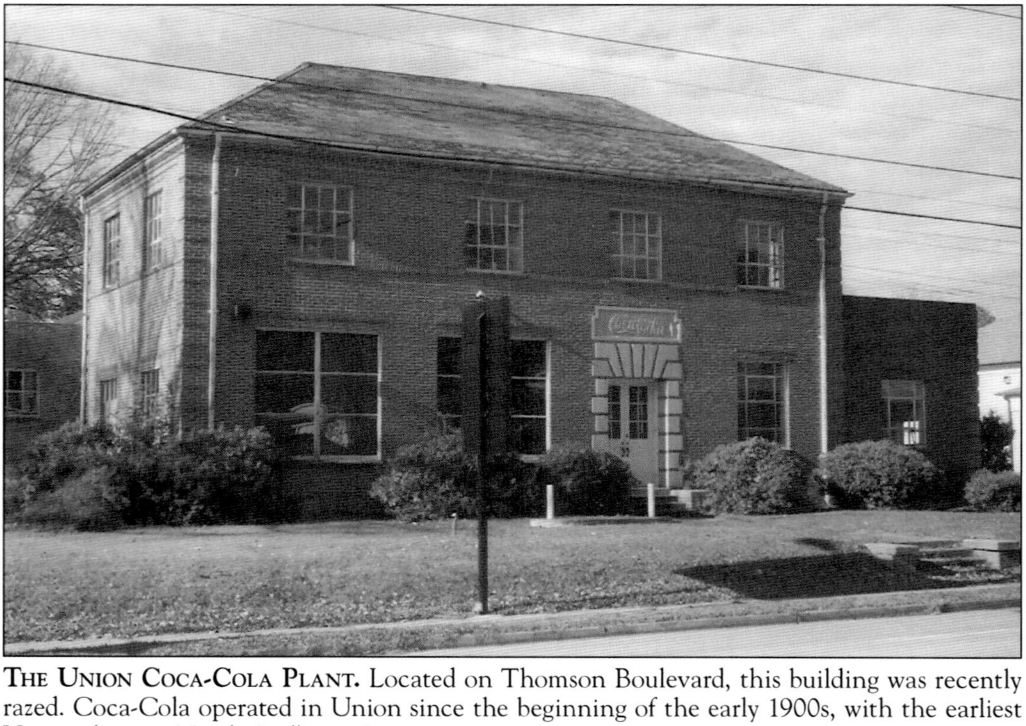

The Union Coca-Cola Plant. Located on Thomson Boulevard, this building was recently razed. Coca-Cola operated in Union since the beginning of the early 1900s, with the earliest Union plant on North Gadberry Street.

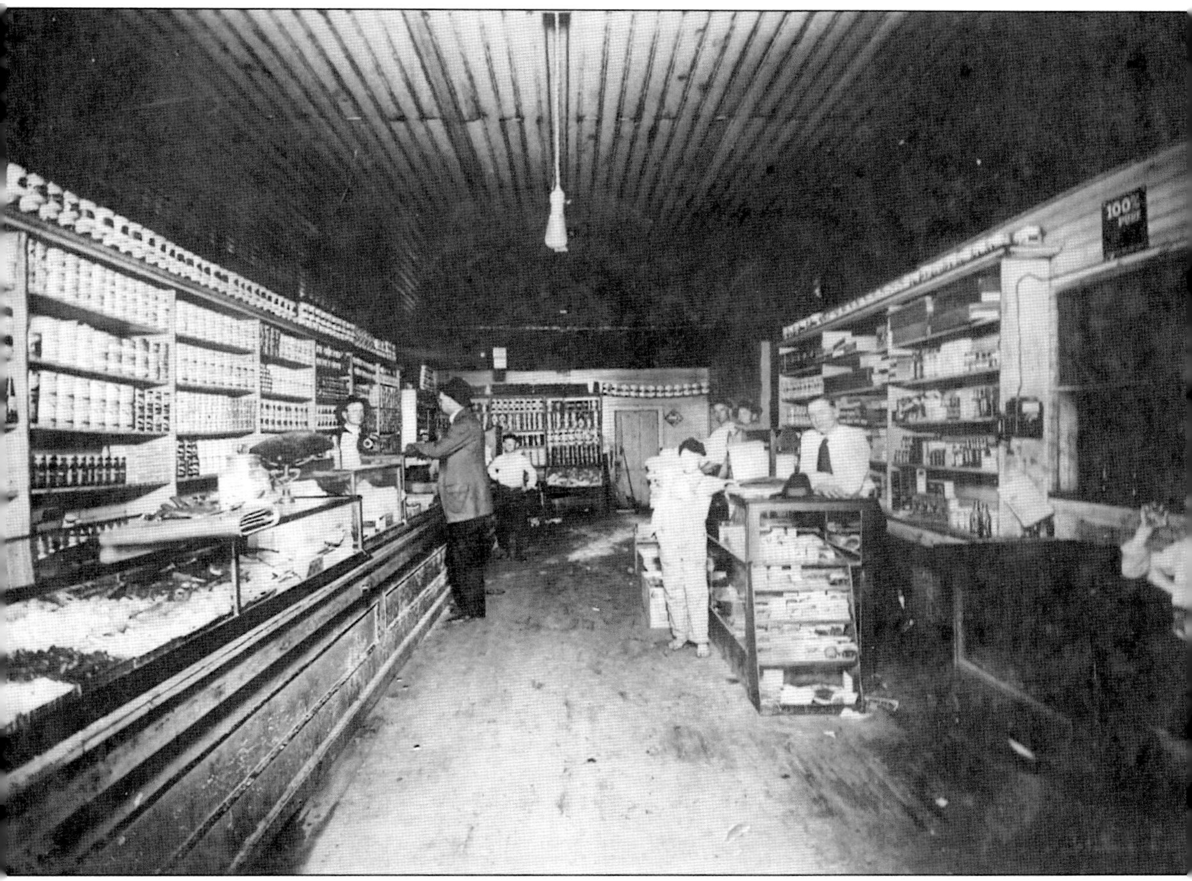

The Godshall Store. Ernie Godshall is pictured here on the right. With the development of many new textile mills, workers had money to spend with local merchants, and these businesses flourished. Godshall was a victim of the 1918 flu epidemic, which unfortunately took his life in December of that year.

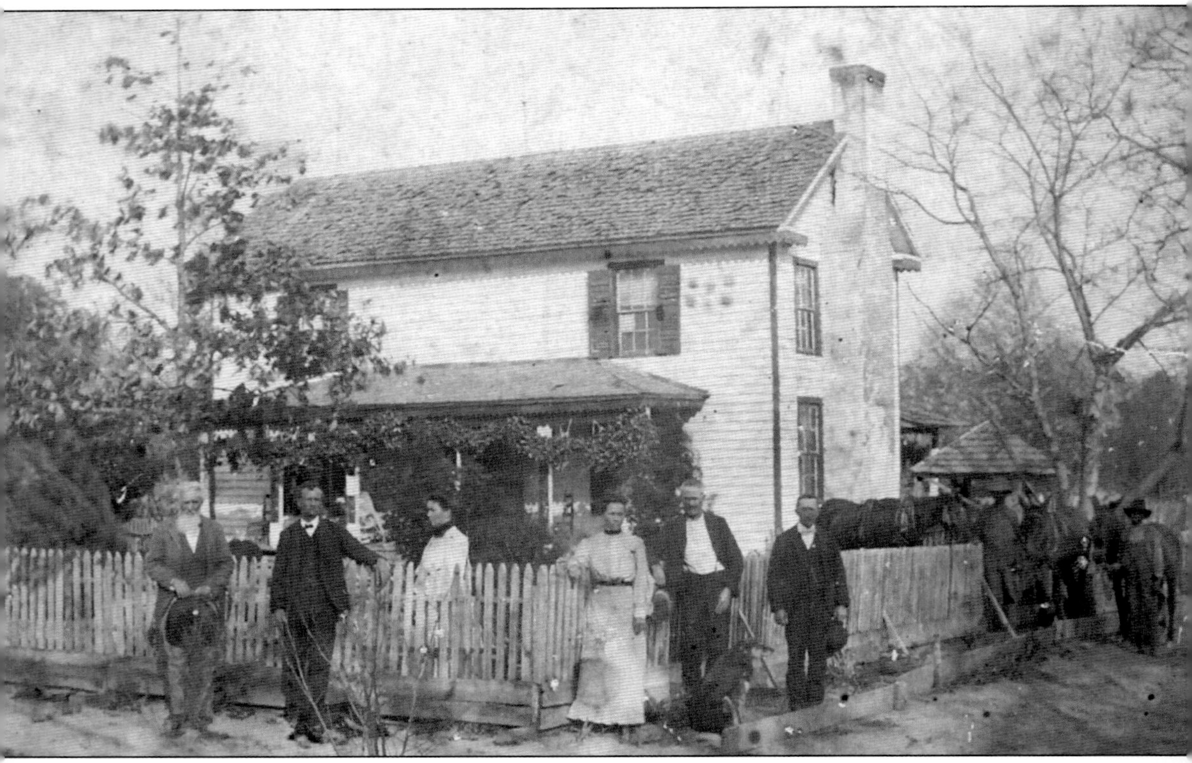

The Gault Home Place. In the Pea Ridge Community, many Gaults recognize this home as their ancestral homestead. With farmers and war heroes as their kin, the Gaults had a tremendously large family in Union, and there are multiple Gault family cemeteries located throughout the county.

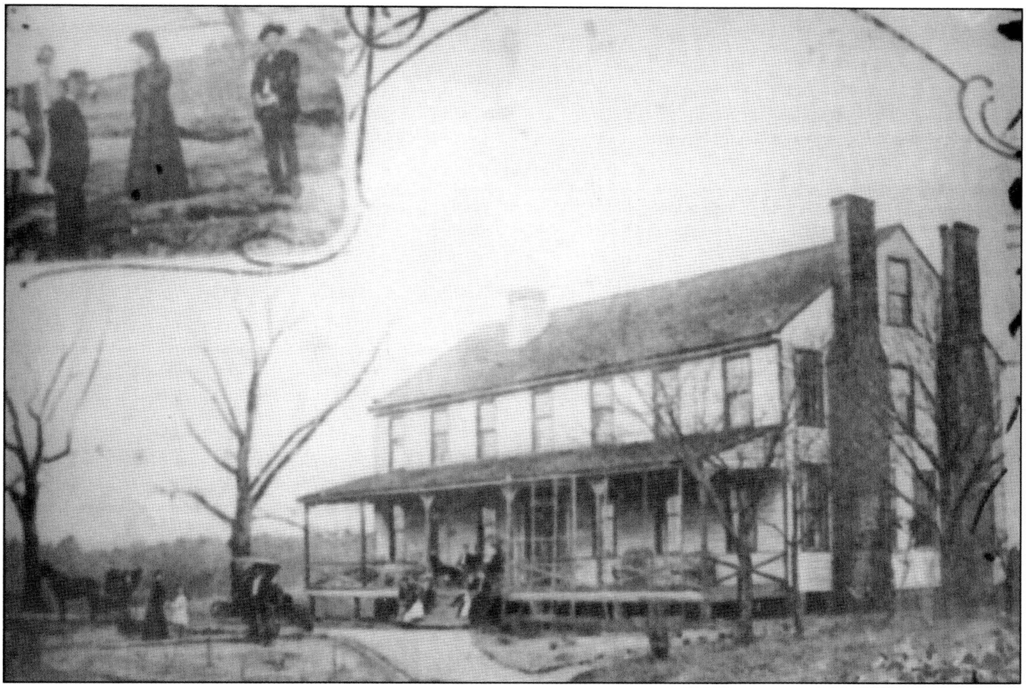

The West Springs Hotel. This image was part of an advertisement for the resort. Announcing that it was open for business in July 1854, the resort touted the water from its nearby spring as a healthy elixir for many physical ailments.

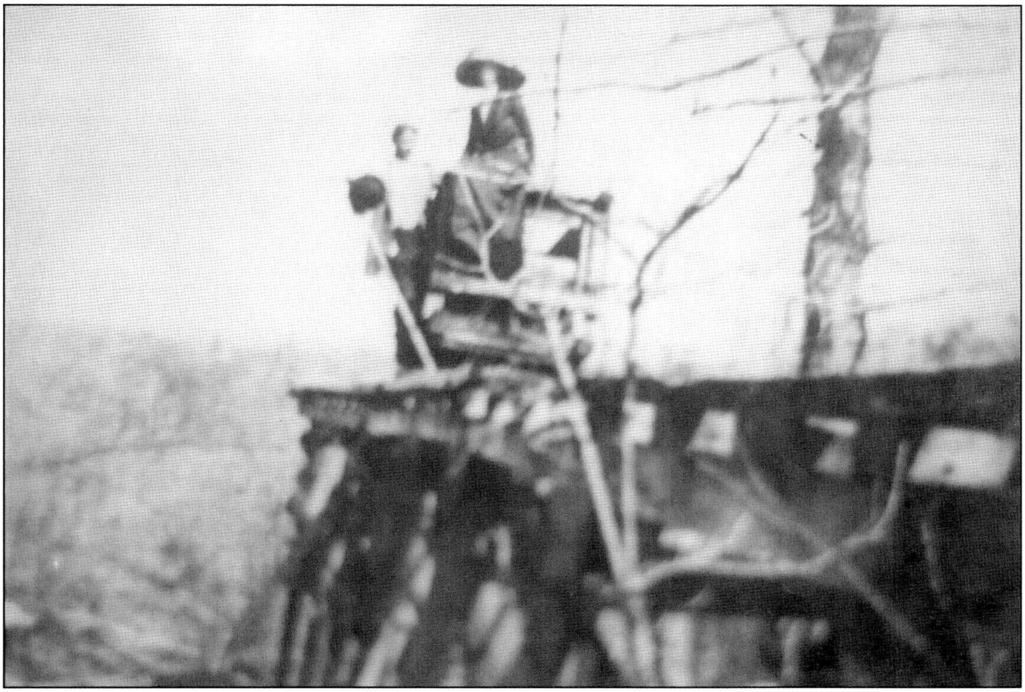

West Spring Gold Mine. A mine car with its leisurely passengers makes its way across a trestle at the West Springs mine. Gold was found in the West Springs community in the early 1800s, giving rise to numerous mines that speckled the area up to the Spartanburg County line.

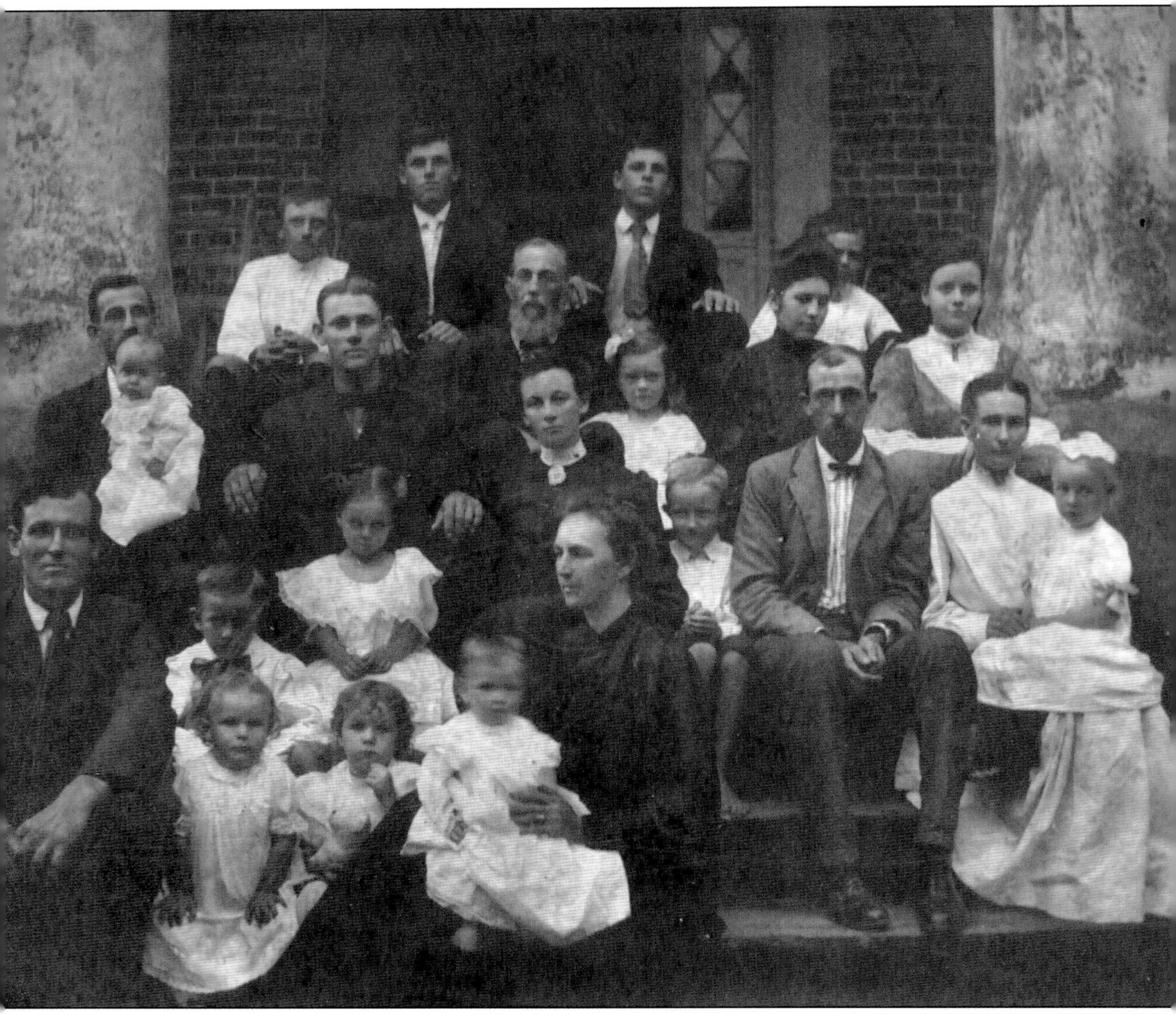

The Meador Family. The Meador family poses for a photograph on the stairs of the Meador Plantation House. With its imposing two-story columns (just visible in the photograph) and Palladian windows, the home was built for John Meador in 1852. At the end of the Civil War, the home became a haven for discouraged Confederate soldiers wandering home on foot through South Carolina.

Three

Local Parades and Celebrations

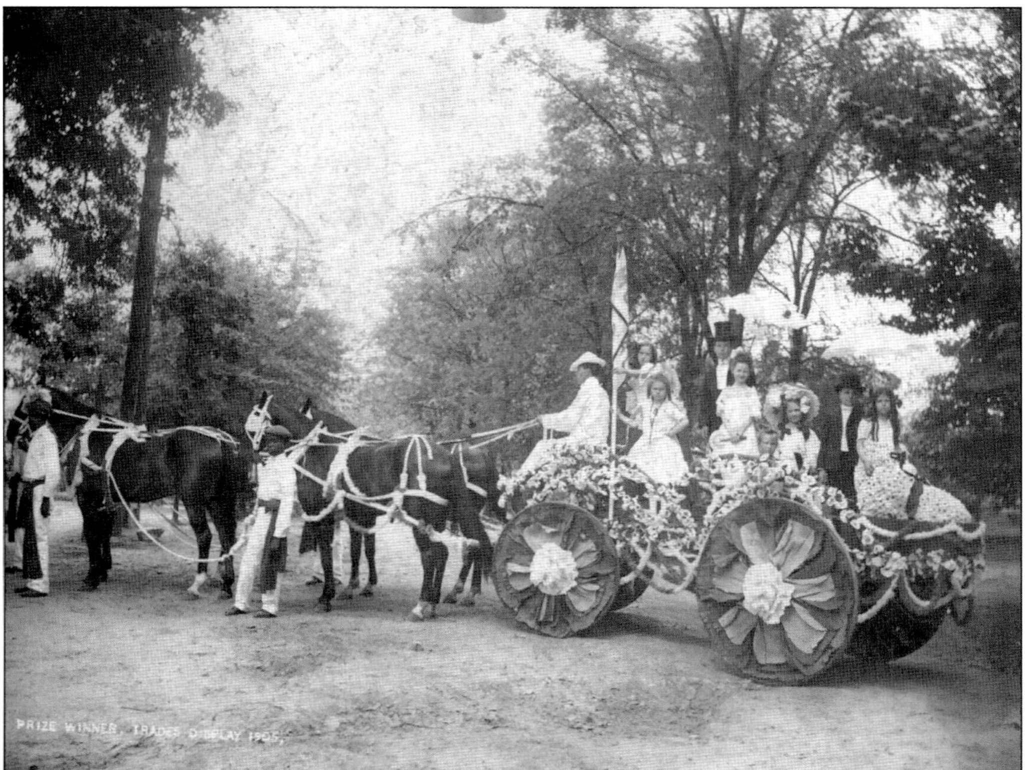

Flower Day Parade, c. 1905. The Union Flower Day Parade had numerous entrants, including this fine carriage of well-dressed young folks. This was an annual parade, and many businesses and individuals took part in the parade competition to win awards. Fireworks and a barbecue were also part of this fun annual event.

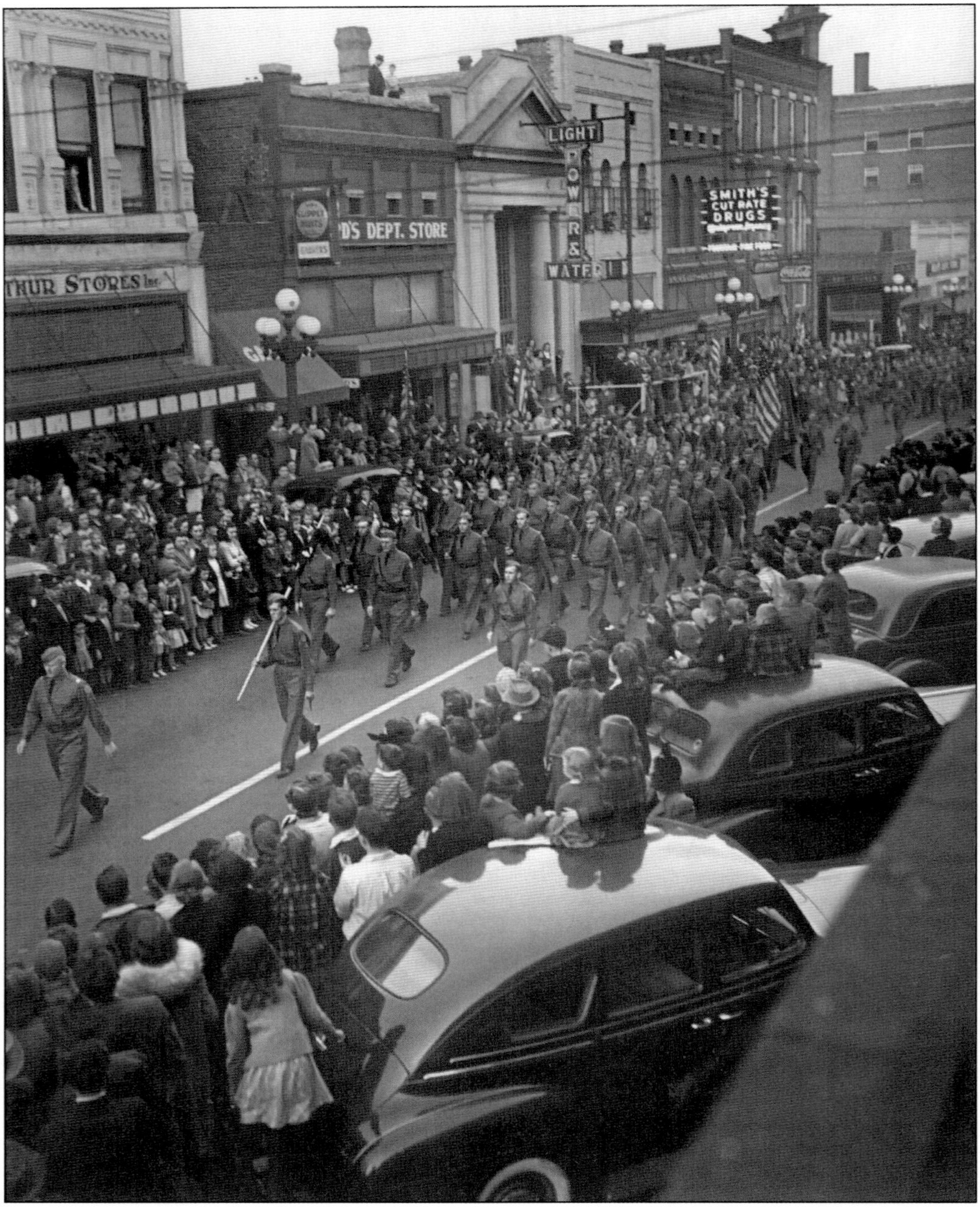

WORLD WAR II PARADE. In this Main Street World War II patriotic parade, Sheriff G. Frank Vaughan, in military attire, leads the Union Home Guard as it marches down the street. The Light, Power, and Water Building (center)—currently Smith's Jeweler's—retains its original two columns in this photograph.

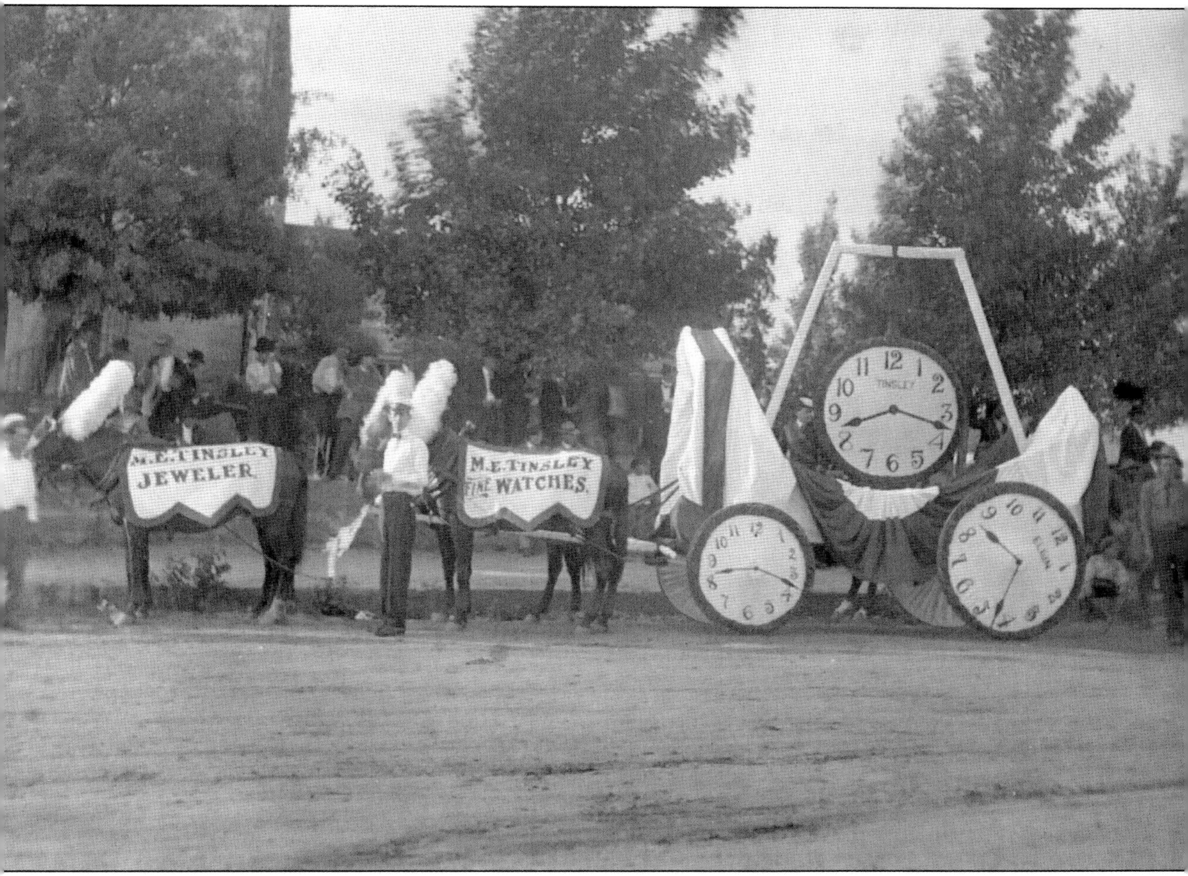

The Parade Winner, 1905. Tinsley's Jewelry parade carriage is depicted as the 1905 Floral Festival parade winner. Carriages were adorned with live flowers and other decorations.

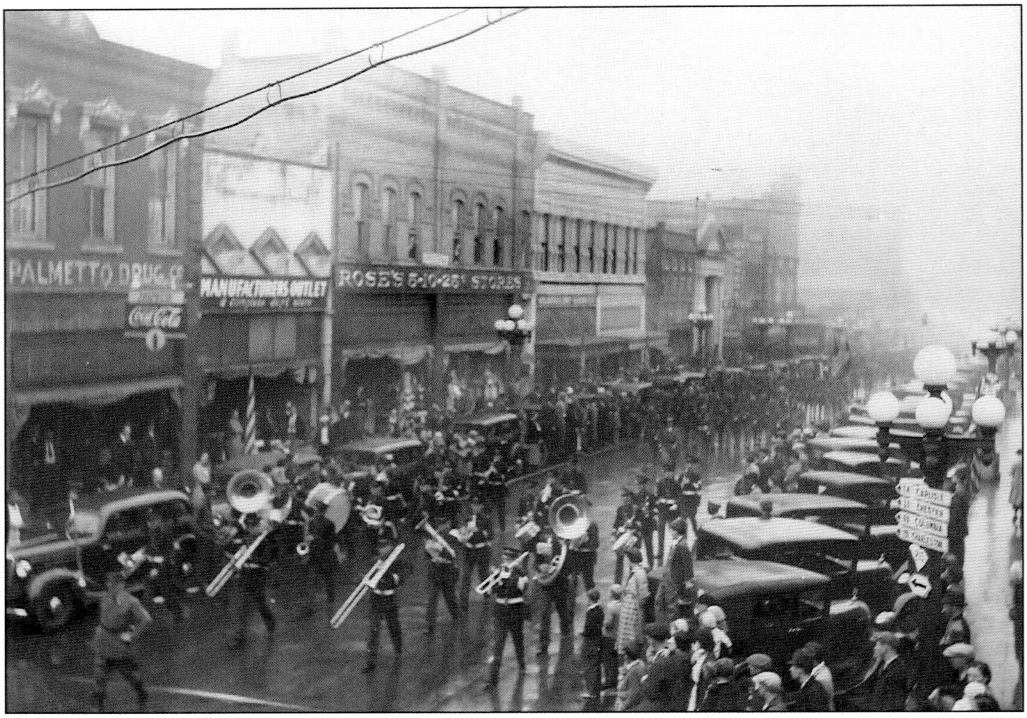

VETERANS DAY CELEBRATION. A Veterans Day parade pushes its way down Main Street. Worthy of notice are the following businesses, Rose's five-and-dime and the Palmetto drugstore.

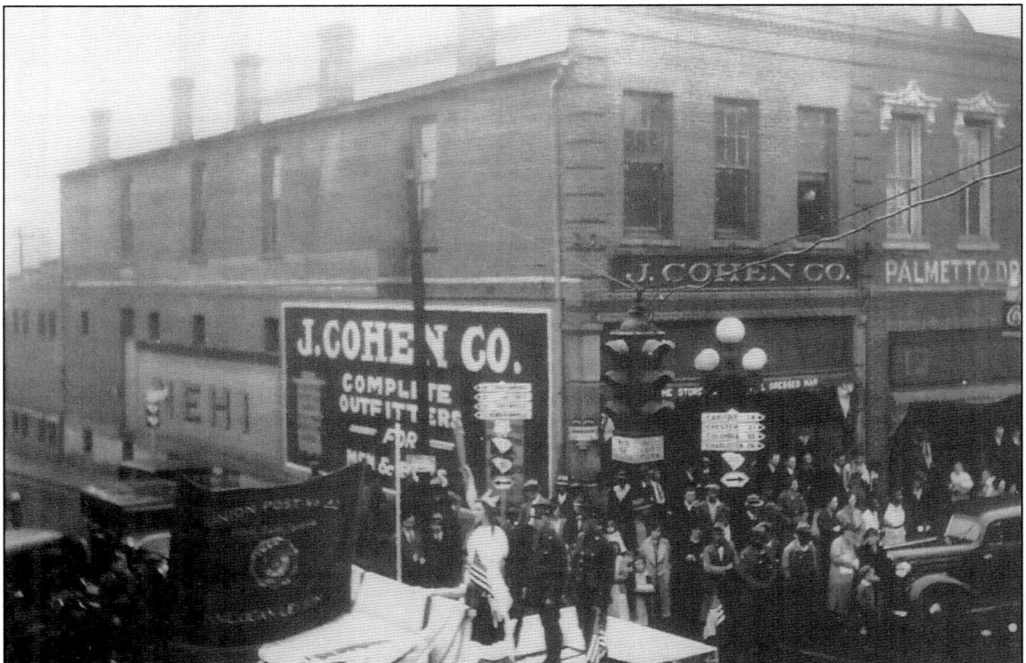

THE AMERICAN LEGION. An American Legion float is pictured here participating in a parade in front of the J. Cohen clothing store. The local American Legion post in Union was Post No. 22, and its headquarters had been in Veterans Park.

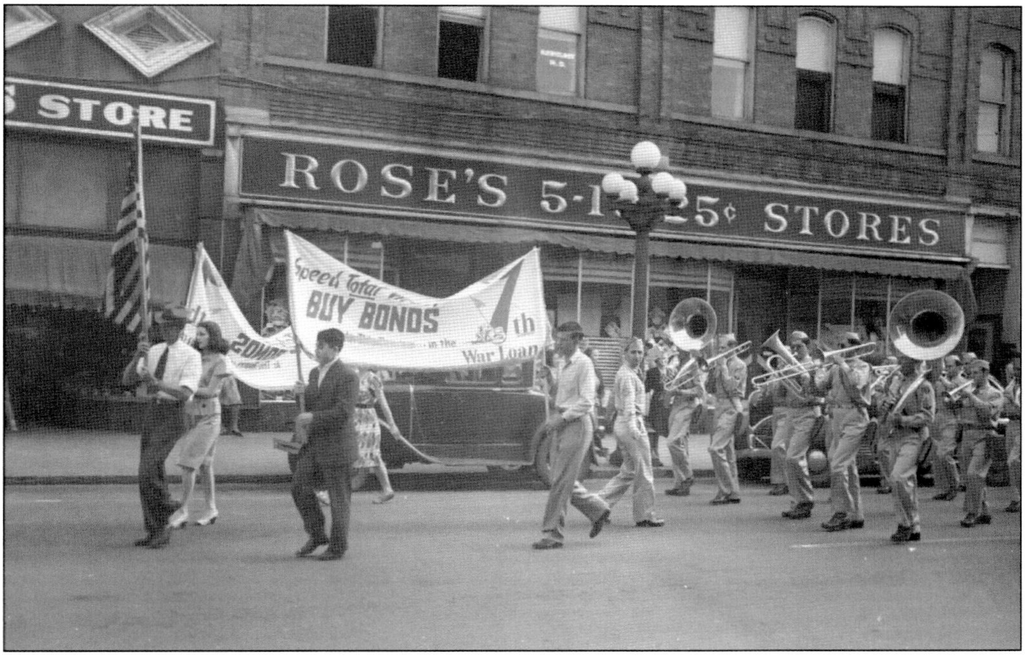

The Seventh War Loan. A 1944 war bond rally parade for the Seventh War Loan makes its way down Main Street. Ed Blackwell of the draft board leads the parade, as he proudly carries the American flag. War bonds financed both World War I and II.

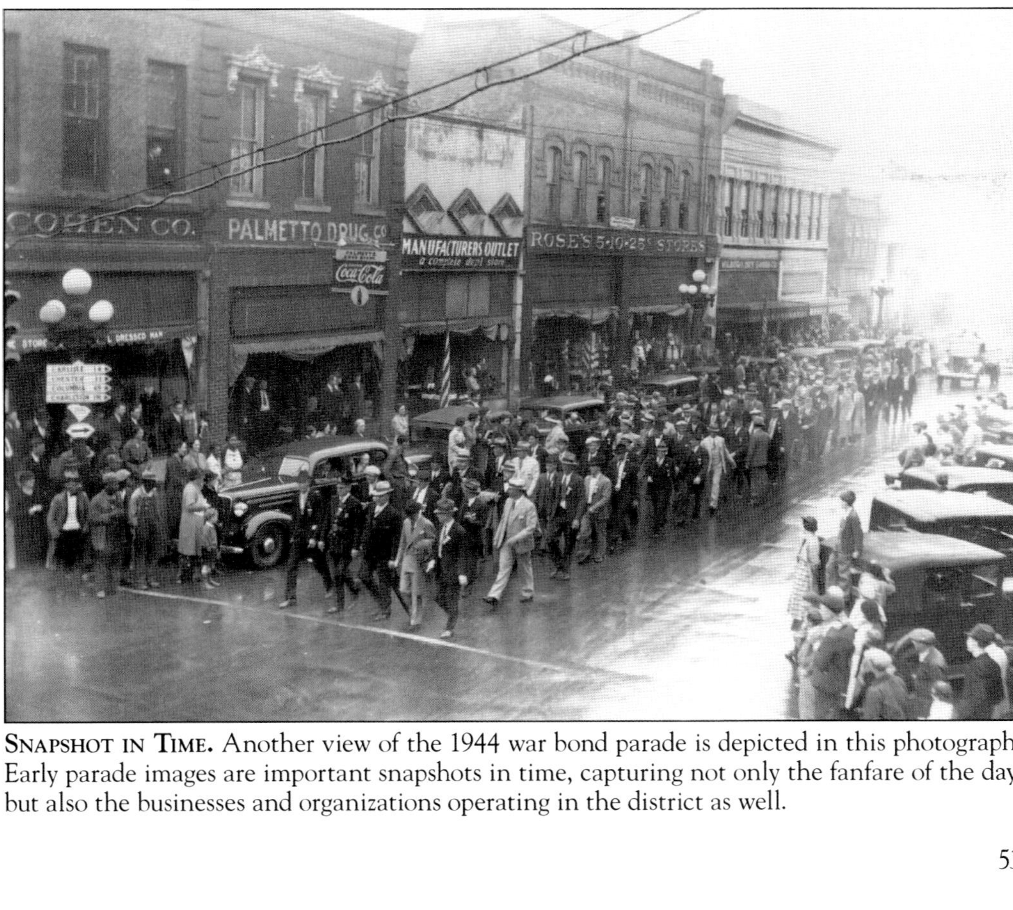

Snapshot in Time. Another view of the 1944 war bond parade is depicted in this photograph. Early parade images are important snapshots in time, capturing not only the fanfare of the day, but also the businesses and organizations operating in the district as well.

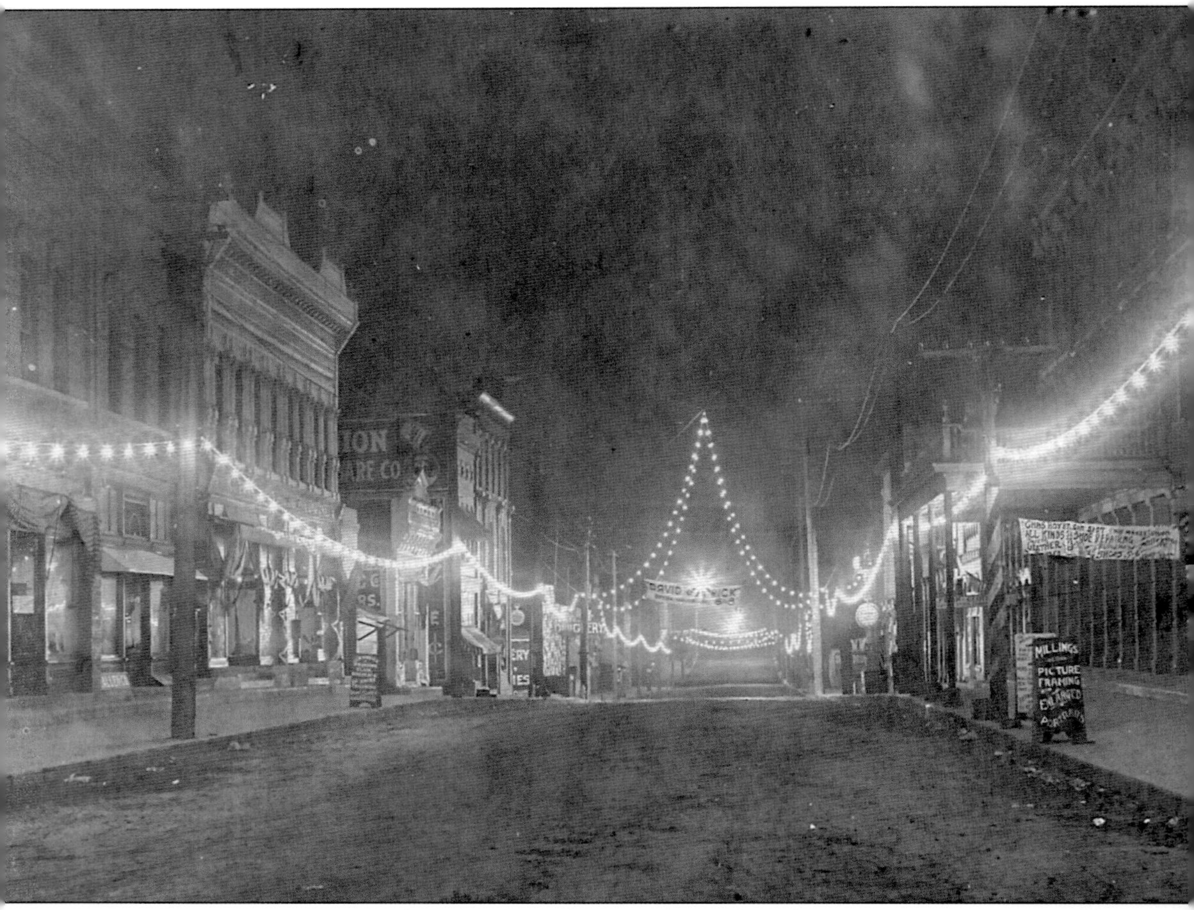

CHRISTMAS IN JULY, 1909. The title of this photograph is "Christmas on Main Street, 1909." The photograph also reads that the photograph was taken during the Fireman's Convention held in Union, but records indicate the convention was actually held in July of that year. The lighting, however, gives the thoroughfare a holiday-like atmosphere.

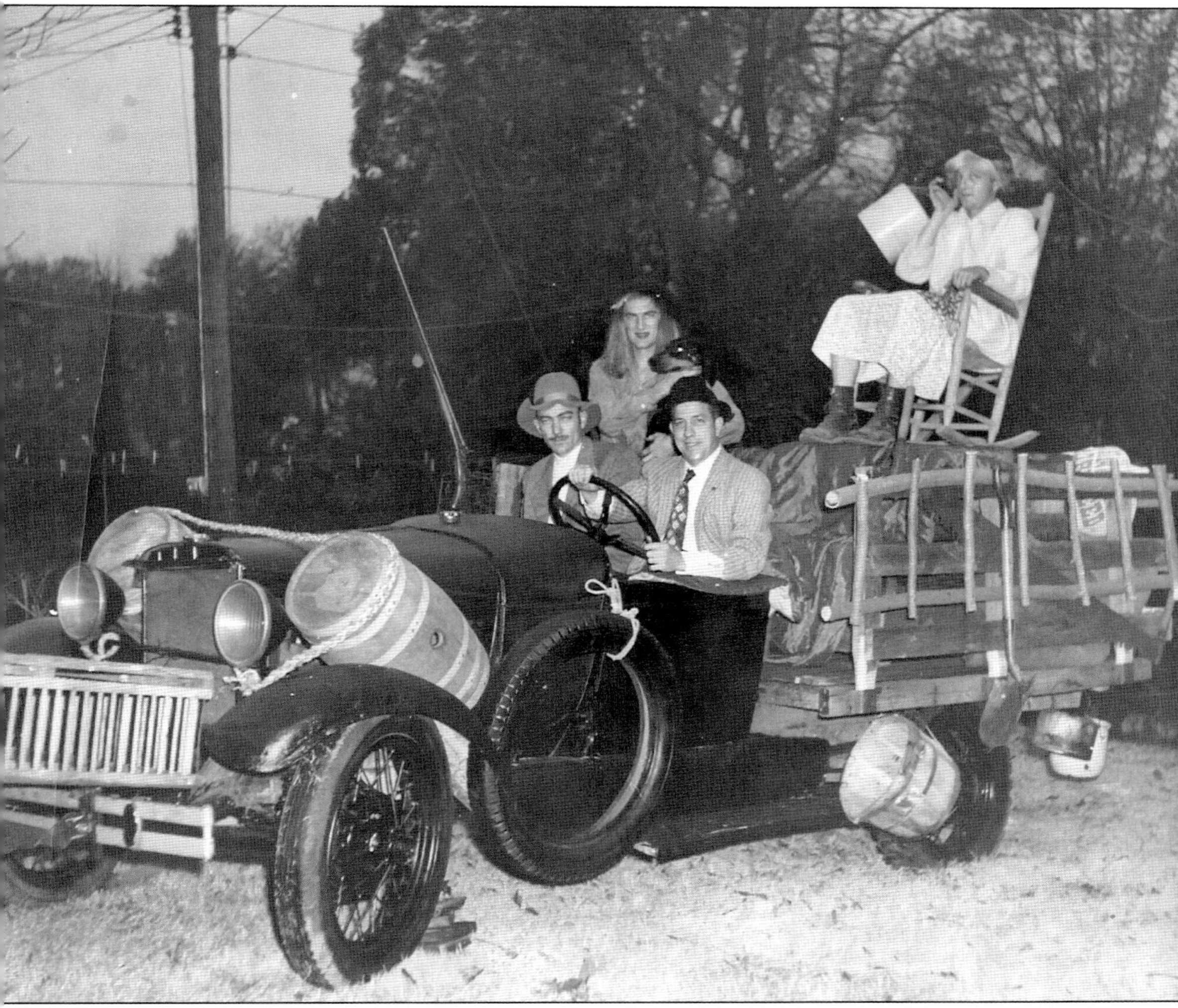

The Beverly Hillbillies. A Beverly Hillbilly parade reenactment is led by Union local George Williford as driver Jed Clampett. Also pictured are his family members: James Lane as Jethro, Harold Lane as Ellie Mae, and J.B. Lane as Granny. It is not known if any of the barrels or jugs actually contained untaxed liquor.

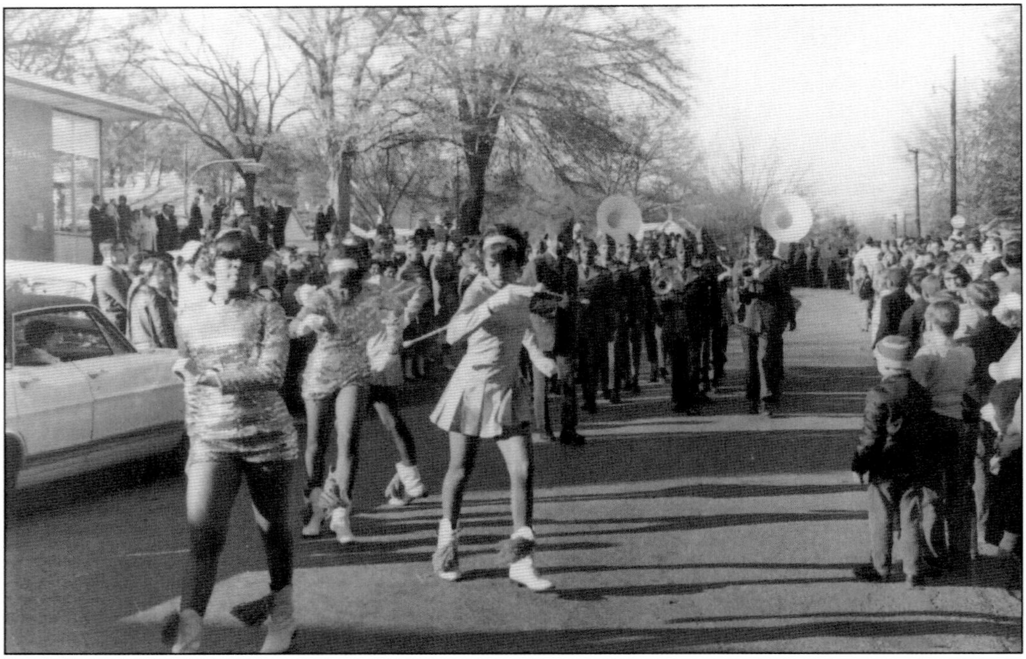

Sims in the Christmas Parade. The Sims School majorettes and ROTC band entertains during a holiday parade. Sims was originally a segregated school for the black community of Union. In 1929, Sims High School was the second black high school in the state to achieve state high school diploma accreditation.

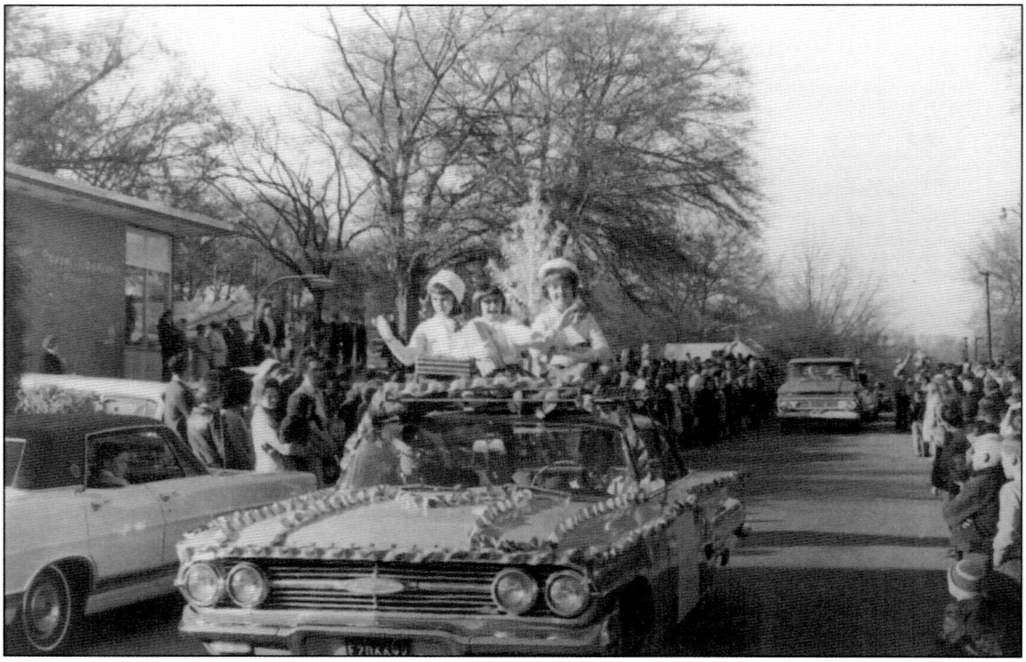

Christmas Parade. A vintage car makes its way down Main Street with its holiday revelers. Classic cars, including old Model Ts, are still a popular treat in contemporary parades. The photograph dates from the early 1960s.

The Bicentennial Parade. In 1976, Union celebrated the country's bicentennial with a Main Street parade. Pictured here are two drummers and a fifer reveling as they cross the intersection of West Main and Church Streets. The Community Cash store sign is partially visible on the right.

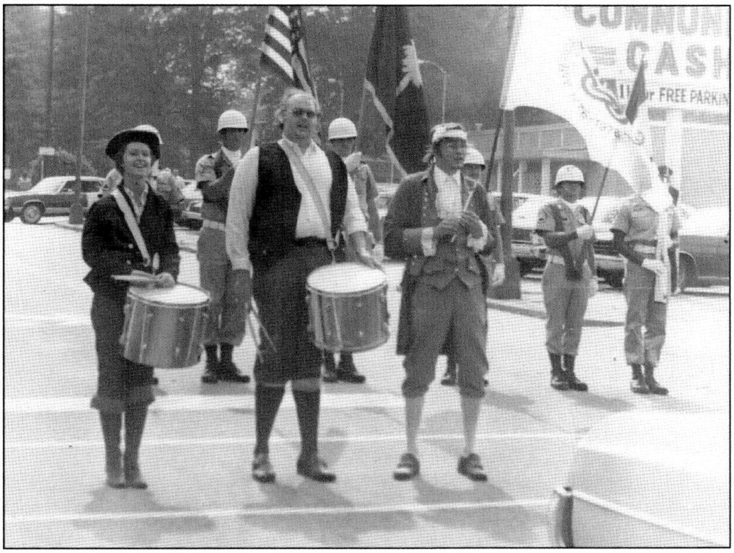

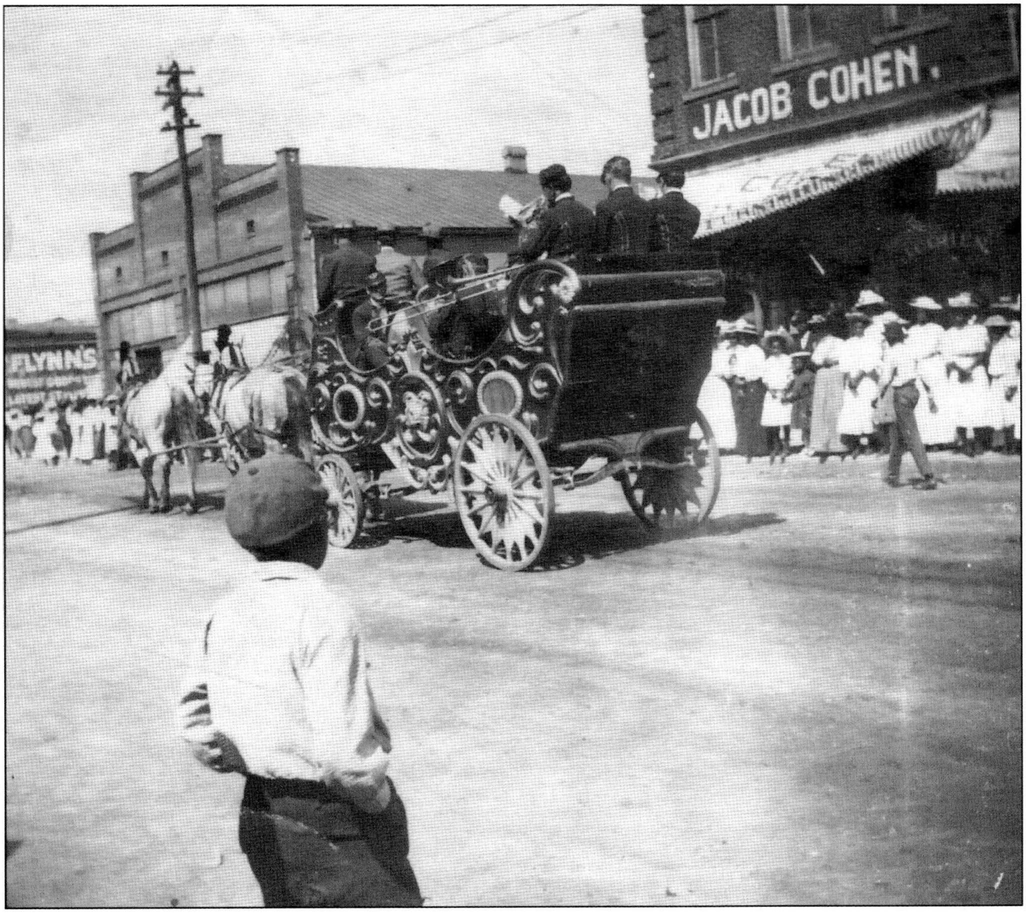

A Circus Parade. A youngster enjoys a circus parade in the late 1800s or early 1900s. The procession had ornate horse-pulled wagons with musicians. Also in the fanfare were a team of elephants parading down Main Street. The intersection visible is that of Main and Pinckney Streets.

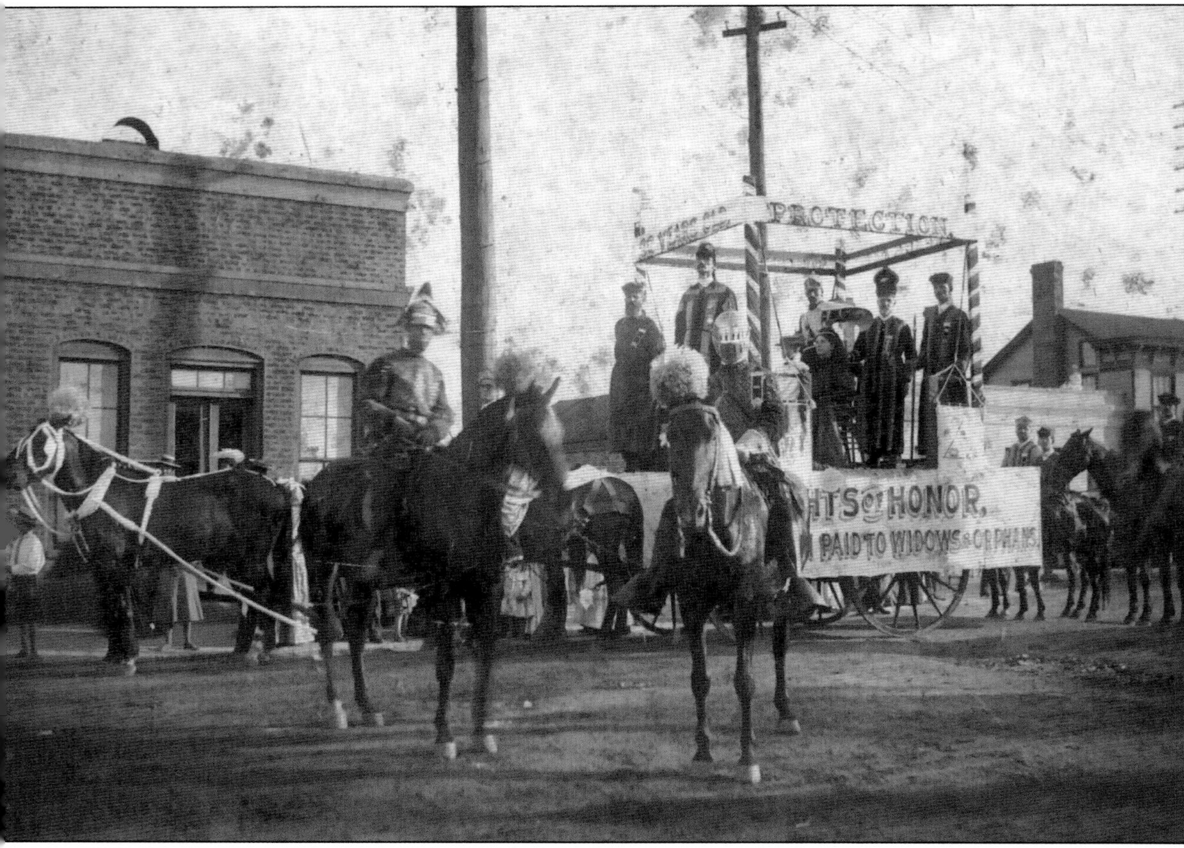

THE KNIGHTS OF HONOR. Members of the Knights of Honor, a local faction of a national fraternal organization and secret society popular in the late 19th and early 20th century, participate in an early Union parade. The intersection visible is the corner of Main and Herndon Streets.

Four

Places of Worship

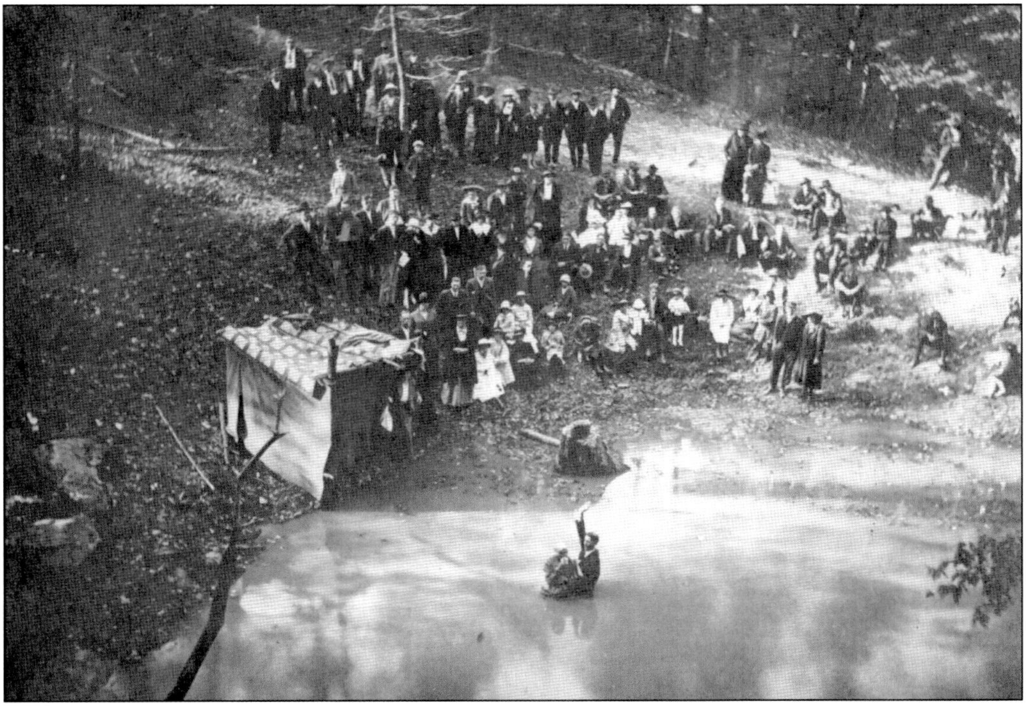

Brown's Creek Baptism, c. 1916. Pictured here is a Brown's Creek Baptist Church baptism in Brown's Creek. The woman being baptized by Reverend Strodgen is Lou Morris, the grandmother of Lonnie Morris.

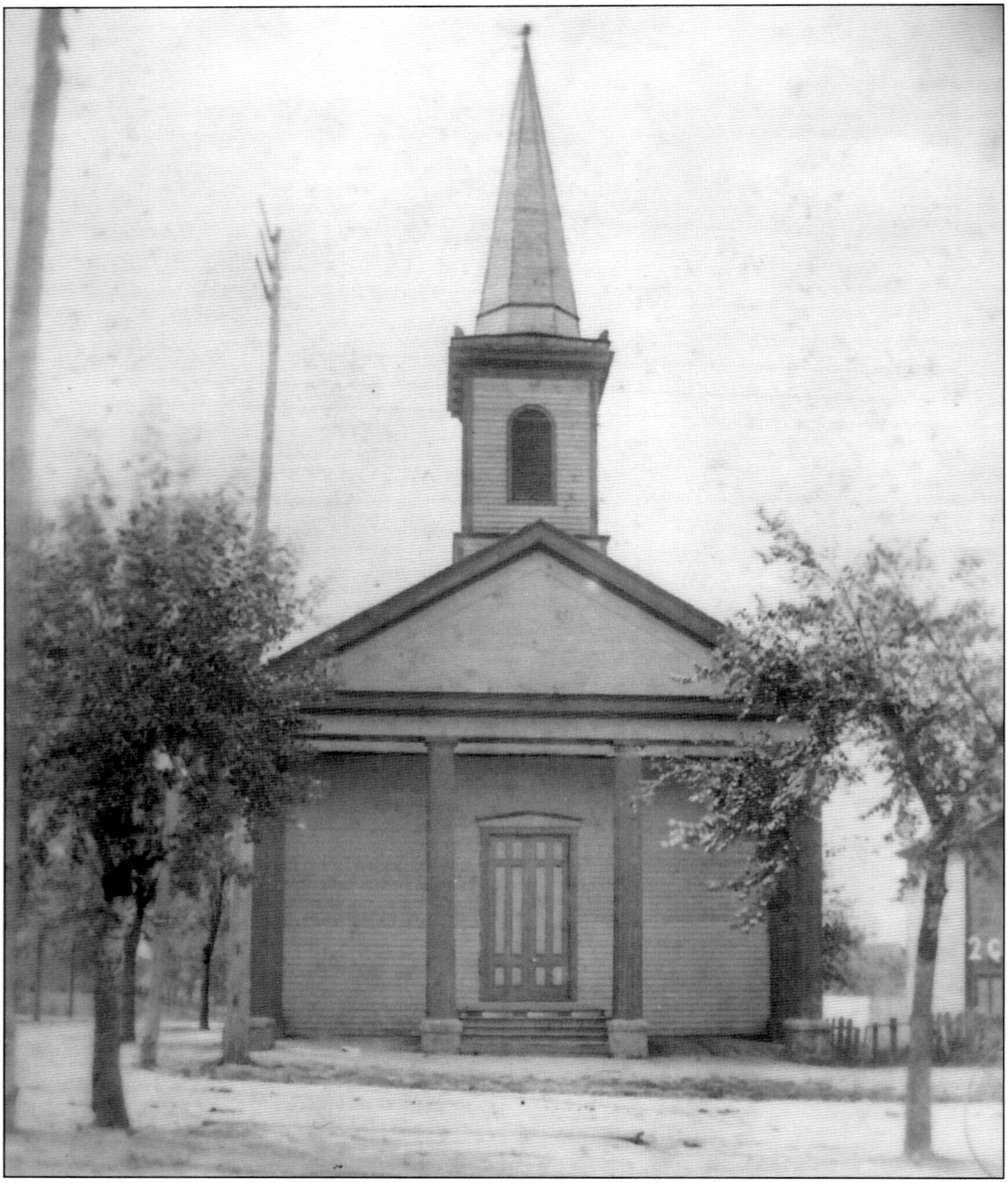

The Original First Baptist Church. The original First Baptist Church, on the southwest corner of Main and South Church Streets, was built in 1855 and burned down in 1905. Another church building replaced the first on the other side of Main Street only to fall victim to another fire in 1952.

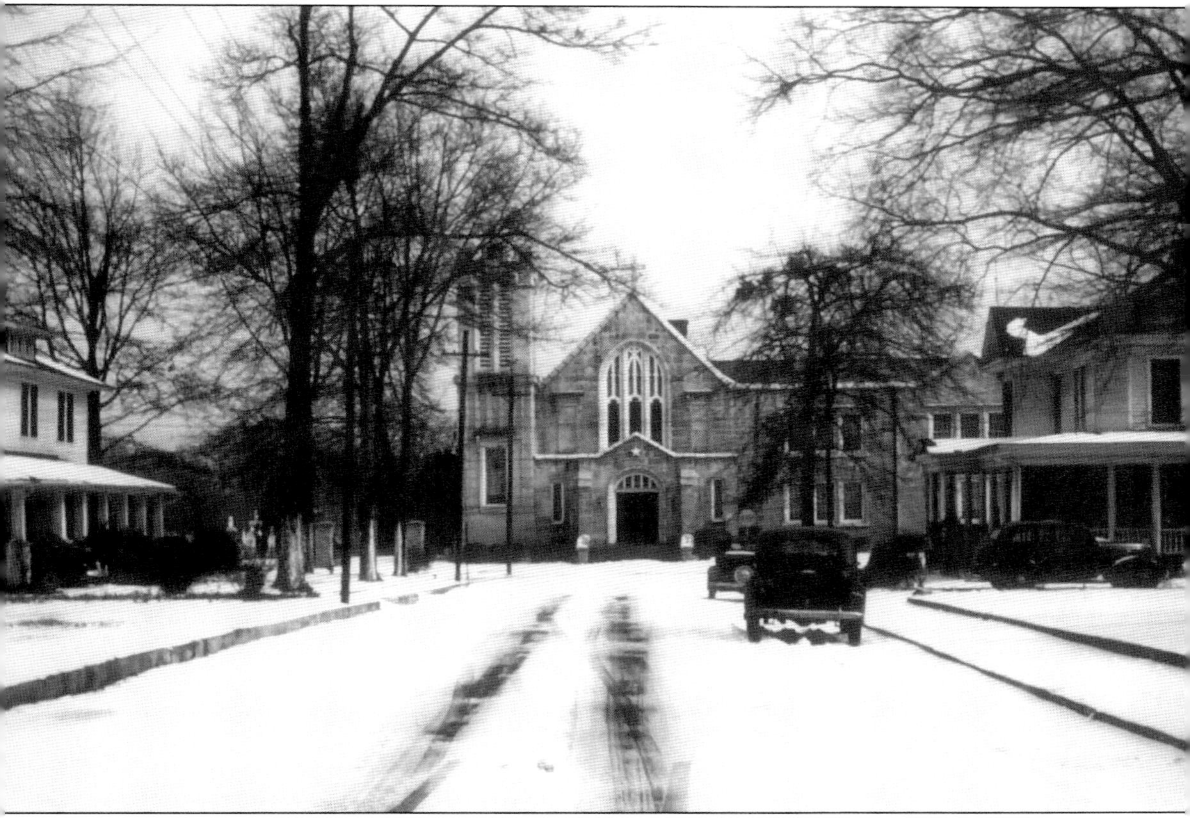

Grace United Methodist Church, 1947. Grace United Methodist Church is located on South Church Street. Construction of this church began in 1872. Benjamin Dudley Culp furnished the rock for the church, free of charge, from his own private quarry. This photograph was taken after a 1947 snowstorm.

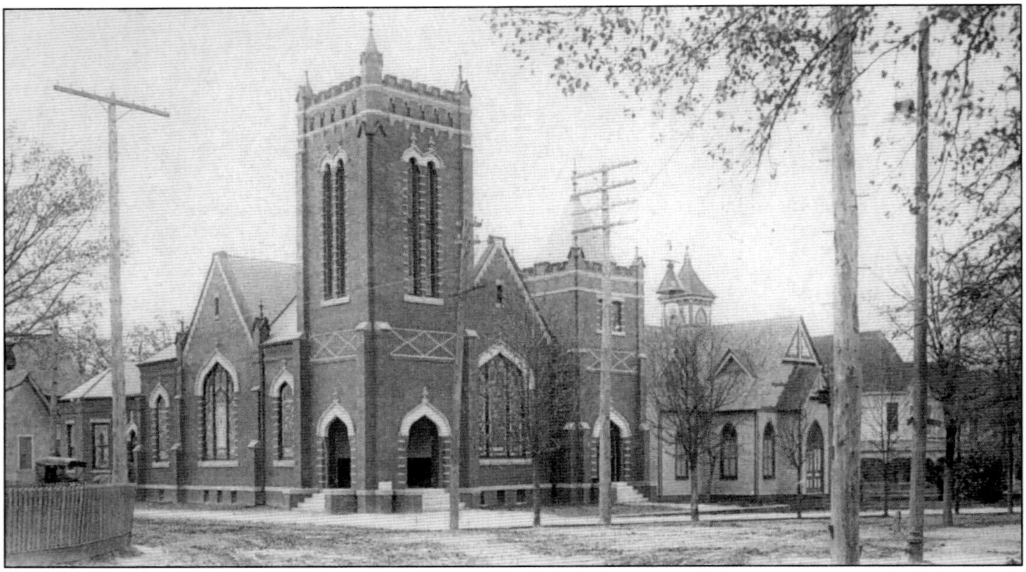

The First Presbyterian Church. The First Presbyterian Church is depicted in a picturesque postcard. The church was built in 1903, and today its parish is still active in the community.

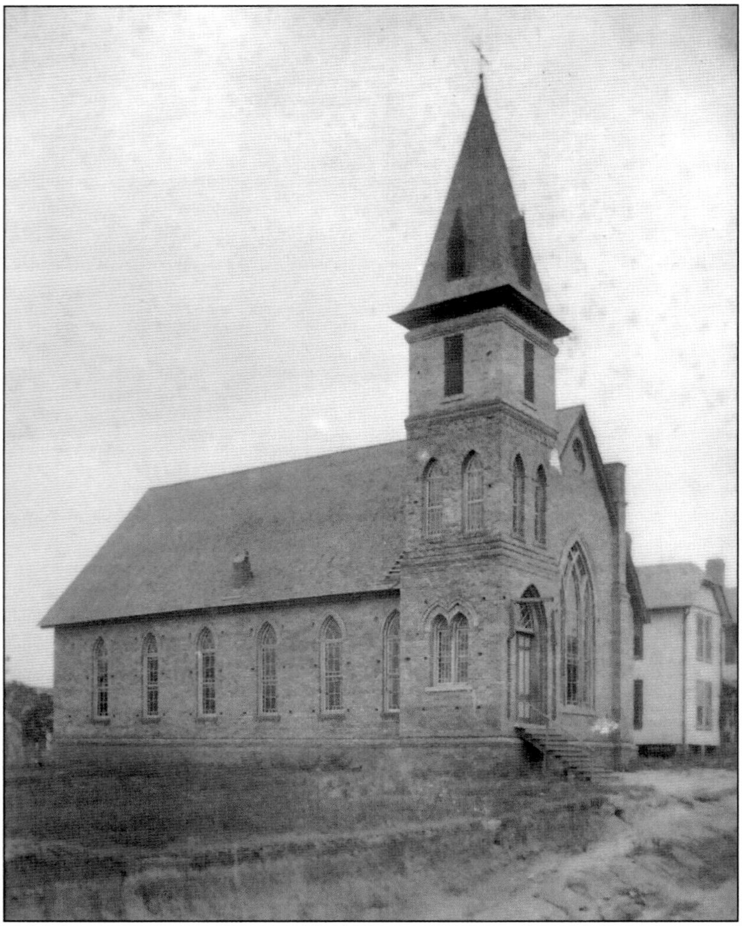

The Corinth Baptist Church. The Corinth Baptist Church was constructed for a black congregation that was organized in 1883. The church pictured here dates to c. 1905. As part of this church was believed to be salvaged from an earlier church, it may contain the core of the original 1817 Union Presbyterian Church.

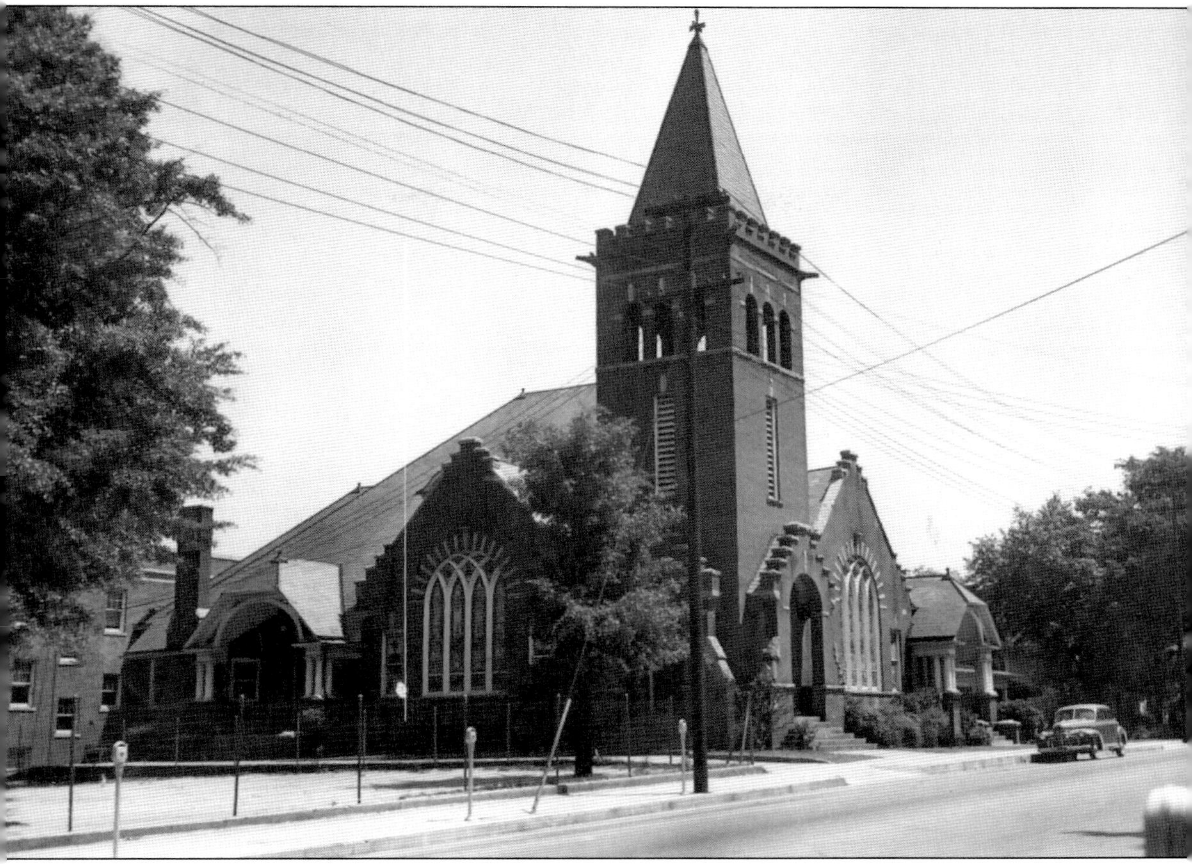

THE SECOND FIRST BAPTIST CHURCH. This First Baptist Church, located on Main Street, was the second building that was constructed after the prior was destroyed by fire. Around 1904, a total of 2.25 acres were purchased for the building of this church on the north side of East Main Street.

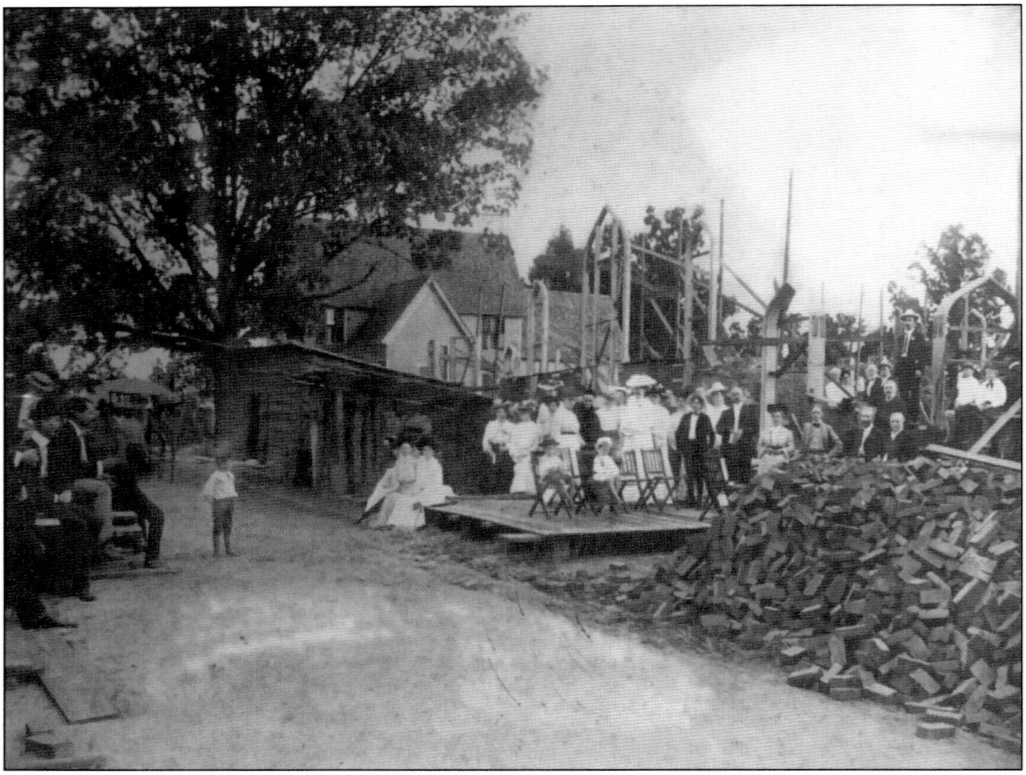

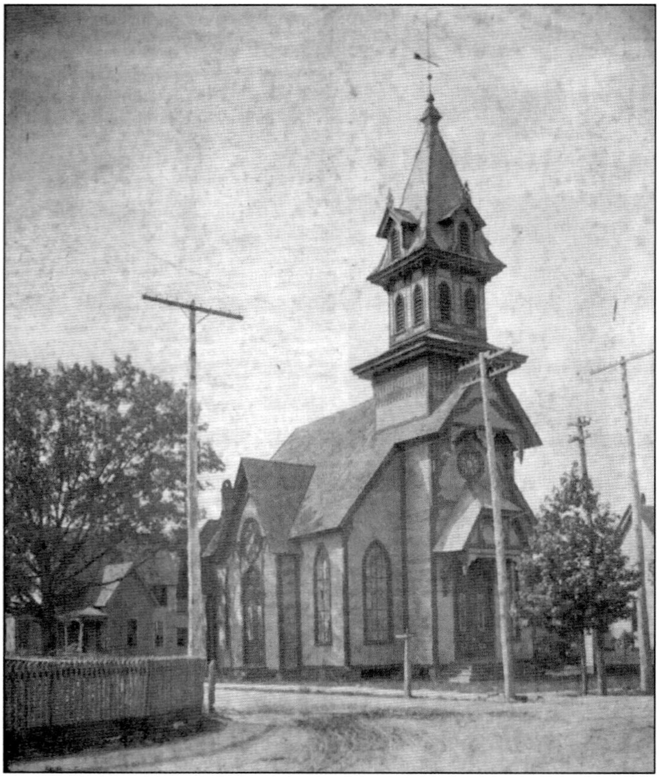

THE NEW FIRST PRESBYTERIAN CHURCH, C. 1903. Parishioners pose for a portrait during the laying the foundation for the new First Presbyterian Church. The new brick structure replaced the congregation's old wooden building.

THE FIRST PRESBYTERIAN CHURCH. The early wooden First Presbyterian Church, located on South Street, was one of the most beautiful churches in Union. Services were held there from 1882 to 1903.

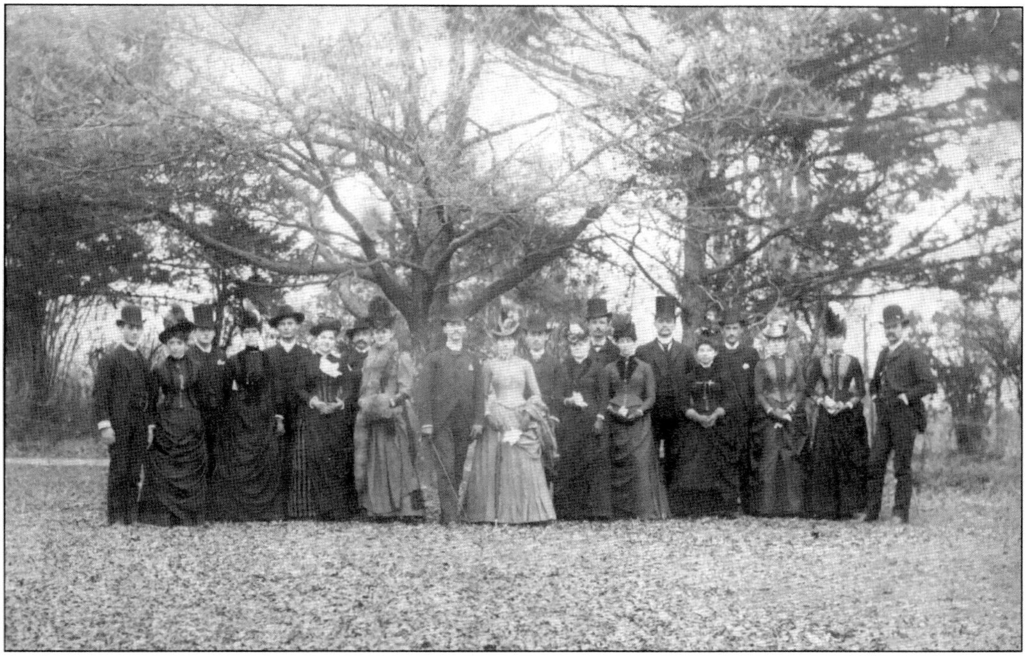

A Union Bridal Party, 1888. Mr. and Mrs. Frank L. Townsend pose with their bridal party. The photograph was taken at 4:00 p.m., Thursday, January 19, 1888, in Union, South Carolina.

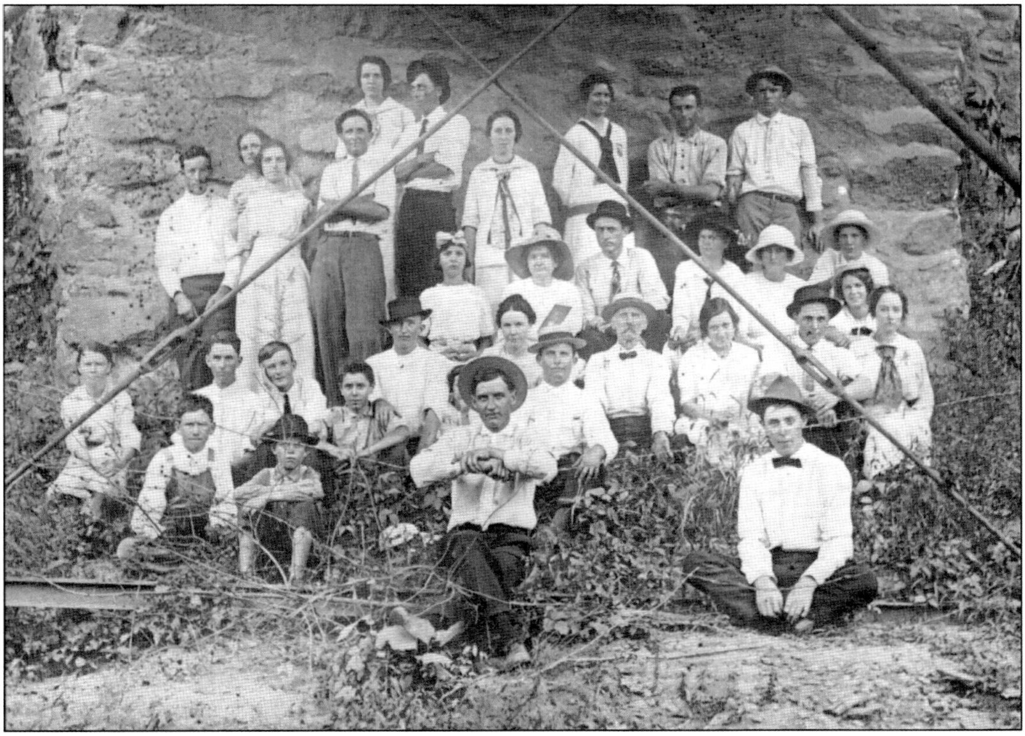

New Hope Methodist Church Picnic, c. 1916. Pictured here is a church picnic in the countryside. Marie Burgess Johns, leaning against the wall (back row, third from right), is the one with the noticeably bright smile. (Courtesy of Amy Garner.)

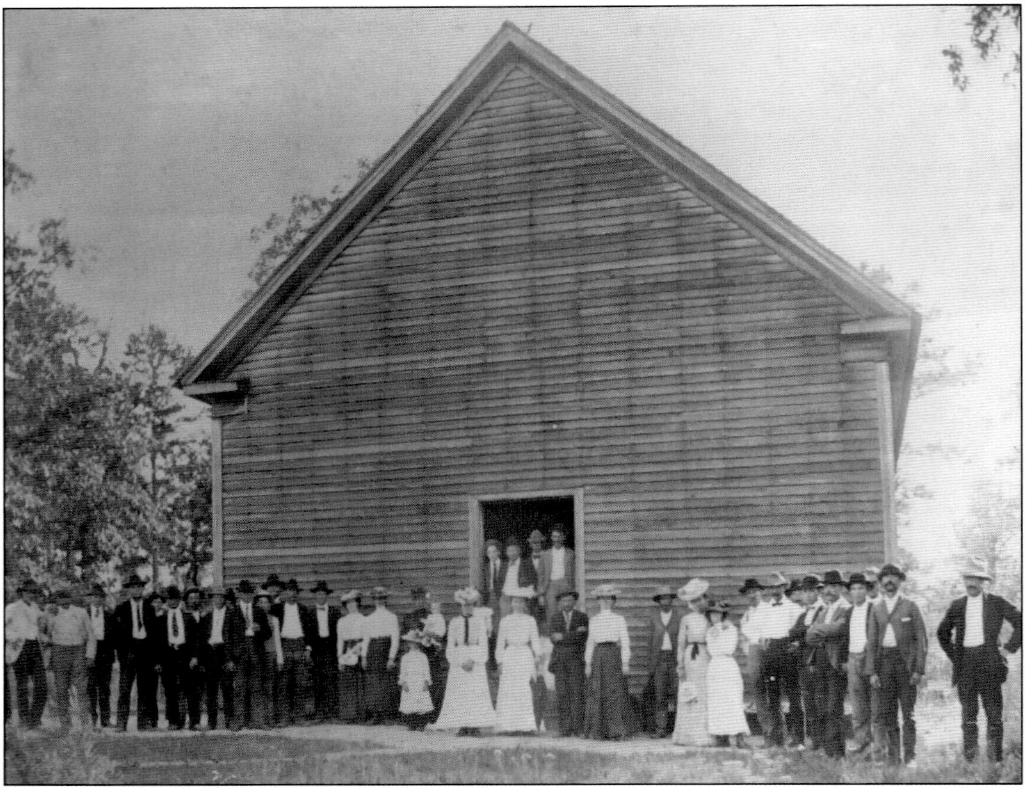

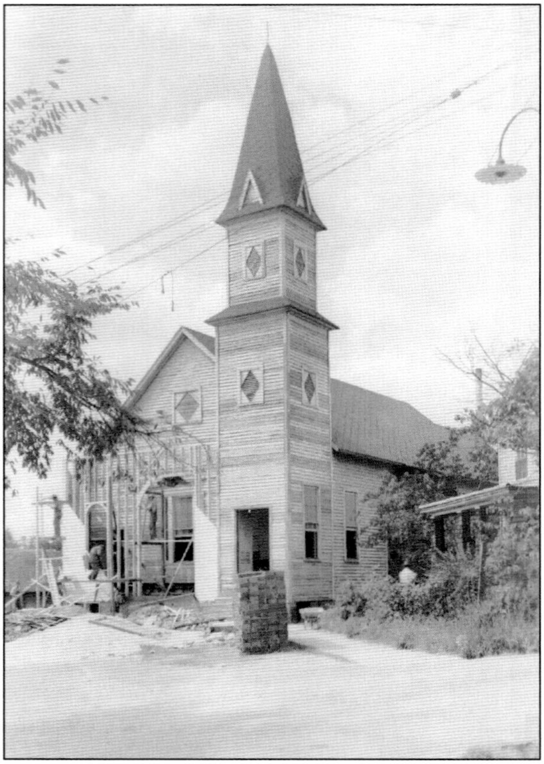

The Sardis Methodist Church. An early photograph depicts the Sardis Methodist Church. Sardis is an unincorporated community located in Union County.

The West Side Baptist Church. West Side Baptist Church was located in the Union Mill Hill community. Built in 1897, this photograph was taken just prior to the church being veneered in brick.

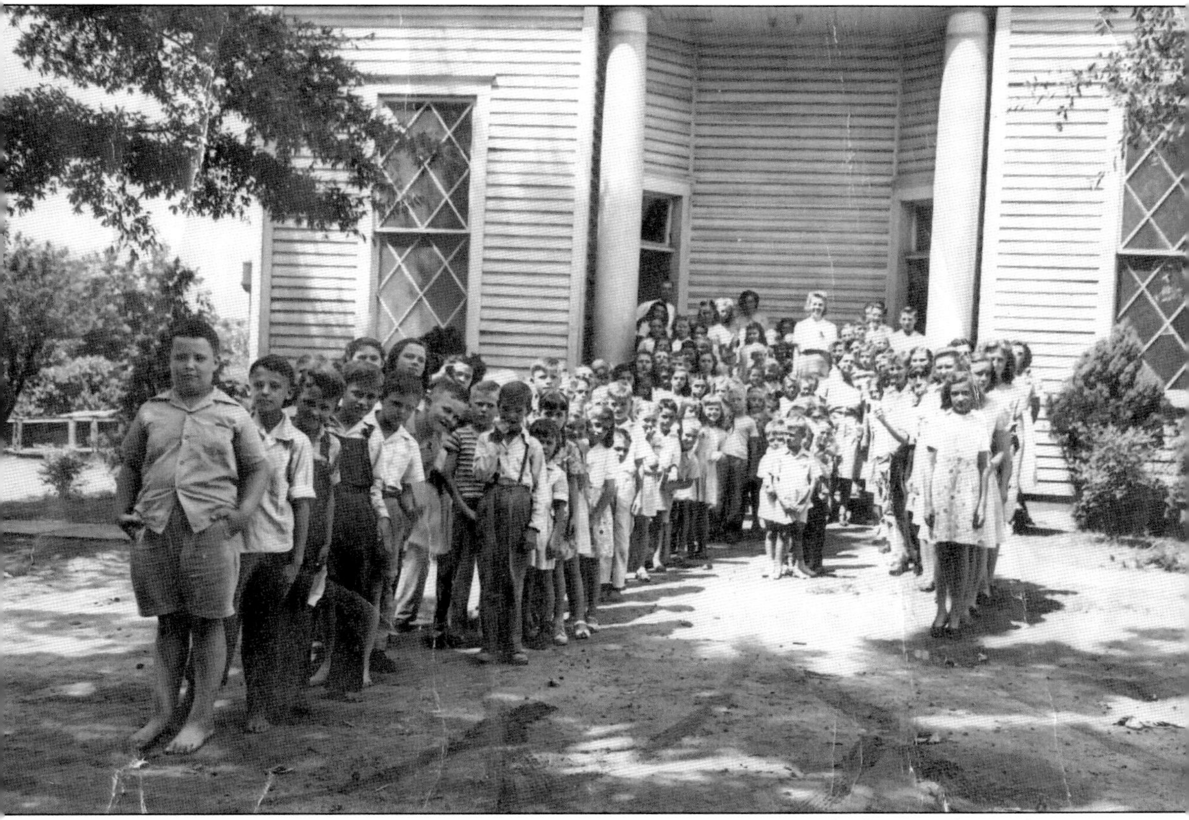

VACATION BIBLE SCHOOL, 1940S. Students line up for Bible school, which was taking place at the McCutcheon Memorial Presbyterian. Harry Orr is the first person on the left line.

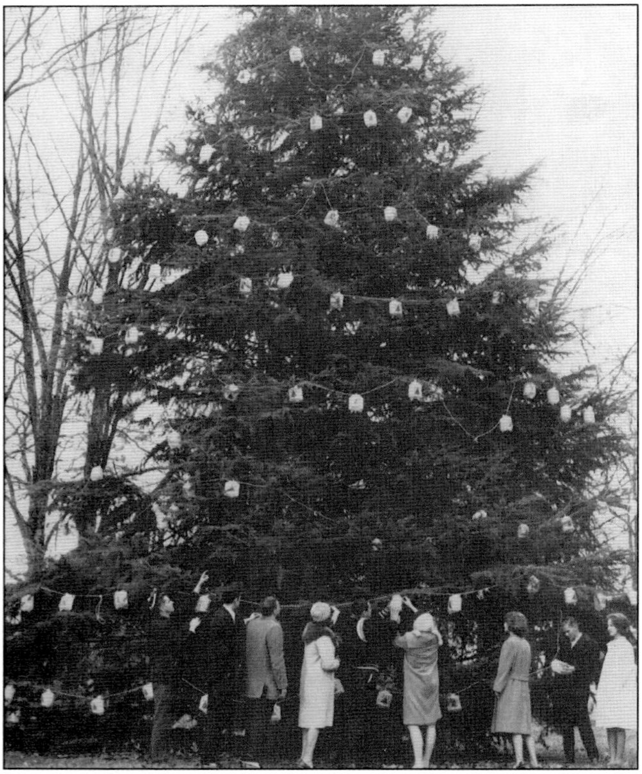

A Local Iconic Christmas Tree. The lighted Christmas tree outside of the Grace Methodist Church is visible each year on North Church Street. As an annual tradition, parishioners decorate their live tree each Christmas.

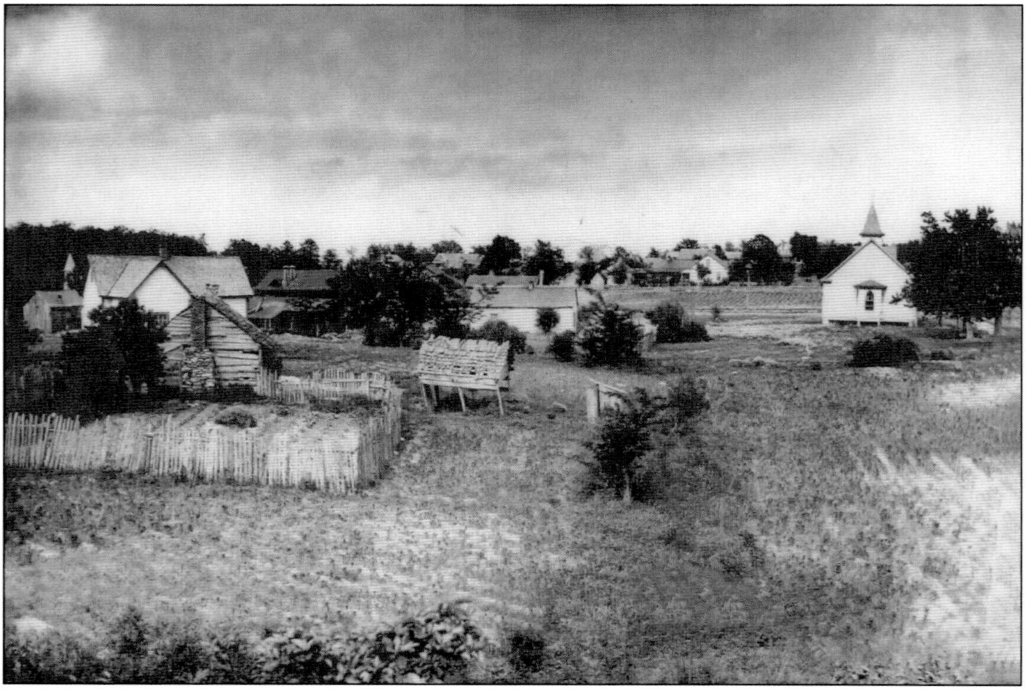

The Old Carlisle Methodist Church. The Old Carlisle Methodist Church is visible on the right side of this photograph. Take notice of the Vernacular log cabin and rustic wooden fencing on the left.

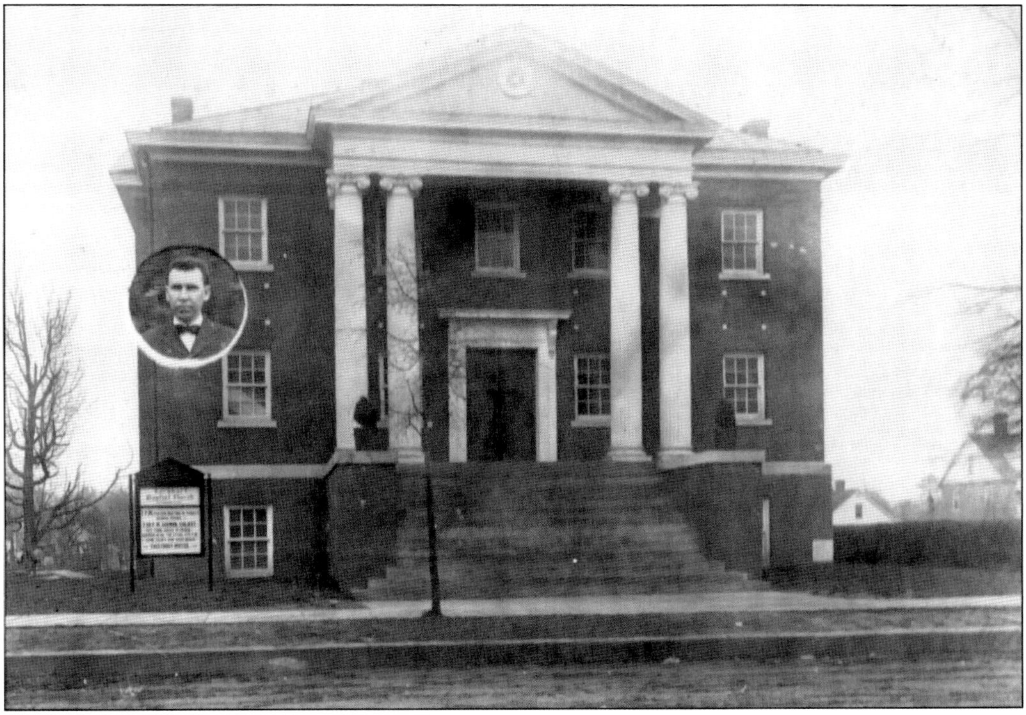

THE LOCKHART BAPTIST CHURCH. The Lockhart Baptist Church was organized around 1896 with the development of the town that was springing up around the construction of the Lockhart Mill.

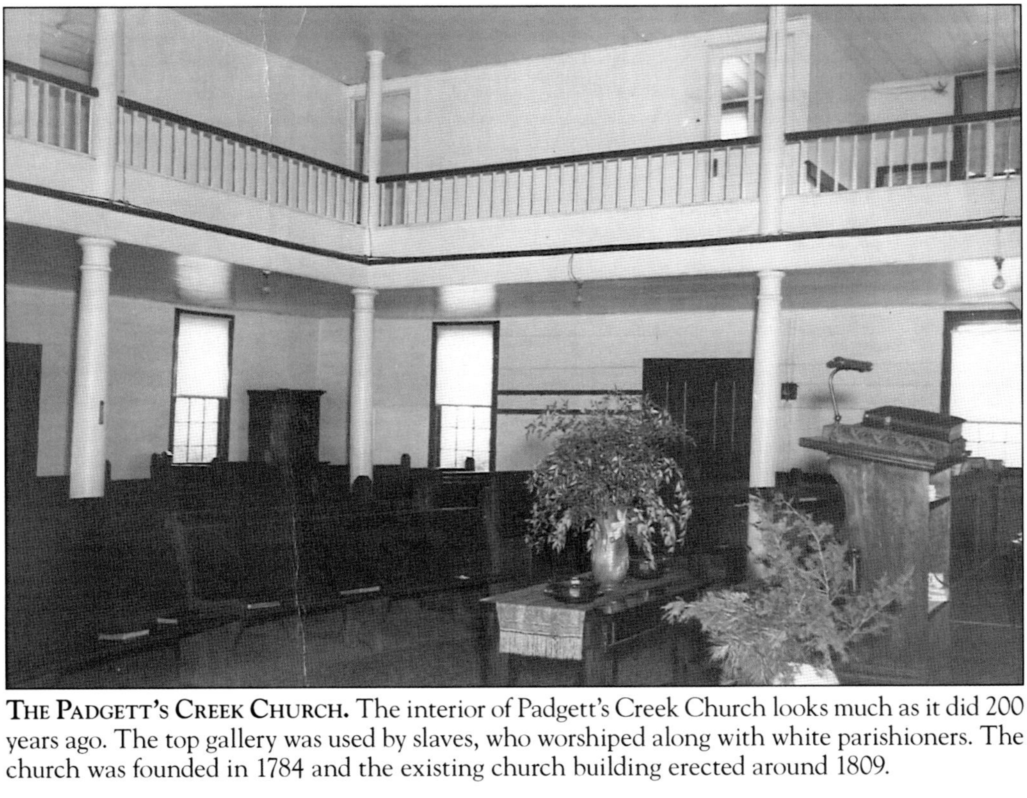

THE PADGETT'S CREEK CHURCH. The interior of Padgett's Creek Church looks much as it did 200 years ago. The top gallery was used by slaves, who worshiped along with white parishioners. The church was founded in 1784 and the existing church building erected around 1809.

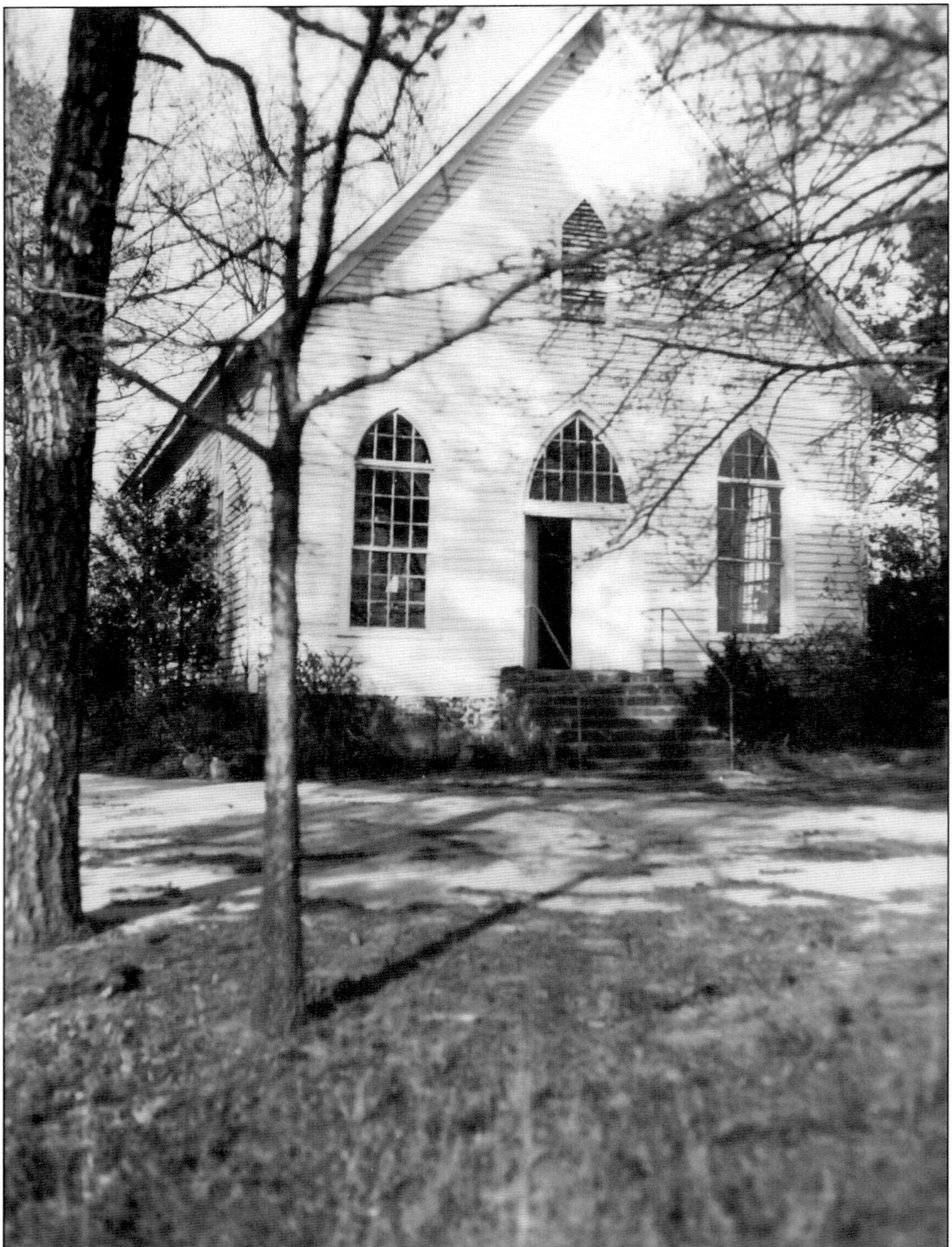

The Cane Creek Presbyterian Church. After the American Revolution, Quakers founded a Cane Creek meetinghouse (church) around 1784. However, when most of the original parishioners moved out of the area by 1805, the church building was subsequently sold, and it found its way to the Presbyterians. The Presbyterians shared the church with various local denominations.

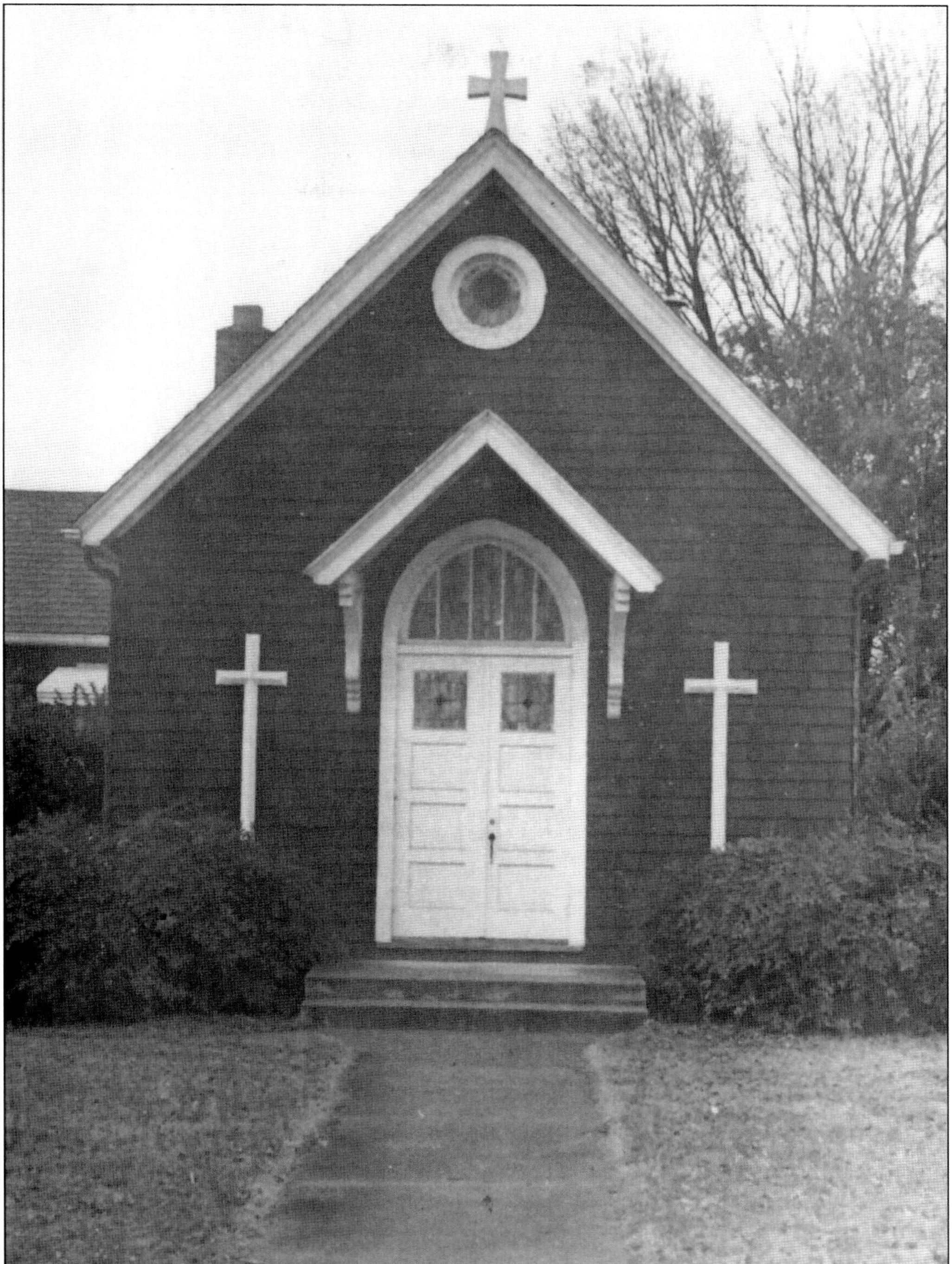

The St. Augustine Catholic Church. Believed to be the smallest Catholic church in South Carolina, the parish dates back more than 150 years. St. Augustine's is located on the corner of South and Pinckney Streets.

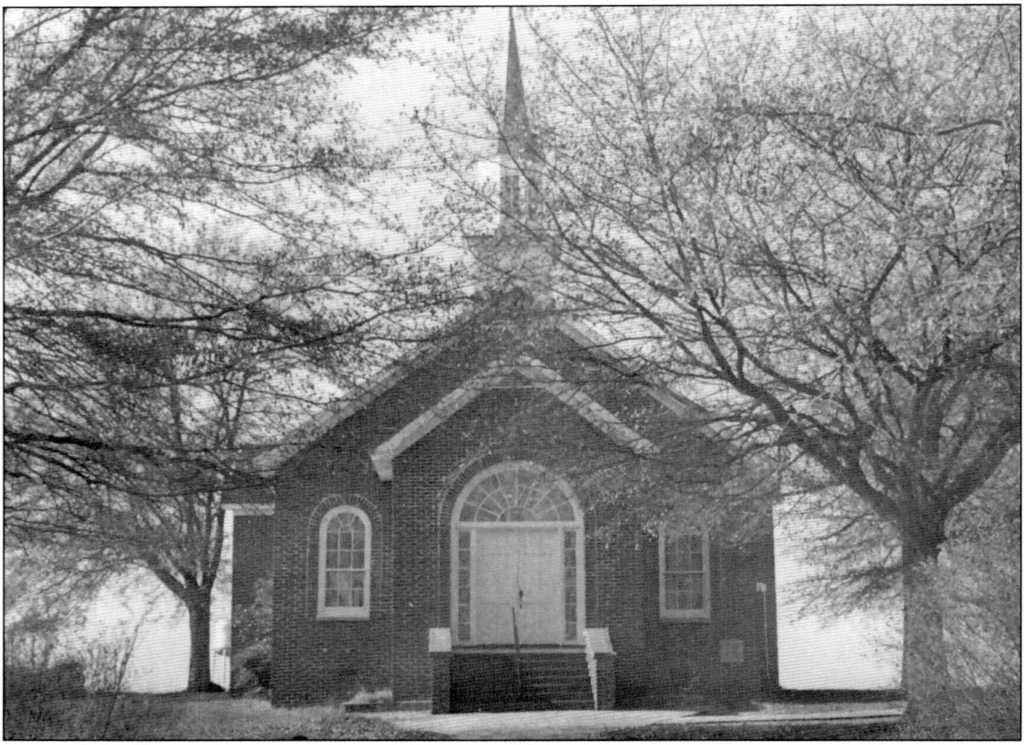

The Lower Fairforest Church. Established in 1762, the church celebrated their 250th year in 2012. Ben Holcomb gave two acres in 1762 for the erection of the first Fairforest meetinghouse; the church was thence built, and it remains the oldest parish in Union.

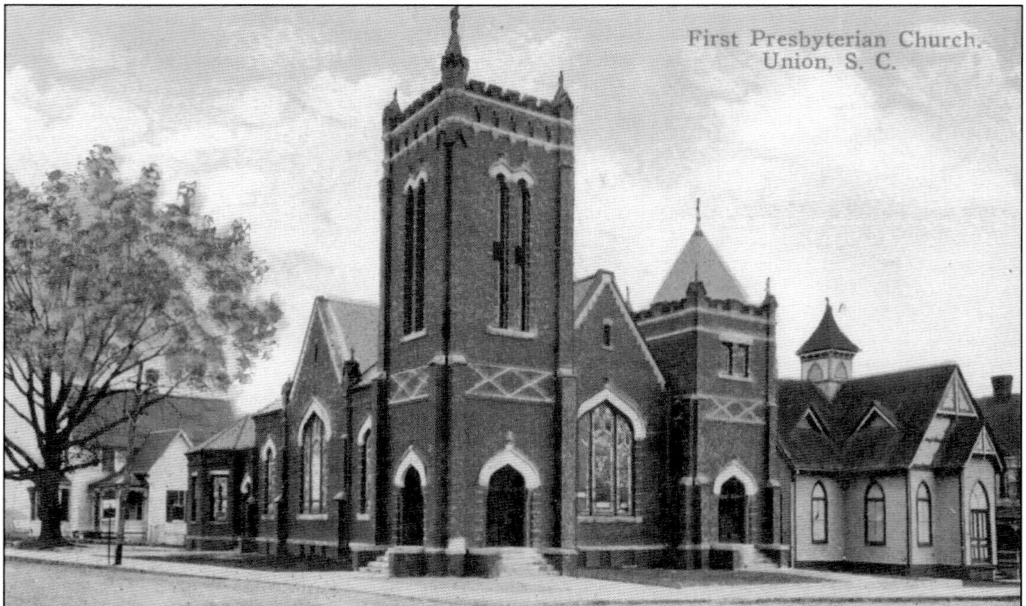

A First Presbyterian Church Postcard. The colorized image of this church made a profitable postcard for local merchants to sell in their stores. The Sunday school building may be seen on the right side of the church.

Five

Union's Railroads

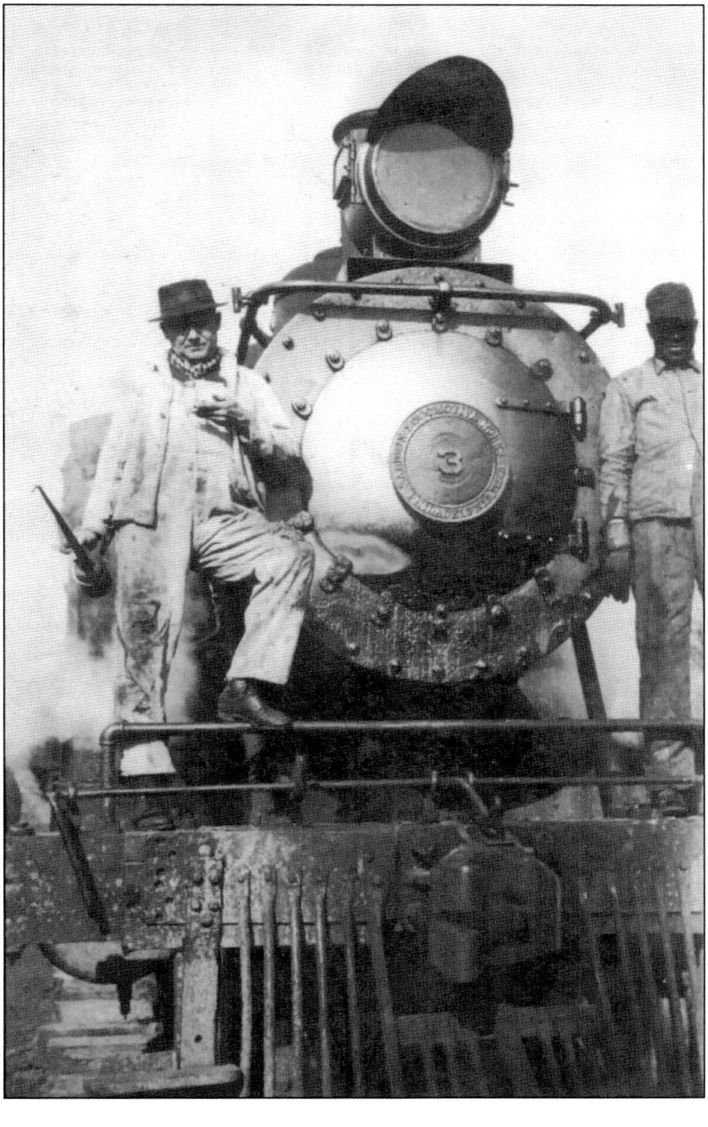

The Iconic Union Railroad. The Union & Glenn Springs Railroad locomotive No. 3 is portrayed with two engineers. Blue Sky, an artist commissioned to make a large mural in downtown Union, used this photograph as his subject. The mural may be seen at its location behind the Main Street buildings off North Pinckney Street. The Union & Glenn Springs Railroad company changed its name to Buffalo Union-Carolina Railroad (known as BUC) in 1922.

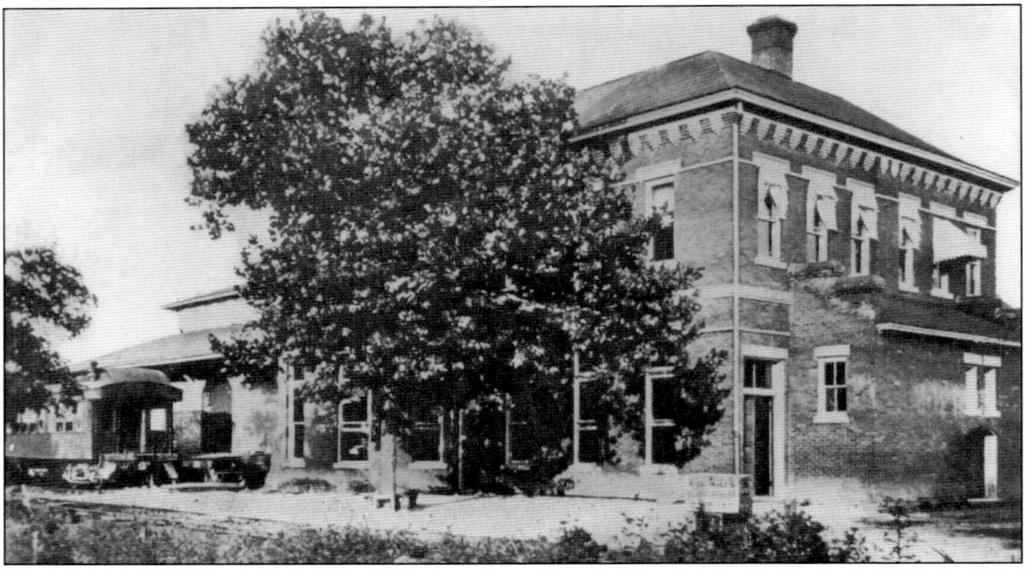

THE UNION & GLENN SPRINGS RAILROAD DEPOT. The Union & Glenn Springs Railroad Company was founded by Thomas Cary Duncan. He realized the need for a railroad to transport goods, raw materials, and commuting employees for his cotton mills. The depot was built directly down the hill from his home, the Merridun Mansion.

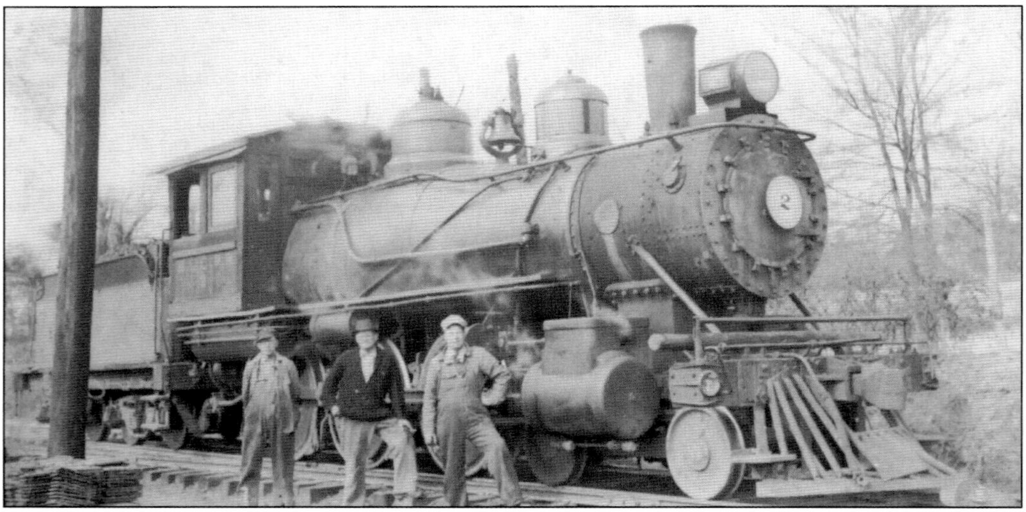

RUEBEN MITCHELL WITH BUC NO. 2. Engineer Rueben Mitchell is pictured here with BUC No. 2, a 4-6-0 locomotive. The BUC ran regularly from Buffalo through Union to Carlisle and all the way to Pride, which is located by the Broad River. It ran, at minimum, three locomotives (No. 2, No. 3, and No. 9), while it is believed the railroad may have possibly owned a total of five engines. However, these additional engines may have been used for spare parts for the operational locomotives. The decision for the railroad to change its name to Buffalo Union-Carolina was purportedly made after the construction of a line from Buffalo to Glenn Springs was abandoned. The reason for this change was likely due to the prohibitive structural cost, which would have been incurred traversing the numerous ravines and creeks between the existing line and Glenn Springs. The BUC was shut down on July 12, 1950, with the last journey being a trip to Pride, South Carolina, undertaken by Engine No. 9. The BUC was afterwards absorbed into the Southern Railway system.

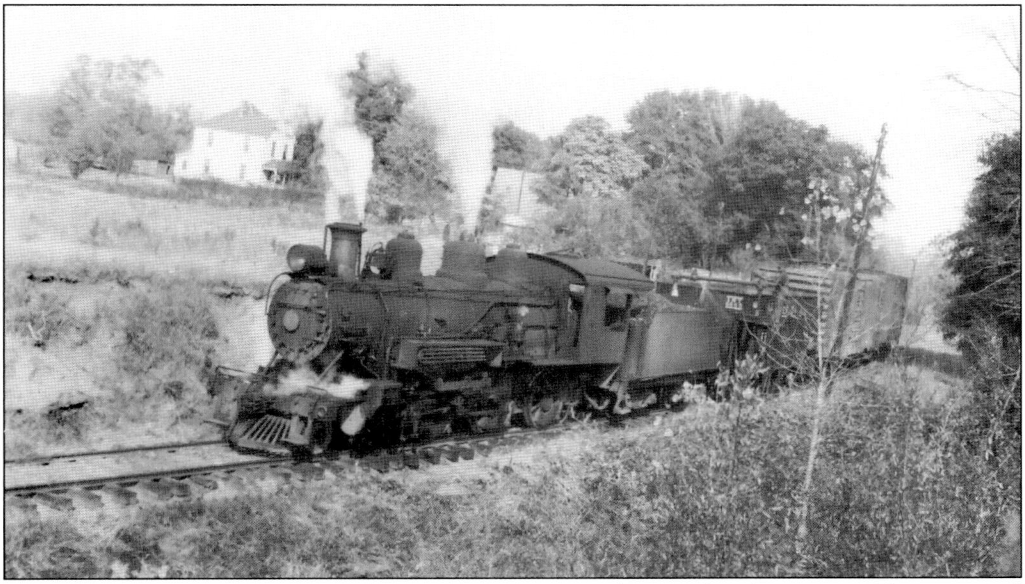

BUC AT NEAL SHOALS, 1948. The Buffalo Union-Carolina Railroad is pictured here at Neal Shoals, South Carolina, on October 30, 1948. Neal Shoals had its own train station, which was located behind the Meador Mansion.

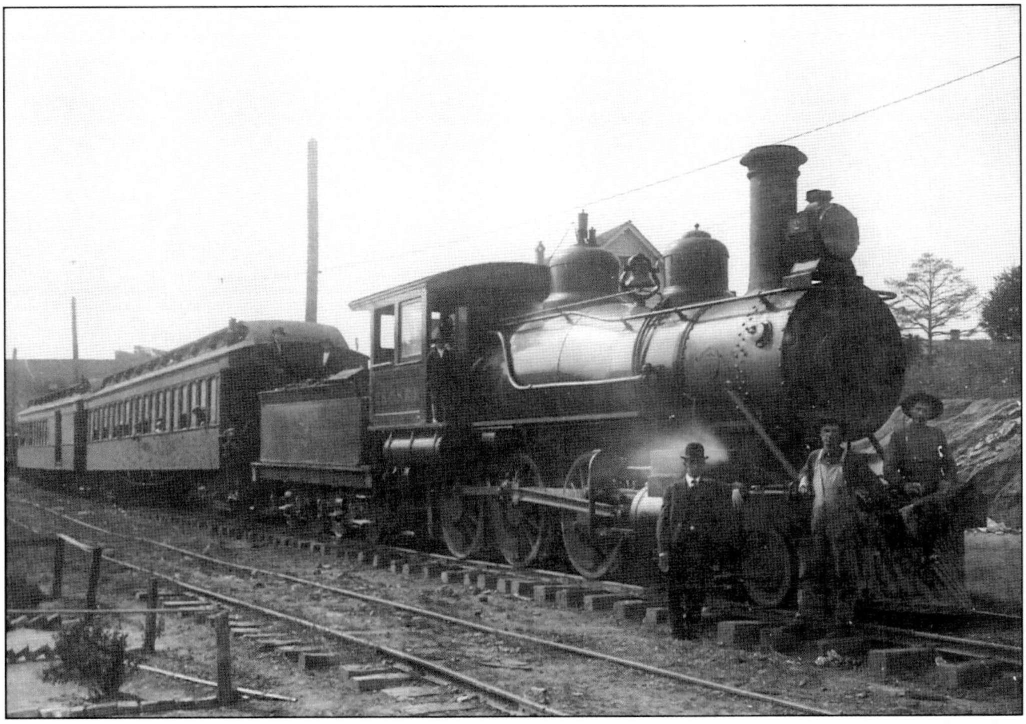

THE UNION & GLENN SPRINGS RAILROAD, C. 1908. The Union & Glenn Springs Railroad is pictured here with one of its locomotives and a typical load of two passenger cars.

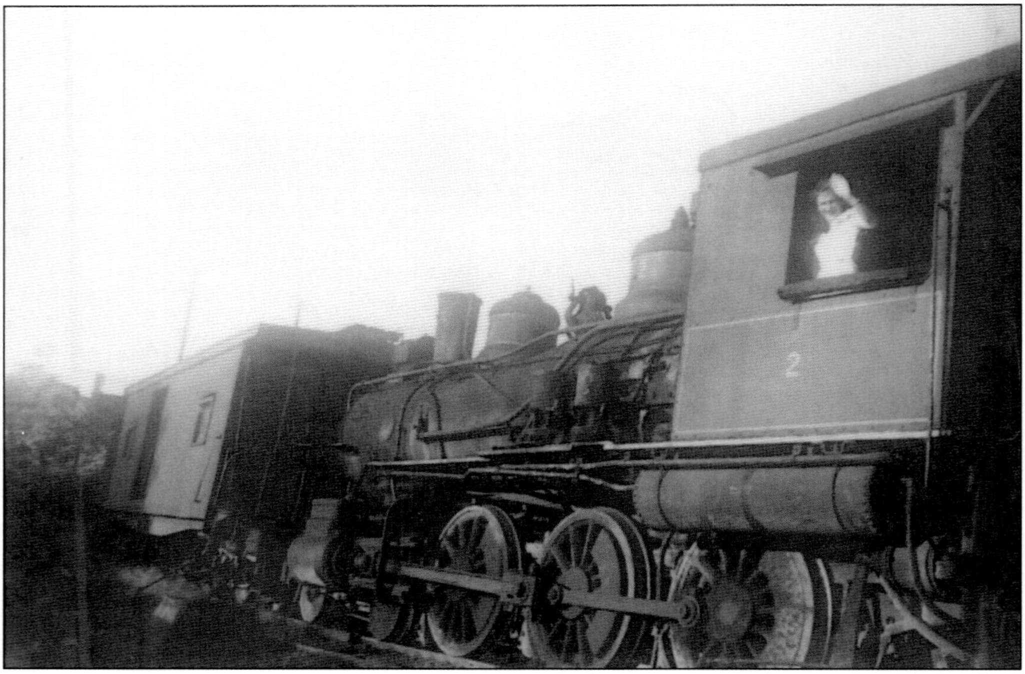

A Locomotive and a Pretty Face. BUC No. 2 is photographed with its photogenic "engineer," the late Betty Jenkins Moore Phillips.

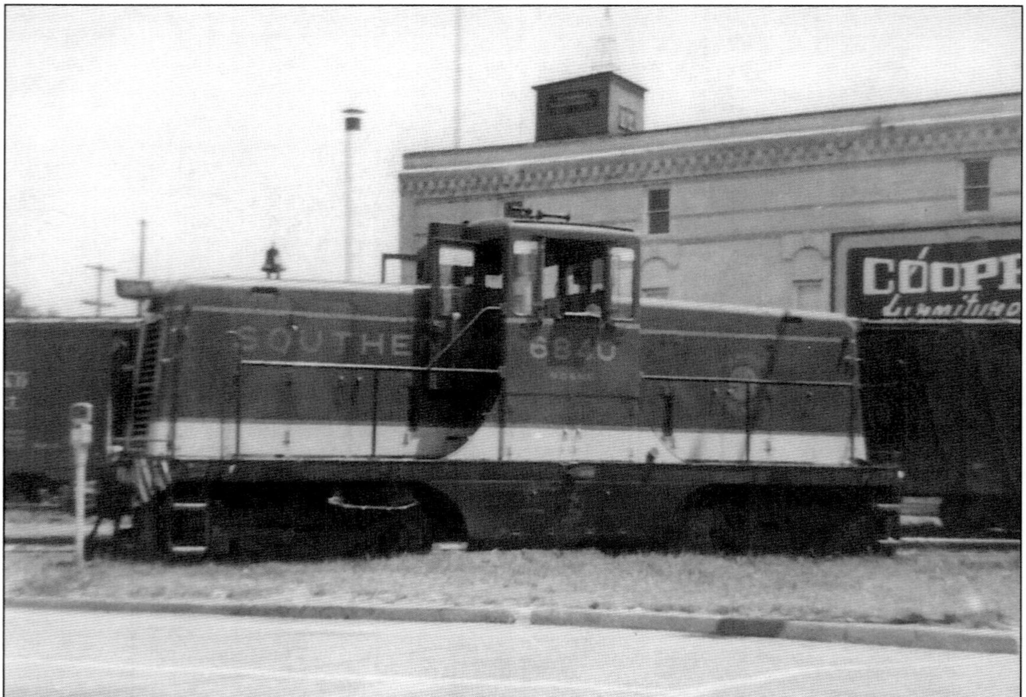

A Southern Switcher. A Southern Railway switch engine is pictured here near Main Street in Union. There was a railroad yard off Main Street, which at one time serviced both the Union Oil Mill and the regular rail line into Spartanburg.

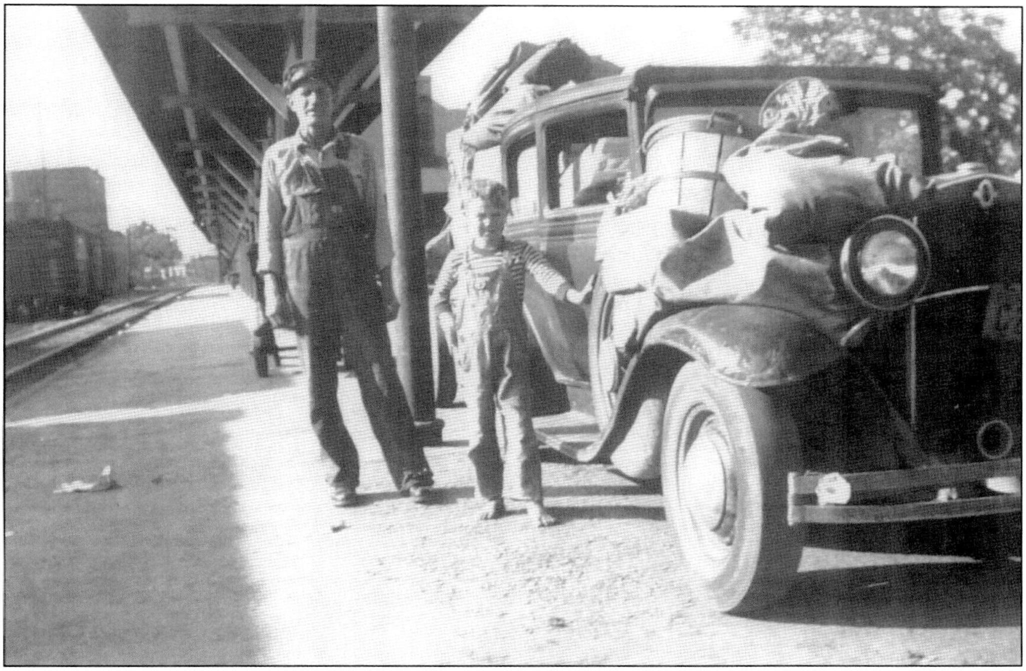

Griffin McAbee and Son J.W, c. 1940. Griffin McAbee was the US Mail transporter between the railroad depot and the Union Post Office. The old Eagle Grocery building is visible on the left, facing north in this photograph.

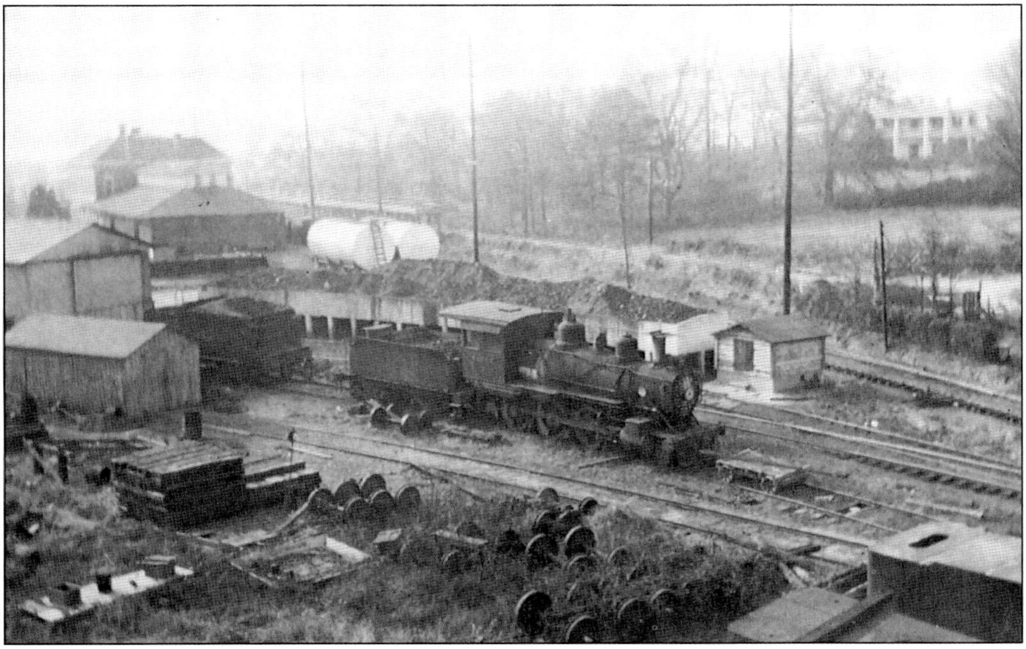

BUC Railroad Yard. In this photograph, the Merridun Mansion, Thomas Cary Duncan's home, can be seen overlooking the rail yard from up the hill. This is the only known photograph encompassing both Duncan's home and his railroad.

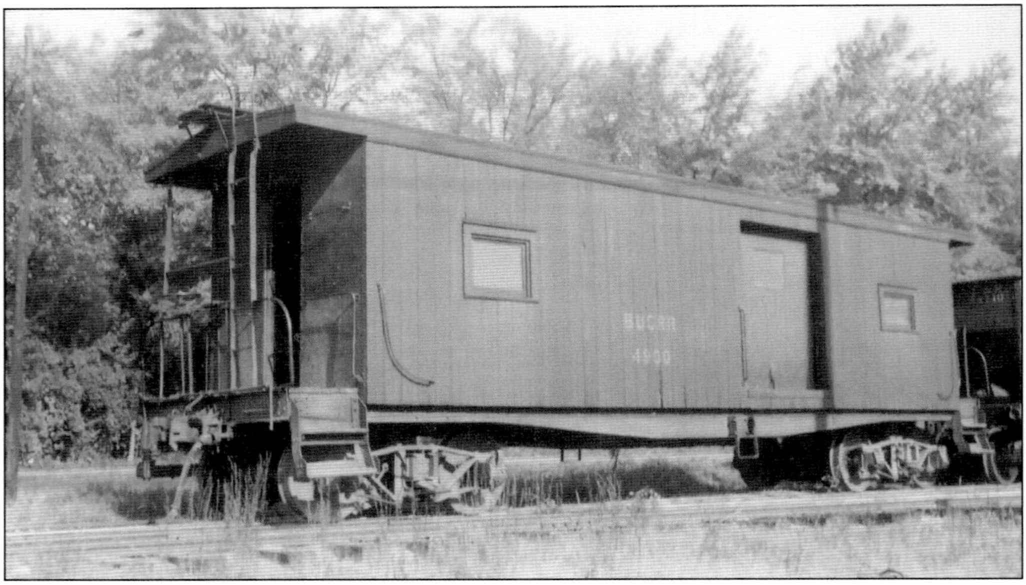

A Wood-Way Car, 1948. BUC's No. 4900 wood-way car is pictured here on October 30, 1948. This railroad car could be used like a warehouse on wheels to transport mail and mill material.

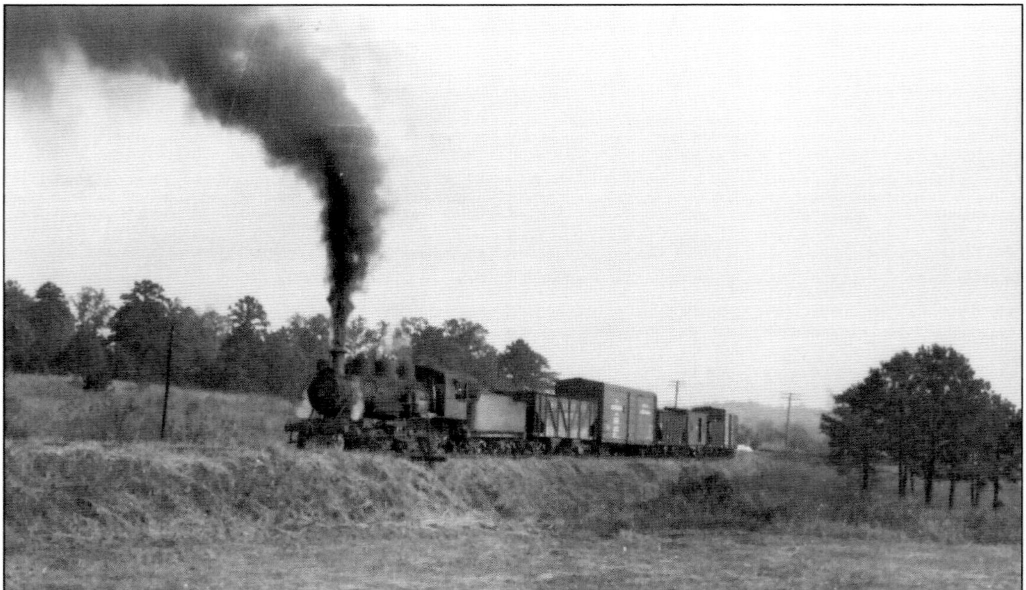

The BUC at Pride. A BUC Railroad train is pictured at Pride, South Carolina, near the end of its line.

A Trestle Collapse. A BUC trestle collapses, but the locomotive made it across. Coal hopper cars strained the trestle with excess weight to the point of collapse. One of the functions of the BUC was to feed the mill's powerhouse with deliveries of coal.

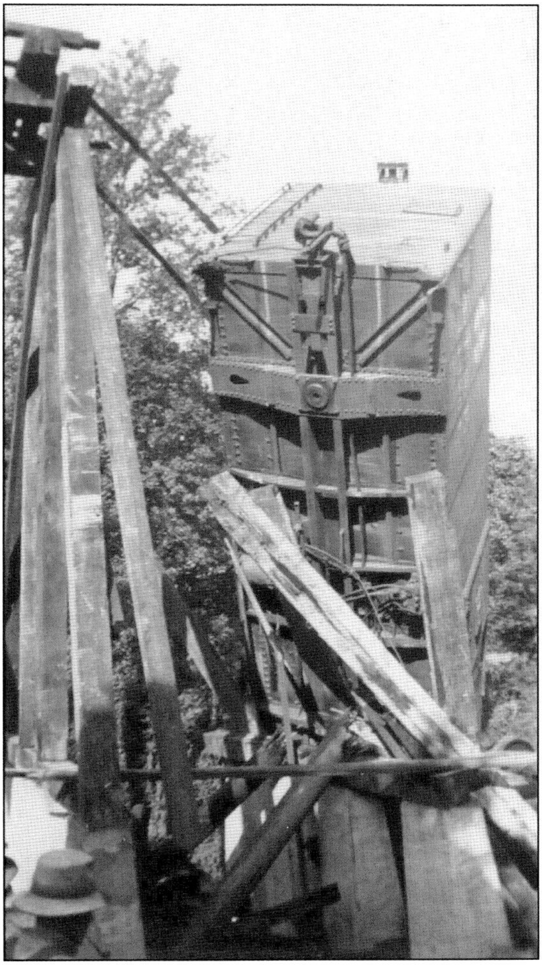

The BUC Rail Yard. A scene from the BUC rail yard shows a locomotive pushing coal hopper cars. The BUC had its own rail yard for the maintenance of its locomotives.

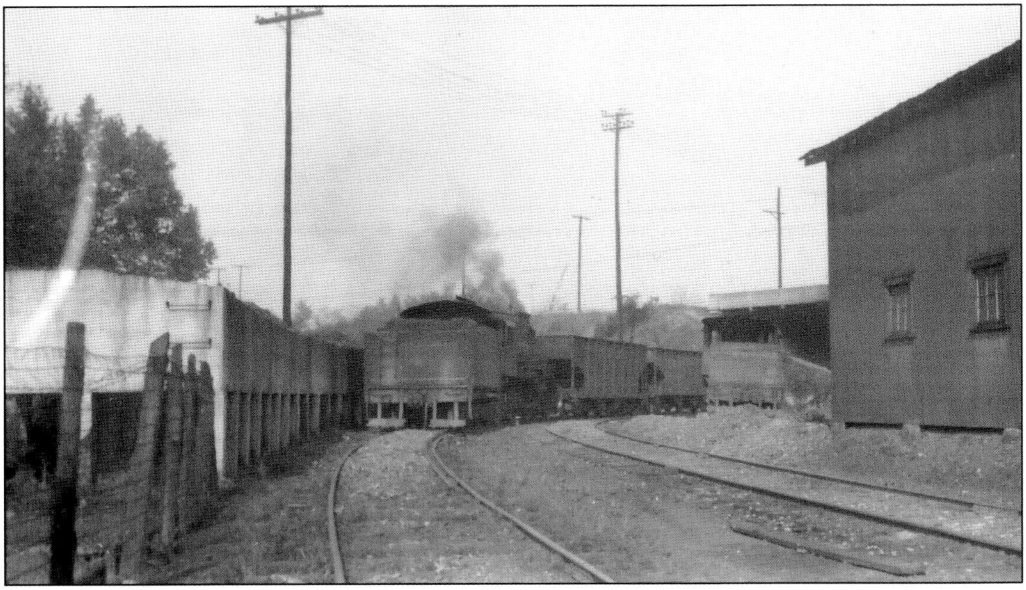

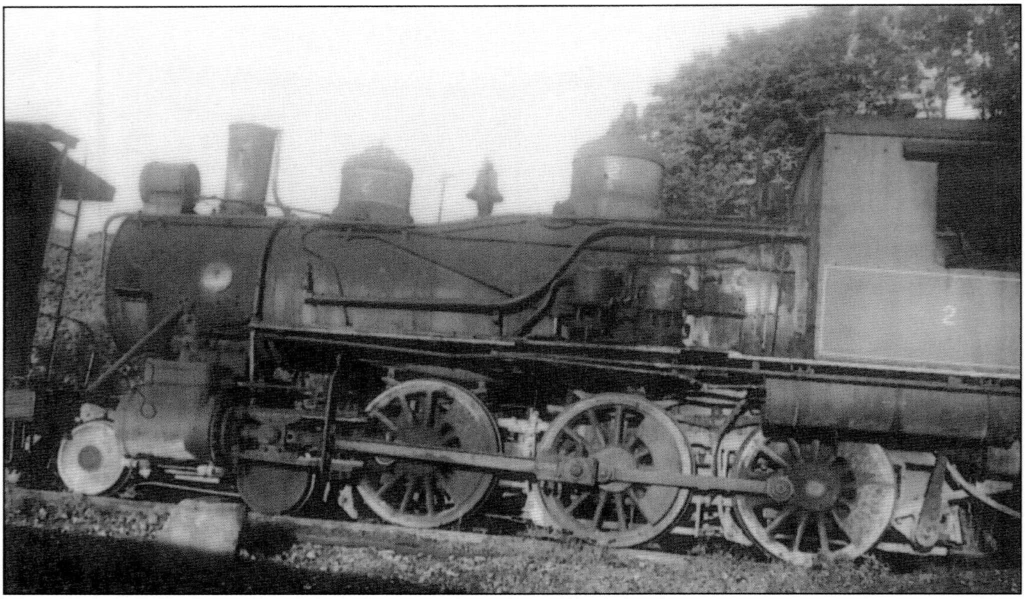

BUC Locomotive No. 2. The BUC operated at least three locomotives and may have owned up to five, inclusive of No. 2. Sadly, all that remains of these locomotives are their circular number plates, two of which are in the Union County Museum's collection. The engines themselves were scrapped.

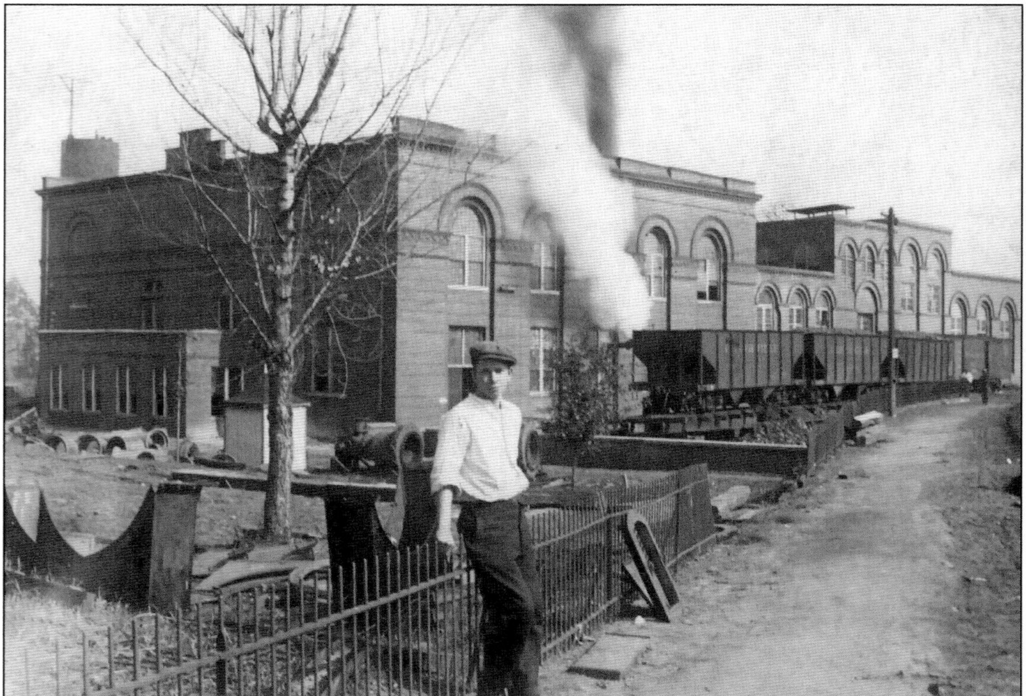

The Buffalo Mill Powerhouse, c. 1913. The mill powerhouse was run on coal, and the railroad was instrumental in supplying its furnace with all the coal required to keep it in operation. Pictured here posing against the iron fence is Furman Haynes.

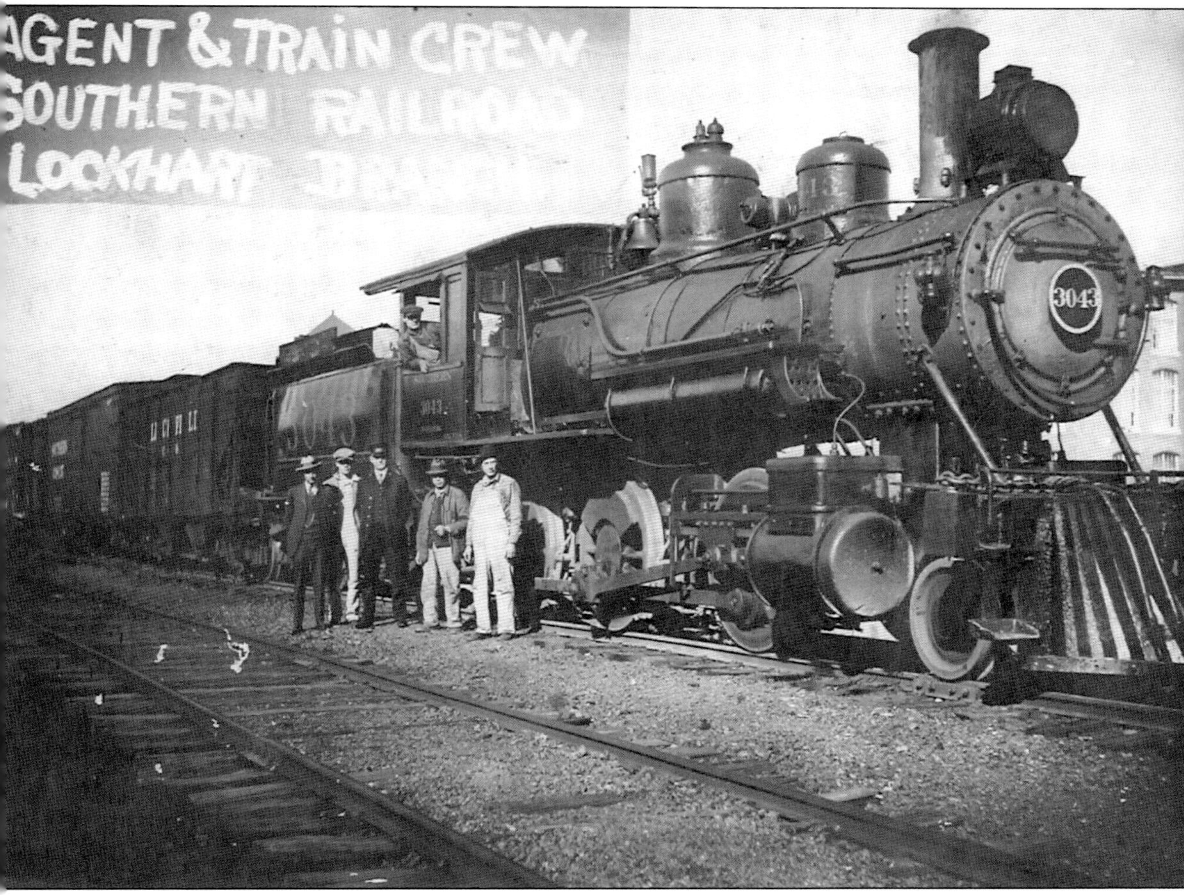

The Southern Railway. A train from the Southern Railway delivers goods to the Lockhart branch of the mill, visible on the right side of the photograph. The Southern Railway began from a conglomeration of railroads in 1894, and after over 100 years of operation, the railroad was placed under the control of the Norfolk Southern Railway in 1990.

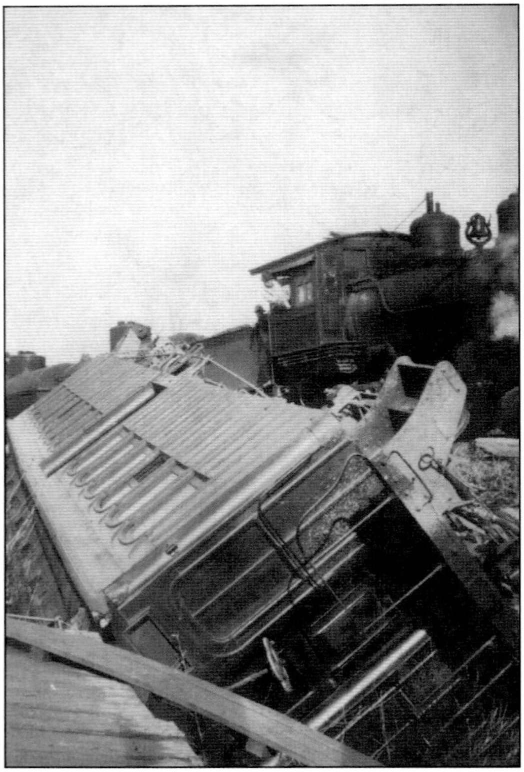

A TRAIN WRECK, C. 1926. A passenger train wreck is pictured here. The rails apparently separated, and a passenger car derailed and overturned.

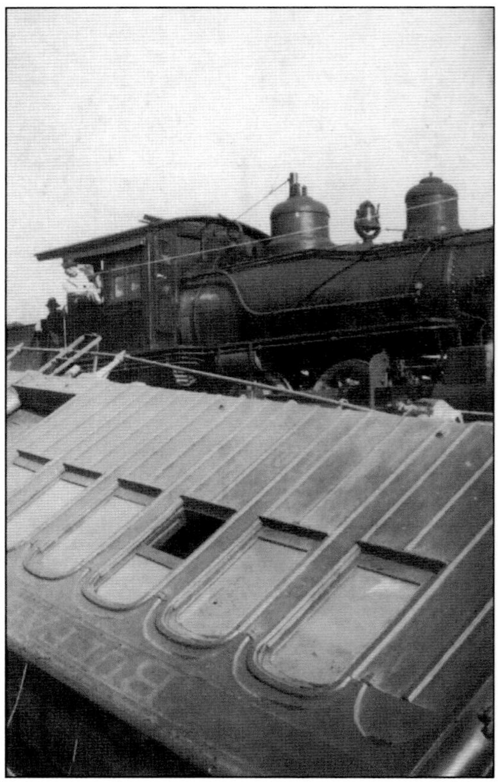

A CLOSER LOOK. An additional photograph of a passenger train wreck goes into more detail. A closer look at the passenger car reveals the word Buffalo as in Buffalo Union-Carolina, which is clearly visible on the overturned passenger car.

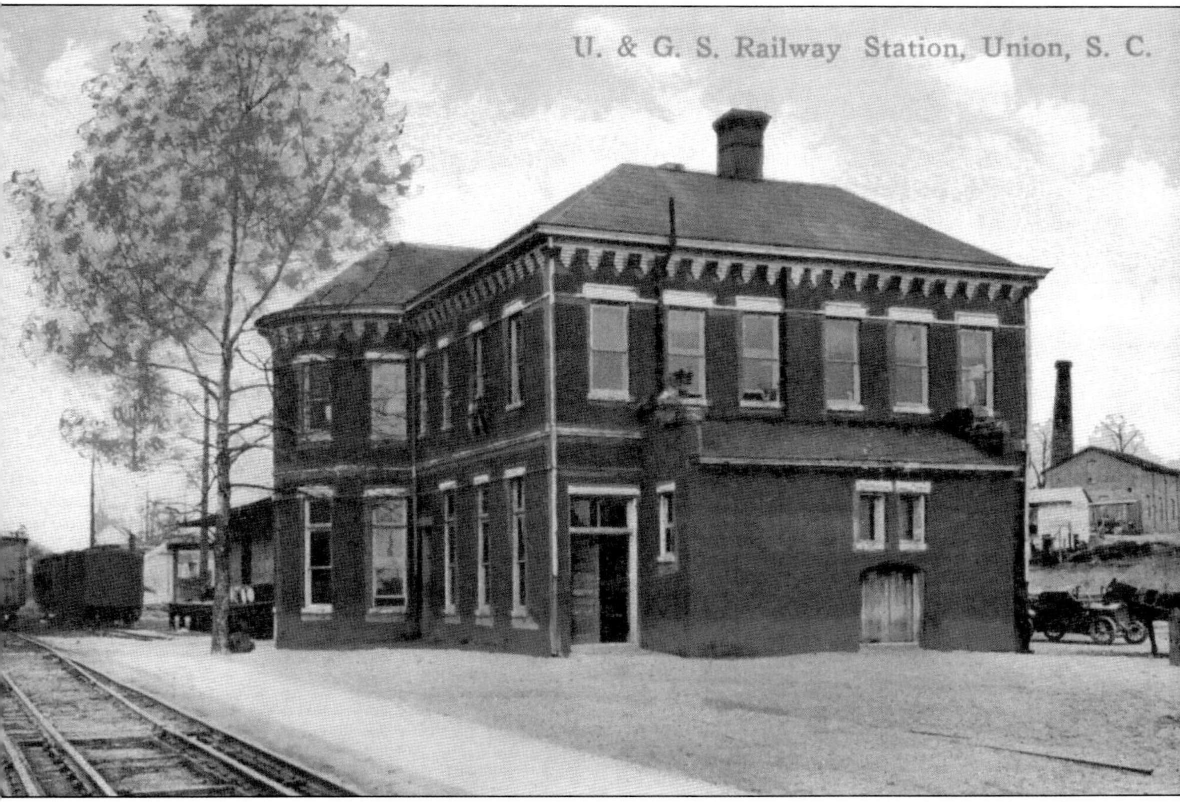

UGS Railroad Station. The Union & Glenn Springs Railroad station is depicted in this postcard. In the background, there is an early roadster and a horse wagon.

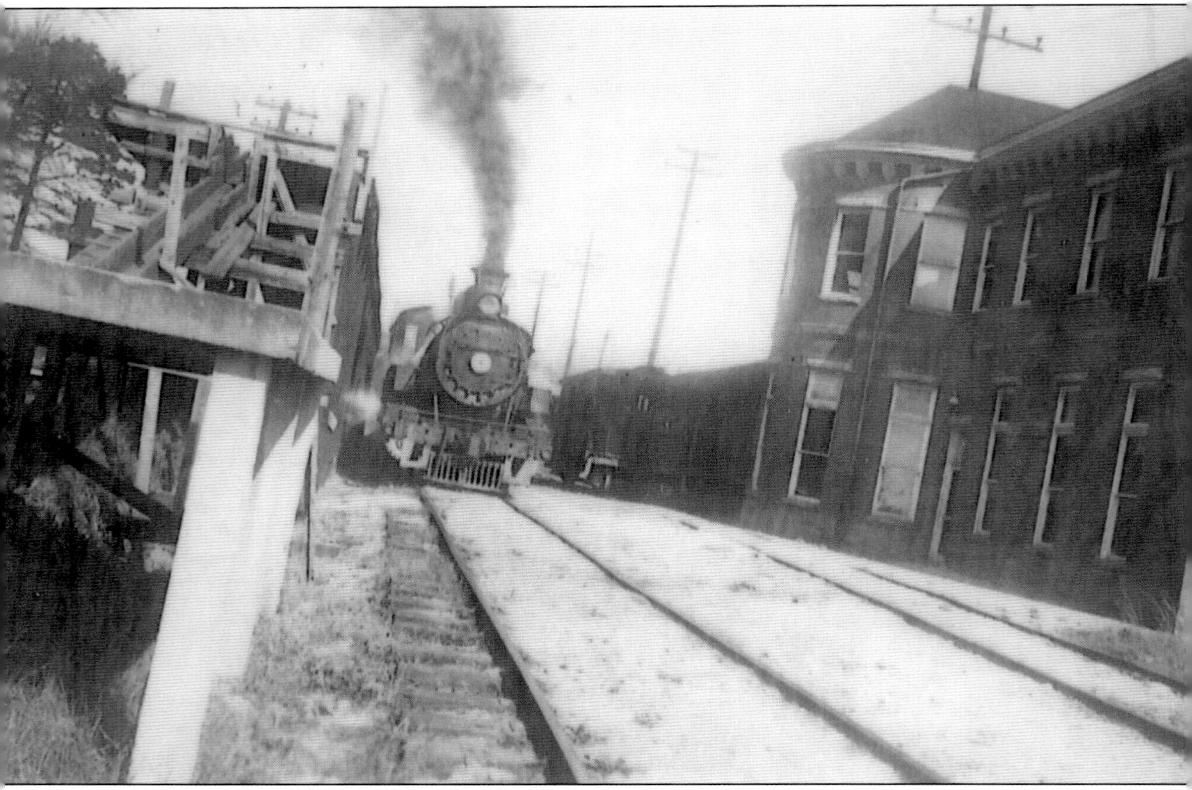

BUC. The BUC train arrives into the station. The most recently built two-story train station on the right hand side still exists.

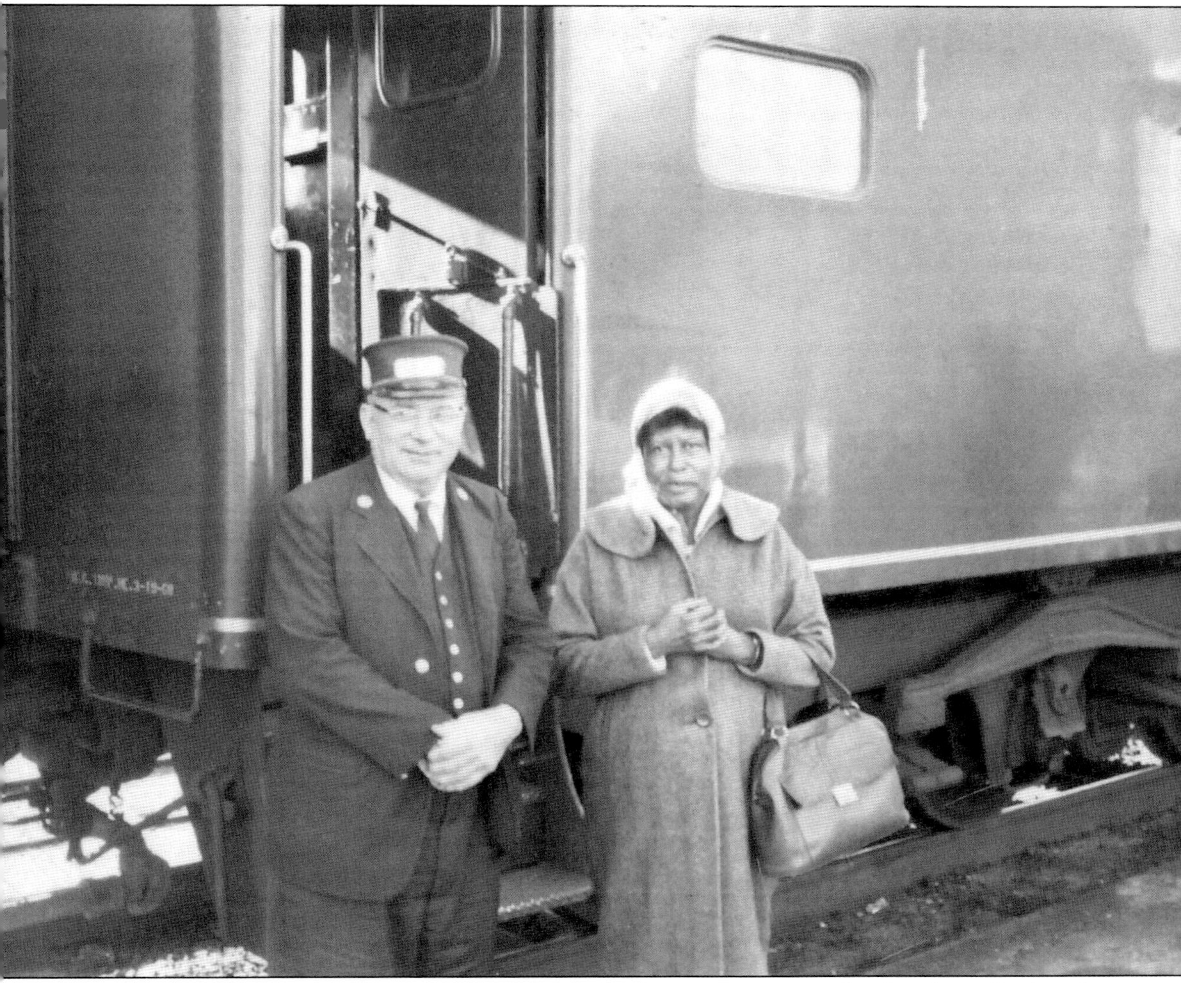

The Last Passenger. Annie M. Johnson was the last passenger on the Southern Railway's passenger line from Union to Carlisle in 1968. The Southern Railway had taken over the BUC passenger line when the railroad ceased operations.

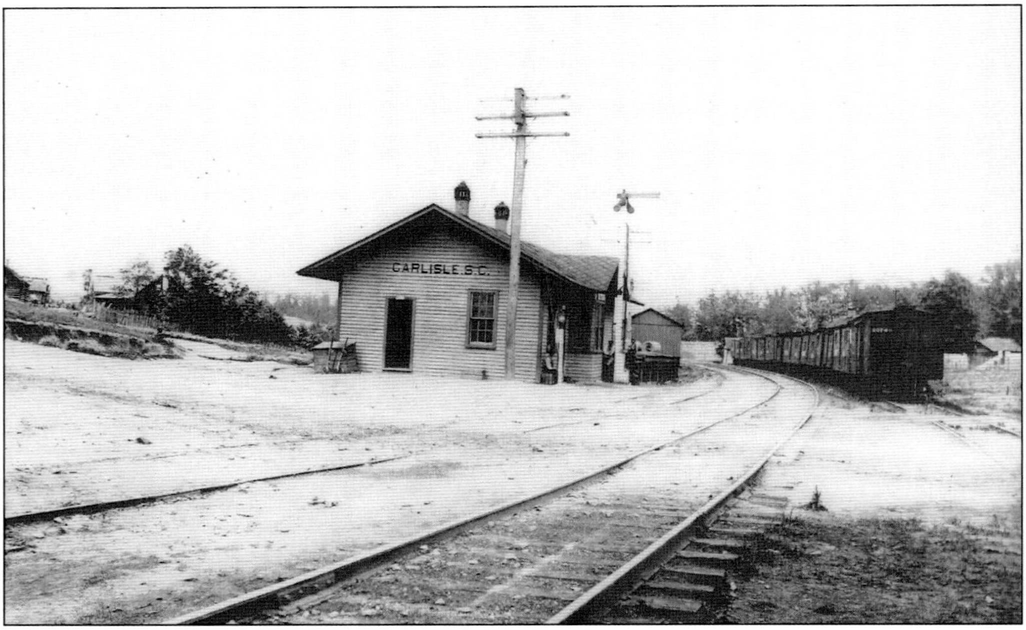

The Seaboard Railway, 1905. The Carlisle Seaboard Railway station is seen in this 1905 photograph. The Seaboard Railway spanned from Atlanta, Georgia, to New York. Duncan's BUC Railroad made a junction with the Seaboard Railway in Carlisle.

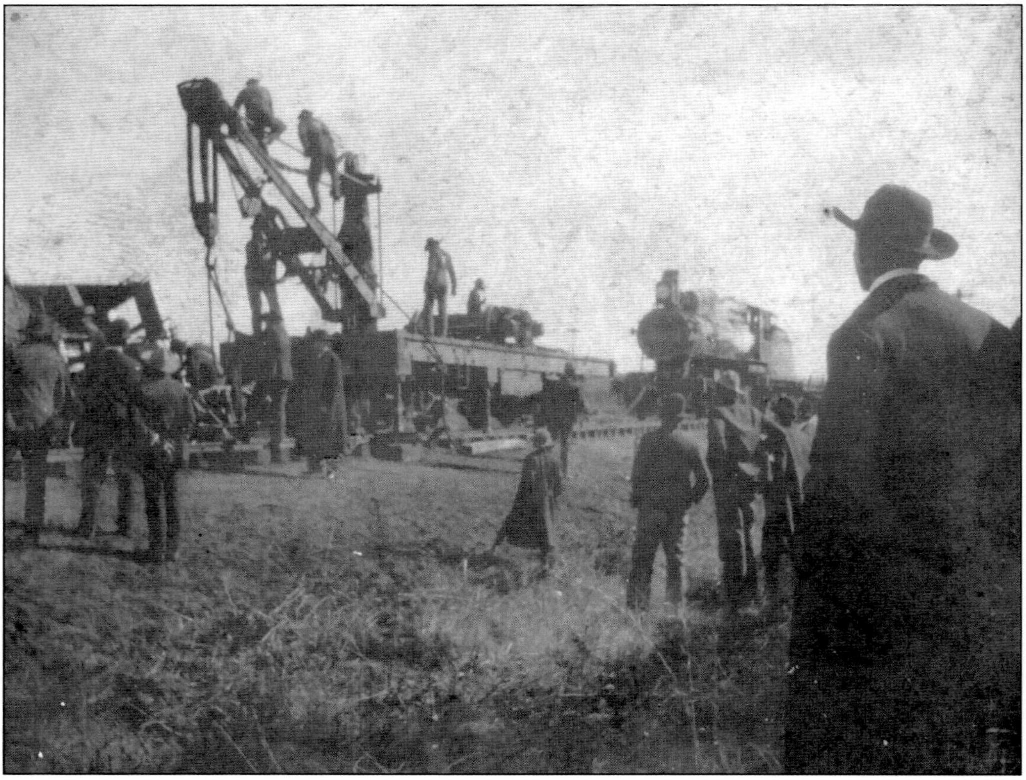

A Railroad Crane. A crew works a railroad crane. Based on the square head lamp on the locomotive, it is not a BUC train but perhaps a Southern Railway locomotive.

Six

Antebellum and Main Street Architecture

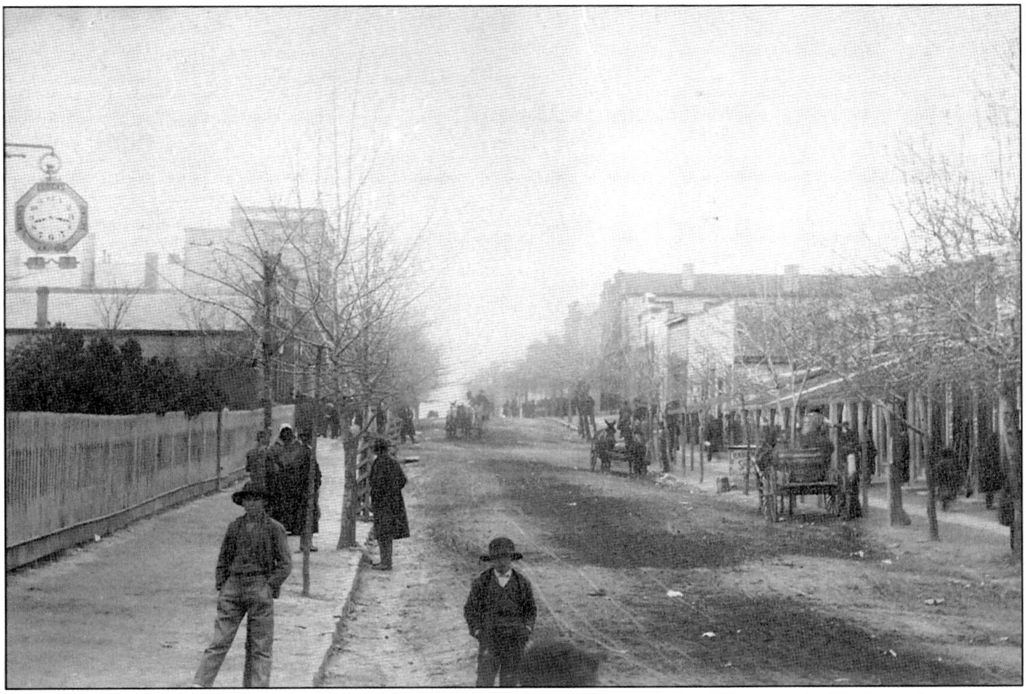

Main Street, 1882. This iconic photograph of Main Street was taken in 1882. Local residents pose for one of the earliest known images, captured on the unpaved dirt road of Union's main thoroughfare. The tallest building to the left is the Hotel Union. The clock visible at left is a nonfunctional advertisement for Tinsley's Jewelers. This early advertisement still exists, and it is displayed at the Union County Museum.

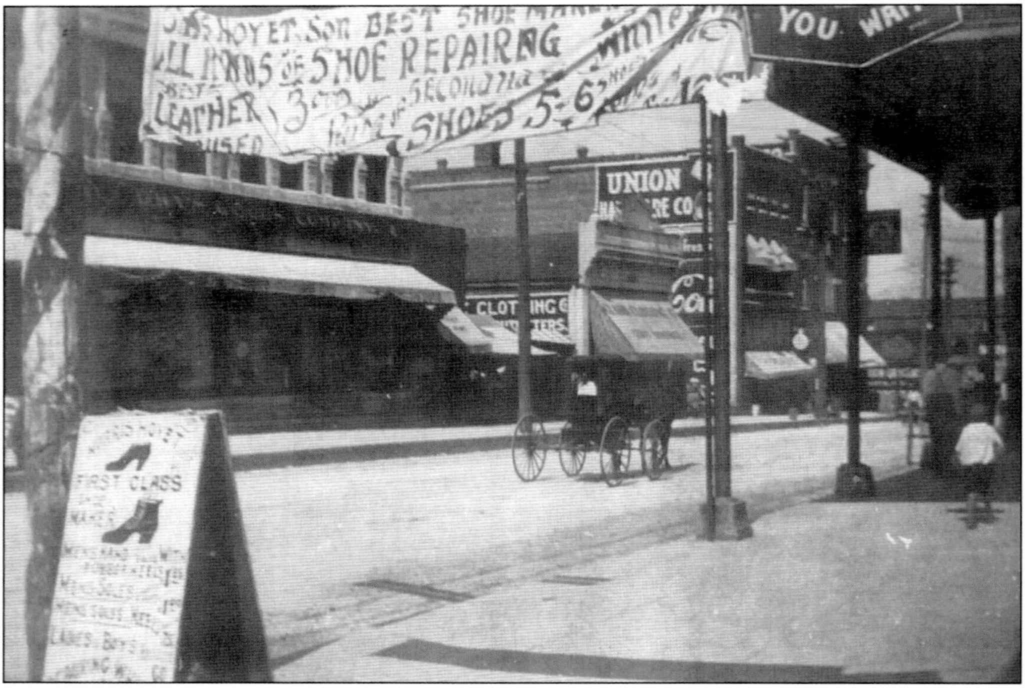

SHOT FROM THE UNION HOTEL. A Main Street scene is recorded in this image, which was taken from the side of the Union Hotel. This snapshot portrays local business advertisements around the north side's 100 block of East Main Street in the early 1900s.

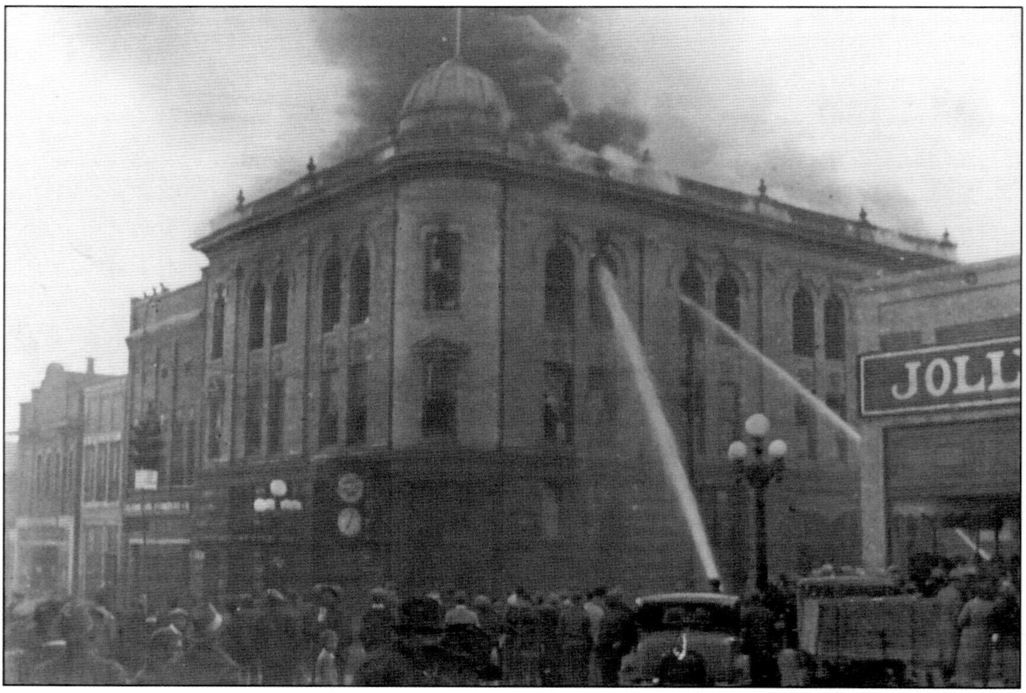

A TERRIBLE FIRE, 1934. The Nicholson Bank Building fire took place in January 1934. The bank was founded in the 1880s and had moved into this new building 30 years prior, on December 31, 1904. Afterwards, this landmark was rehabilitated, but eventually the structure was torn down.

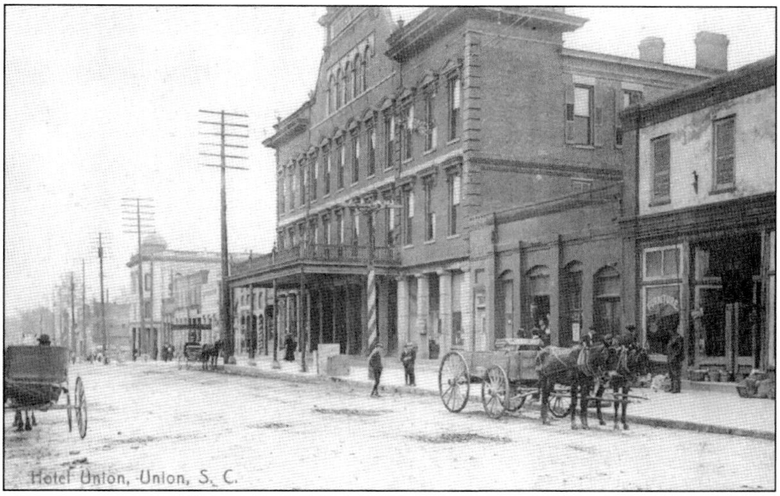

The Hotel Union. Hotel Union is displayed in a wonderful postcard image from Union's Main Street. The hotel, constructed after the fire of 1887, was three stories high, making it one of Union's largest early buildings.

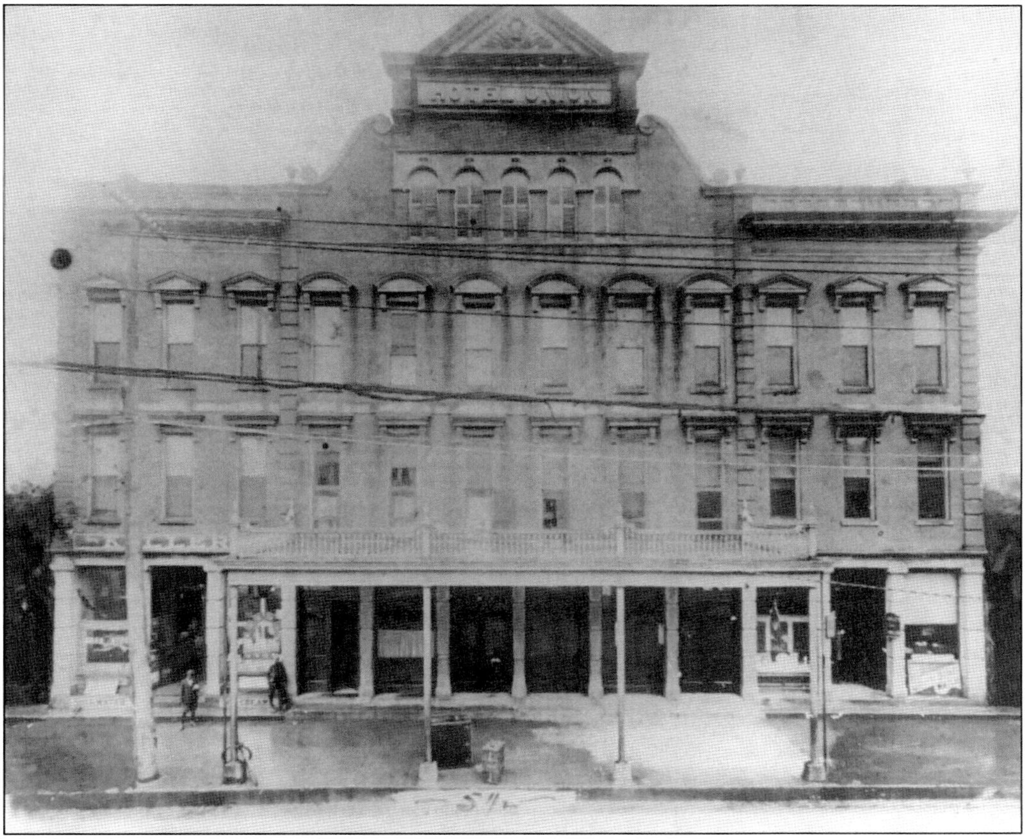

The Facade of Hotel Union. A rare frontal image of the Hotel Union's facade is depicted in this early photograph. A fire later ravaged the upper floor of the hotel, and it was subsequently remodeled by removing that upper floor and dividing the remainder of the building into three separate business units.

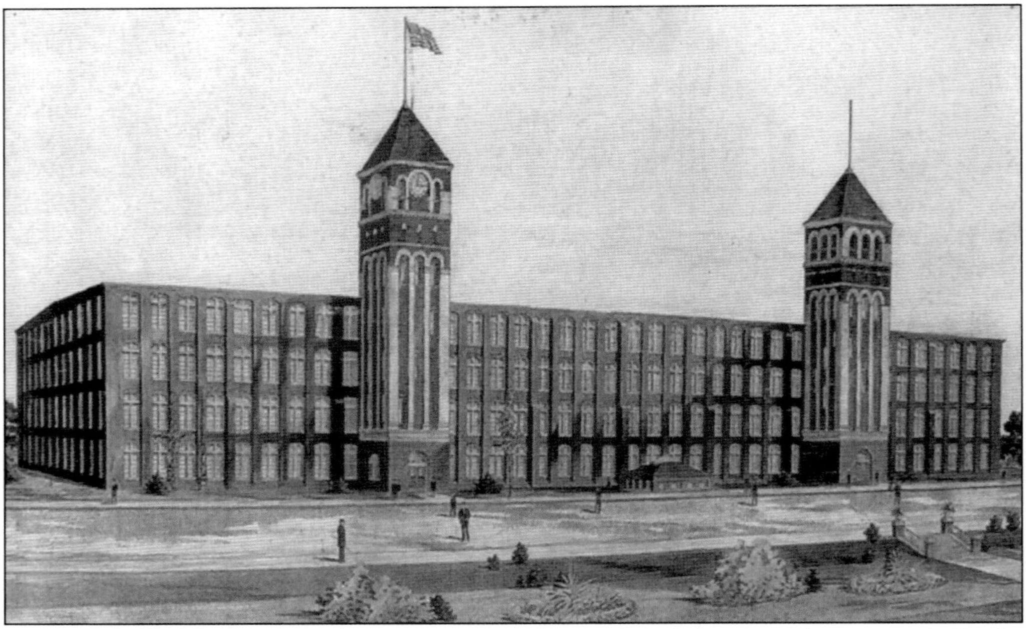

THE BUFFALO MILL CONCEPTUAL DRAWING. This is a copy of the original concept art for the Buffalo Mill. The Buffalo Mill was Thomas Cary Duncan's second mill facility, and it was once deemed the largest cotton mill in the world. A purchase order was authorized for the acquisition of one million bricks for the construction of the building.

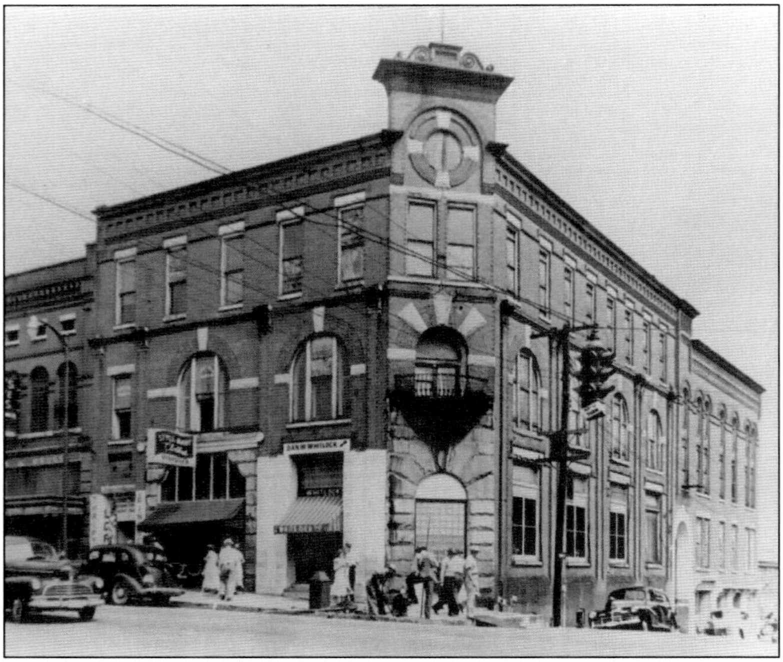

UNION'S OPERA HOUSE. The Main Street Opera House was located on the northwest corner of Main and Gadberry Streets. The opera house was a stage for many performers, from vaudeville actors to touring companies whose performances encompassed both drama and comedy. Built in 1892, the structure was torn down in 1952.

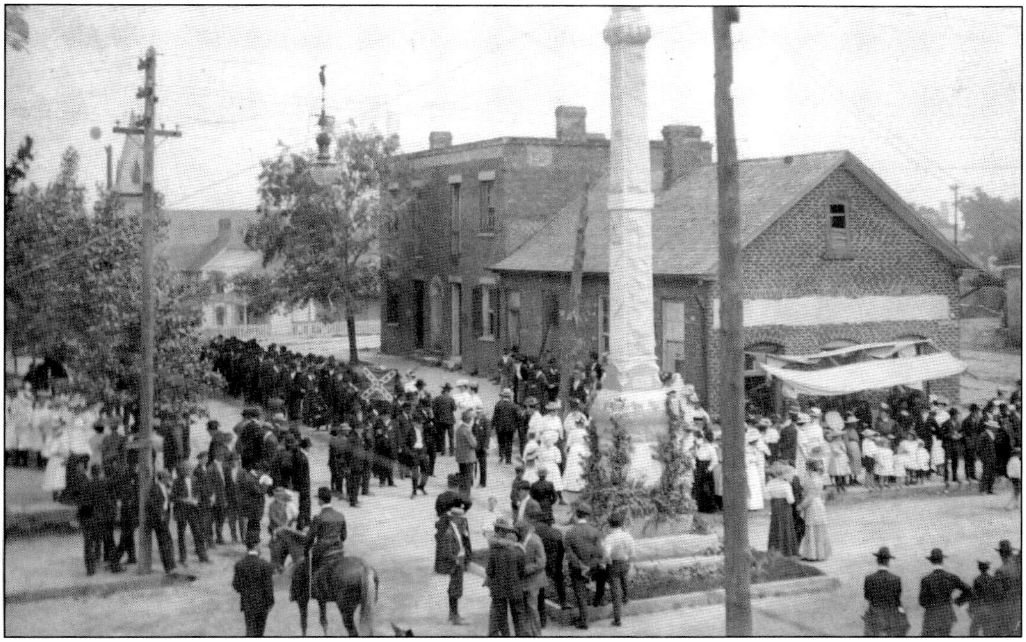

The Confederate Monument. The Confederate monument was unveiled on May 25, 1907. Robert Mills's courthouse can be seen in the background, and the J.B. Porter Grocer is visible on the right.

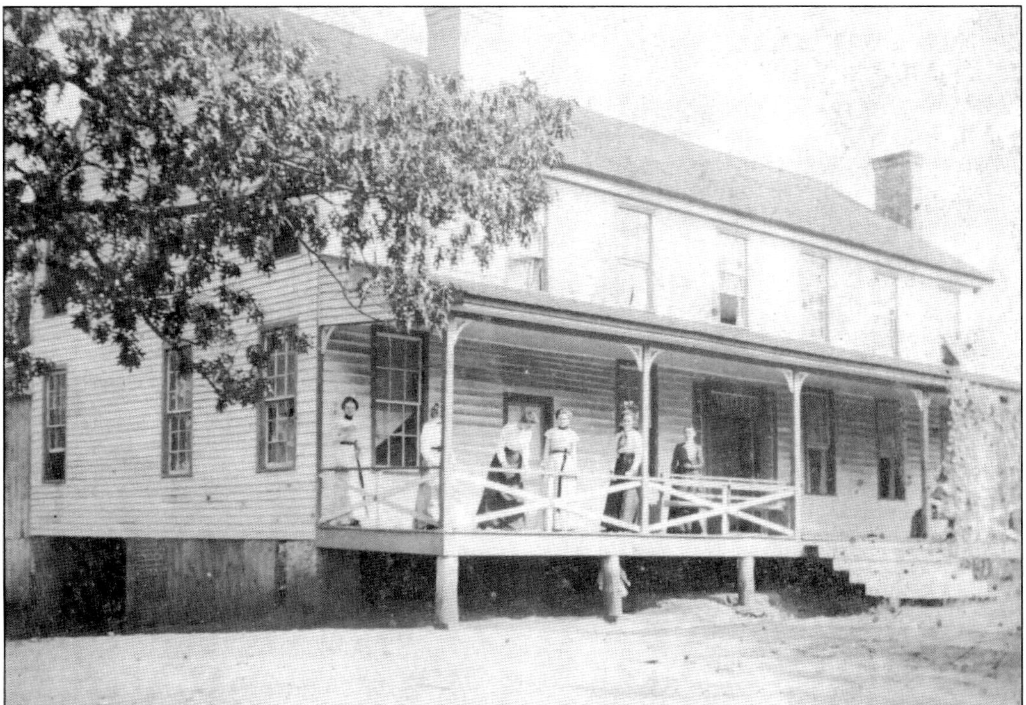

The West Springs Hotel. This rare snapshot details the West Springs resort hotel. The West Springs Hotel began operation as a hotel and spa around 1854, though it ceased operations around the time of World War I. The building survived for decades but was demolished in the 1970s.

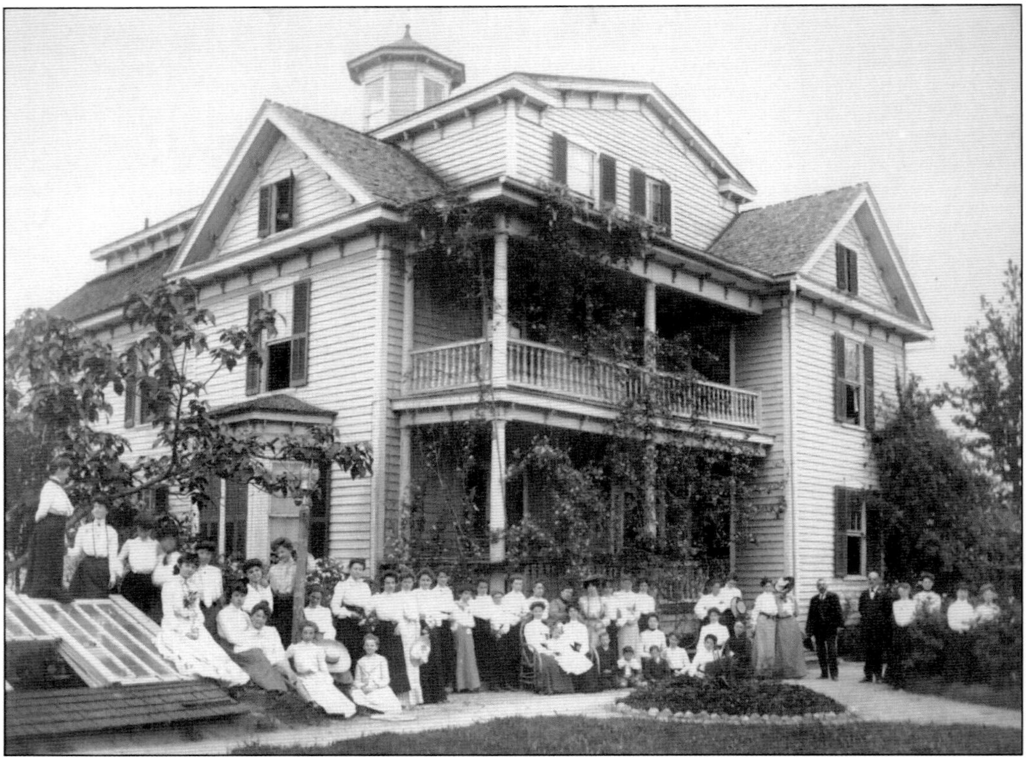

The Clifford Seminary. Organized in 1881 and granted a regular college charter by the State of South Carolina in 1884, the Clifford Seminary was founded by the Reverend Branch Greenleaf (B.G.) and Mary Scofield Clifford. For almost 50 years, they were engaged in religious and educational work in Union. Their college was a home and girls' school, which also served as an institution of learning and culture. For this reason, it attracted students from South Carolina, North Carolina, Georgia, and Florida. Upon the death of Dr. Clifford in 1910, Mary Clifford took over the management of the school, and she continued educating young women for a number of years. The seminary closed around 1920, and a portion of the original building was used as part of the Union High School facilities up until the 1950s. The structure has since been torn down. The YMCA on East Main Street currently stands on the location formerly occupied by this institution for higher learning.

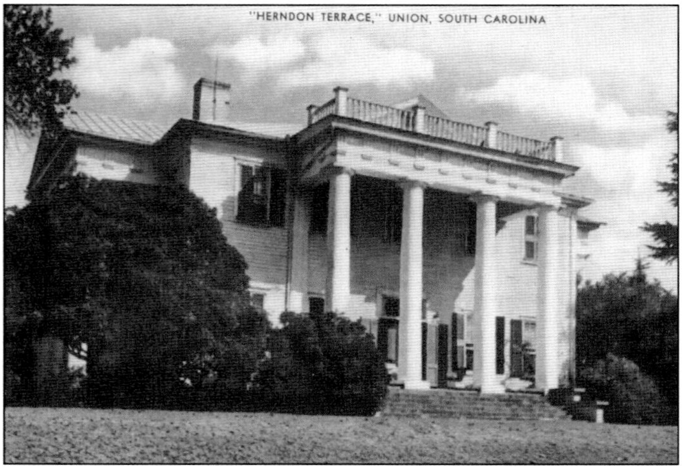

Herndon Terrace. This Greek Revival home was designed by John Pratt for Zachariah Herndon. Pratt was also known as an inventor of a precursor to the modern typewriter. The residence was built during the period between 1845 and 1848, and its massive porches present identical facades on three sides. This mansion is an exemplary sample of Union Antebellum architecture.

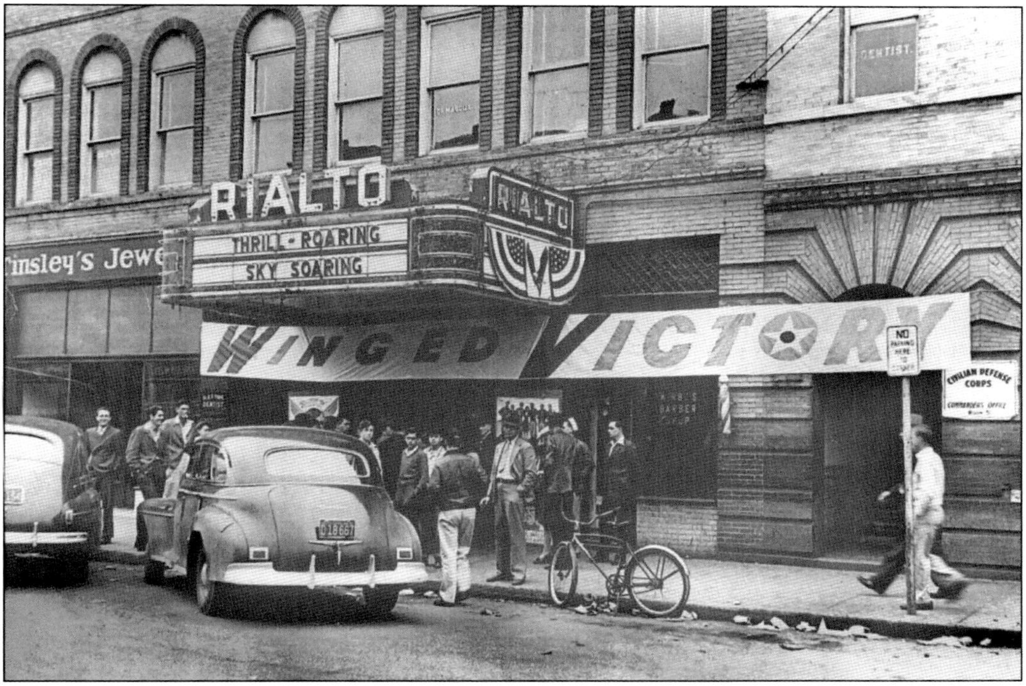

The Rialto Theatre. Union's Rialto Theatre is pictured here during World War II. Tinsley's Jewelers is visible on the left side of the photograph. To the right of the theater is the entrance to the local Civilian Defense Corps.

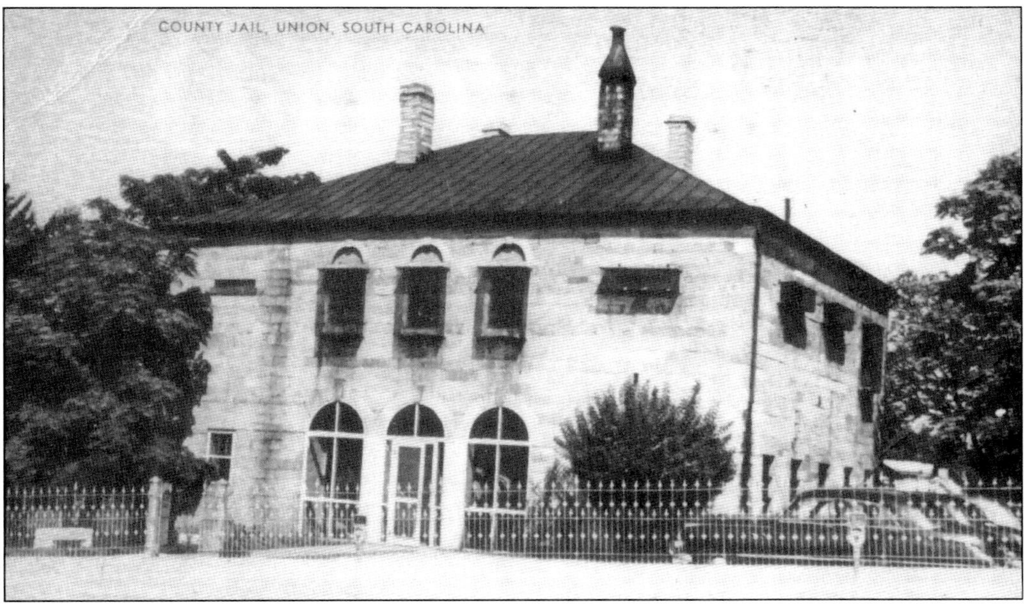

The Union County Jail. Designed by Robert Mills, the famous American architect, the jail was built in 1823. This was actually not the original jail known to have been built on the site. Mills also designed the Union Courthouse, which was torn down and replaced around 1912. Mills was a prolific early American architect, and he designed numerous buildings in South Carolina and for the federal government. These designs include the US Treasury Building and the Washington Monument, located in the US capital.

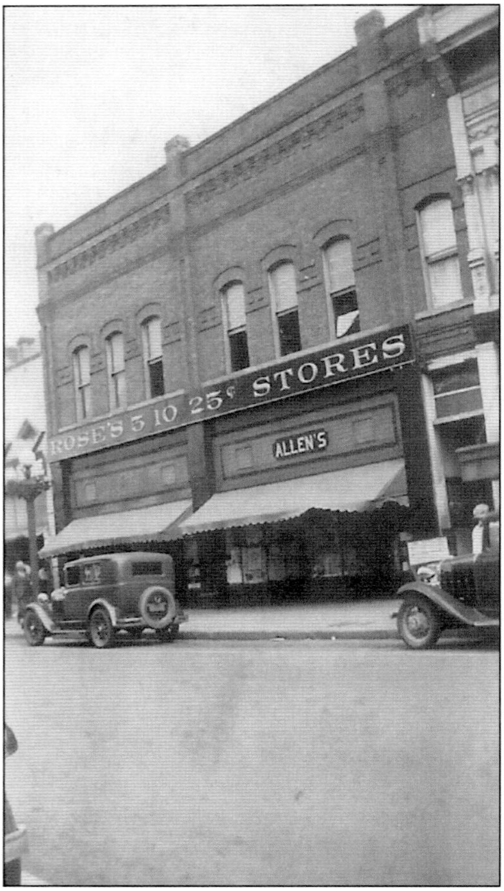

Rose's 5 & 10 Store. Rose's ran a very popular five-and-dime store on Main Street, and the store's 1900s cash register is displayed in the Union County Museum. Due to its age and the monetary values from its day, the register is only able to make sales up to $3.99.

The Gilliam House. This home is located on East Main Street, which was also the location of many fine early Antebellum and Victorian homes. The Gilliam House exists to this day, along with many other intact homes.

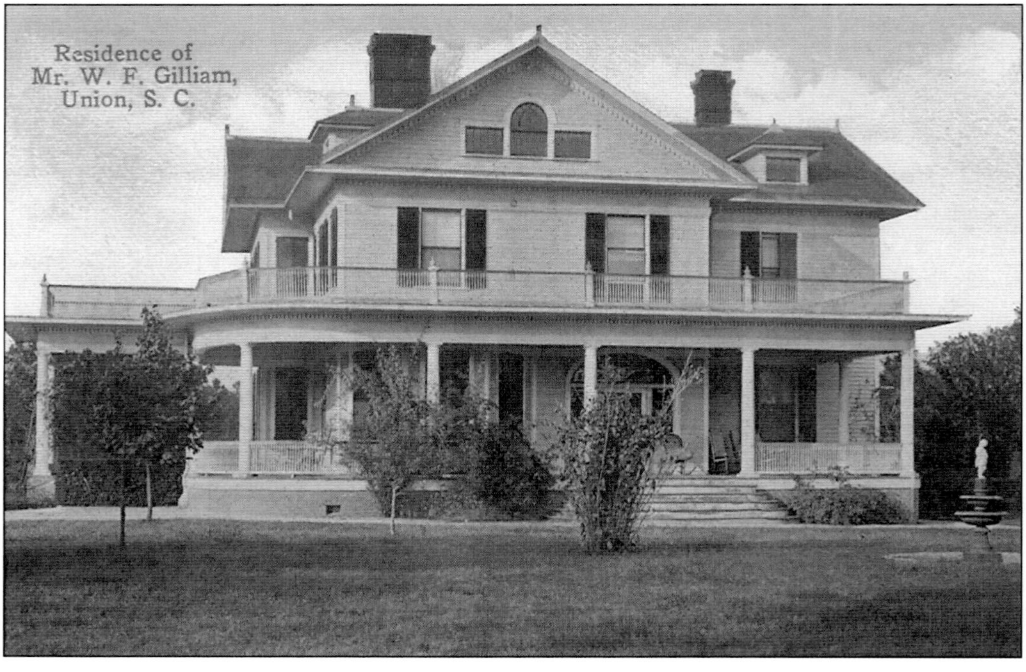

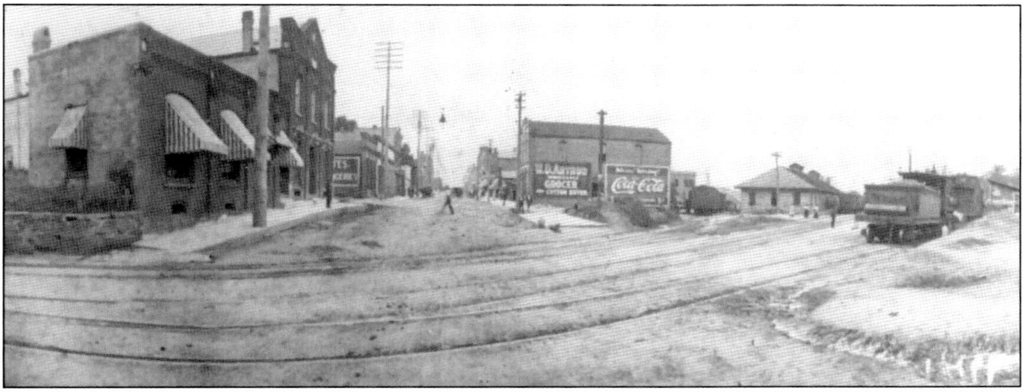

Main Street Panorama. This photograph, facing west down Main Street, was taken over the railroad tracks close to the intersection of Mountain Street.

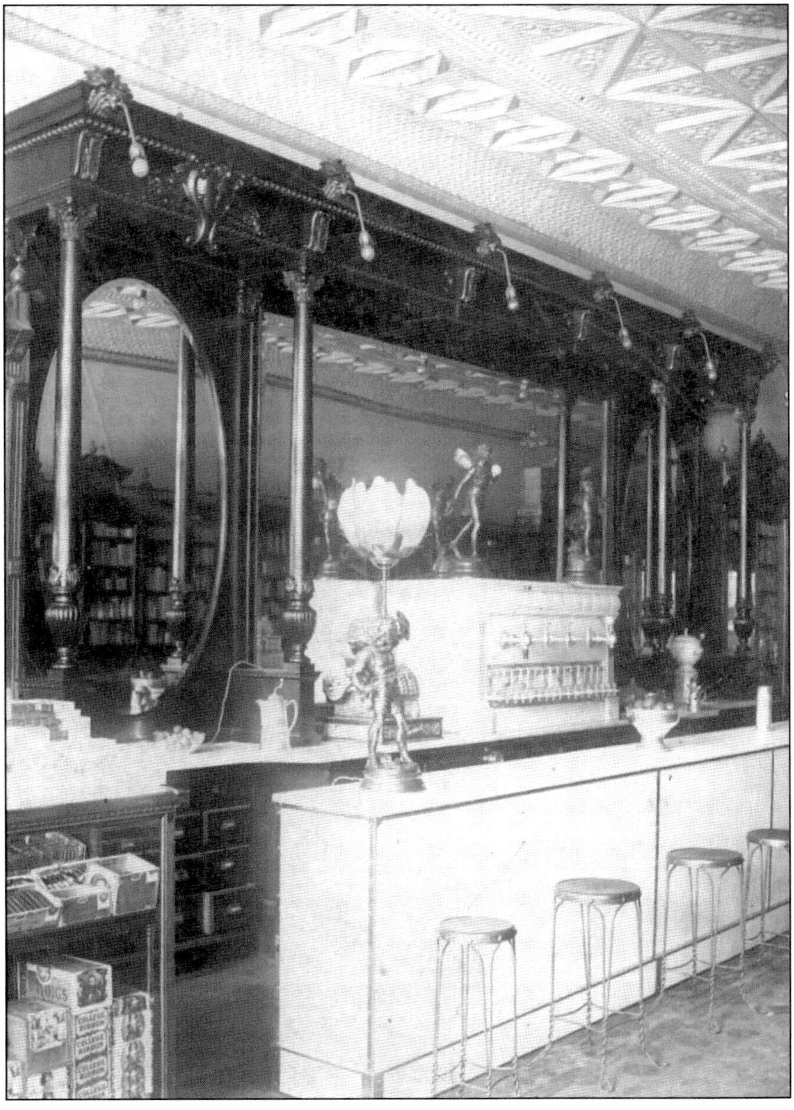

The Union Drug Company. The interior of the Union Drug Company is seen in this photograph. The Union Drug Company was a competitor of the Palmetto Drug Company, which was another local Main Street drugstore.

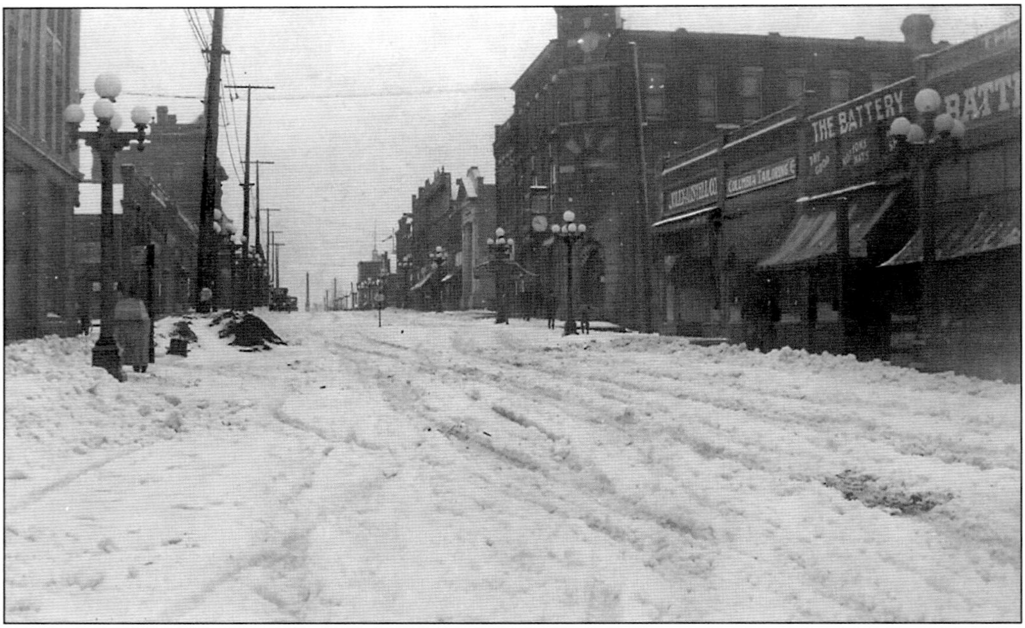

SNOW ON MAIN STREET. Union can experience very cold winters and, on occasion, is susceptible to snowstorms. The opera house, located on the corner of Gadberry and Main Streets, can be seen. The Confederate monument is visible farther down the street at its original location, which was in the center of the street.

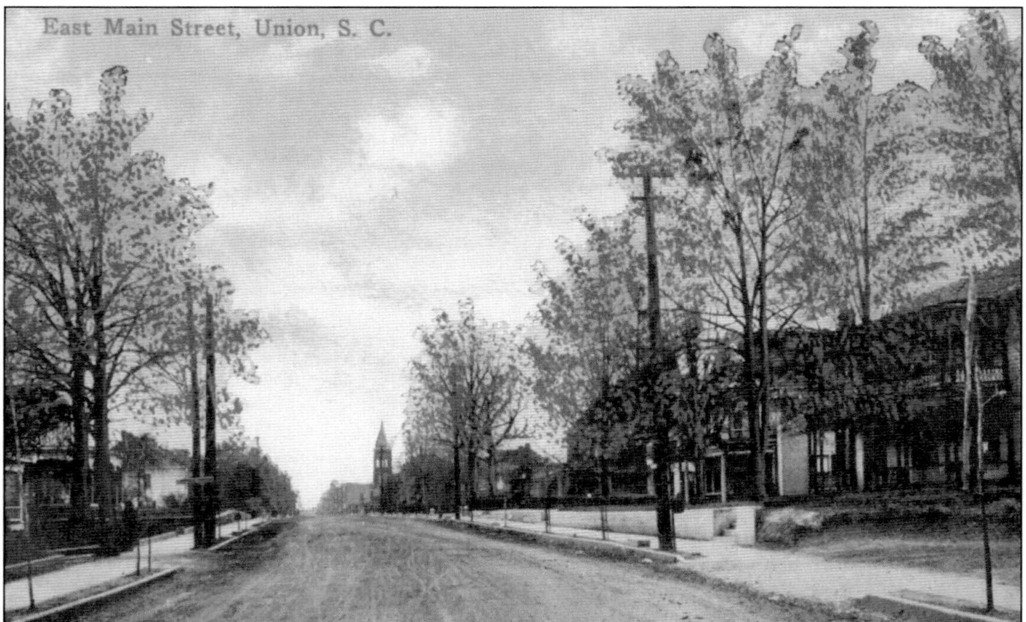

EAST MAIN STREET. East Main Street is seen from a western view, and the First Baptist Church's steeple is visible in the distance. This photograph was taken farther down the street from the business district, in a residential area.

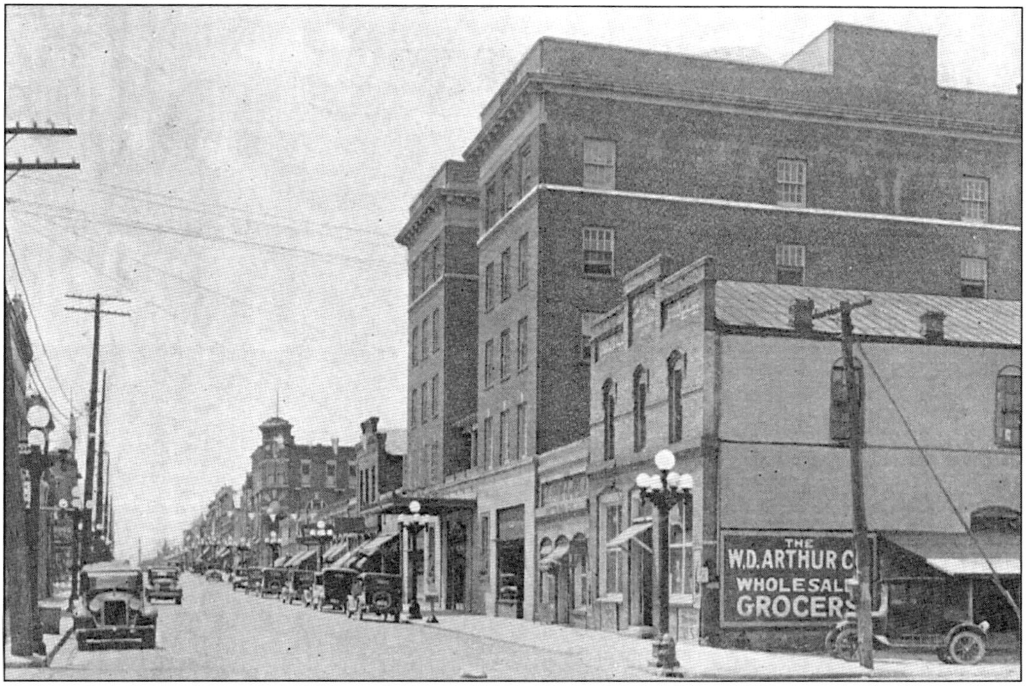

The Fair Forest Hotel. A Main Street photograph depicts the Fair Forest Hotel, which opened its doors for business in 1927. The hotel operates today as rental apartments.

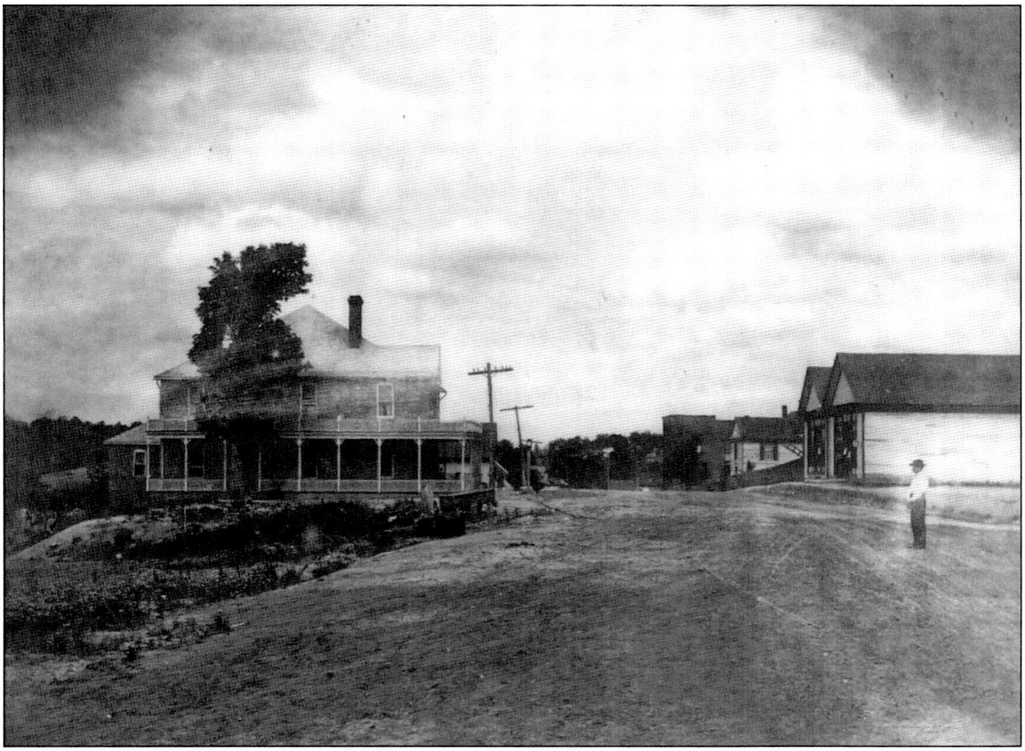

Carlisle Main Street. Pictured here is Carlisle's Main Street, prior to paved roads. The Carlisle Hotel is visible on the left with its large open porch.

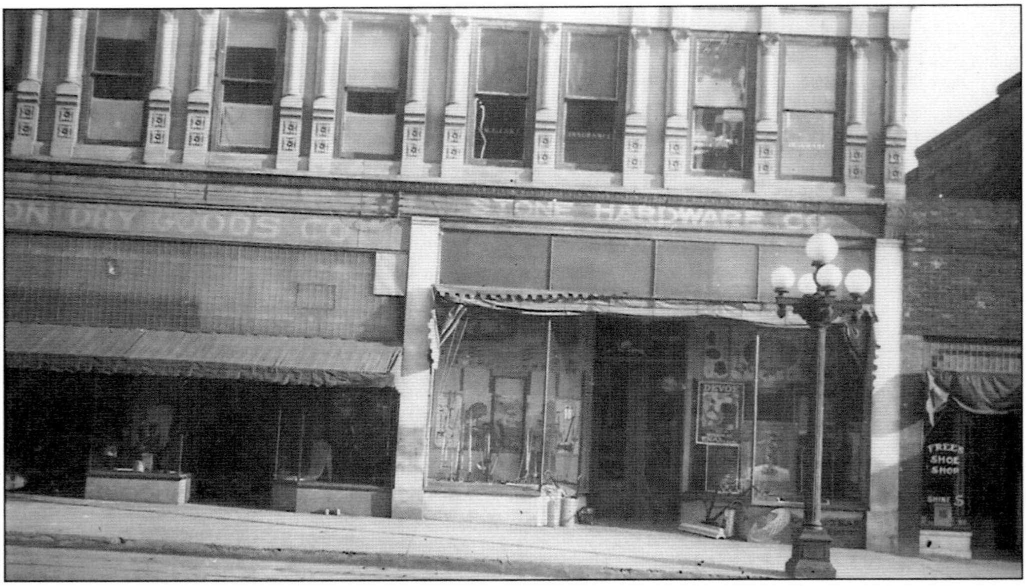

The Business District. Wilburn's Union Dry Goods, Stone Hardware, and Free's Shoe Shop are visible on the north side of 100 Main Street. Early electric street lamps illuminated the downtown area. The electric street lights that exist today are reproductions of these earlier fixtures. The first municipal street lamps were operated using kerosene, and the units were lit and extinguished by hand daily.

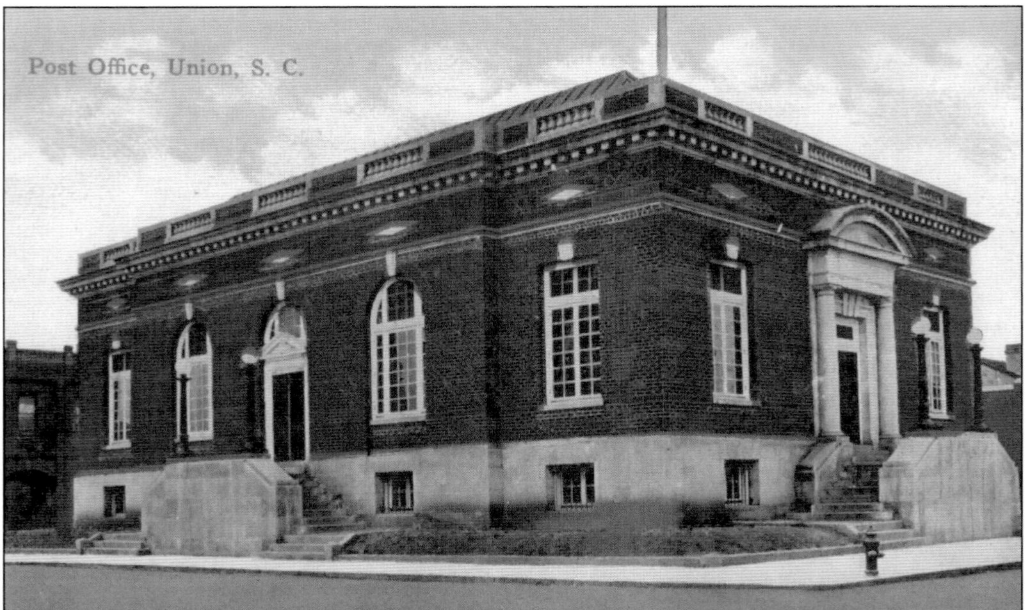

The Thurmond Building. The Thurmond Building was constructed in 1912 as Union's new post office. Currently, the building houses the Union County School administrative offices.

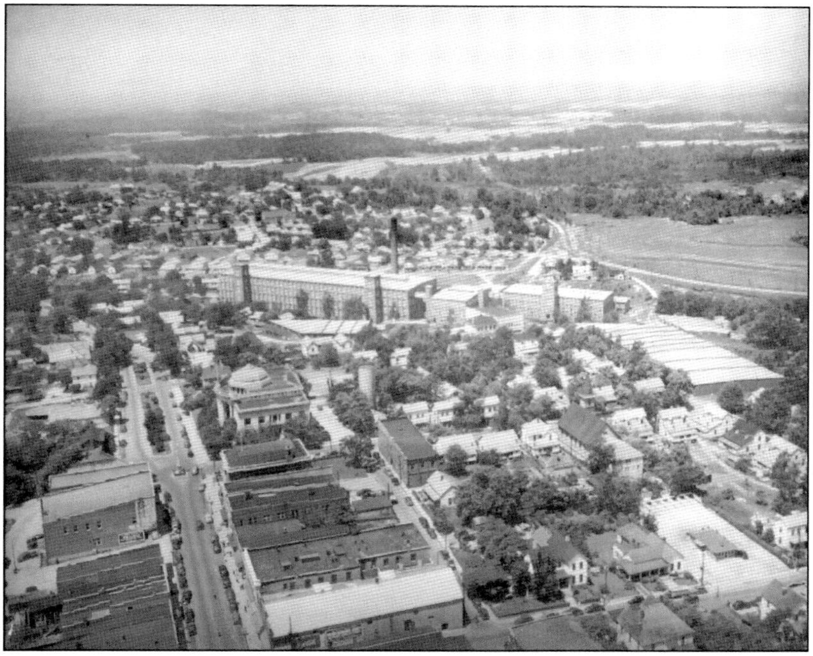

Bird's-Eye View of Union, c. 1946. This image of Union was taken from an airplane. The Union Courthouse and the immensity of the Union Mill complex are easily discernible from the air.

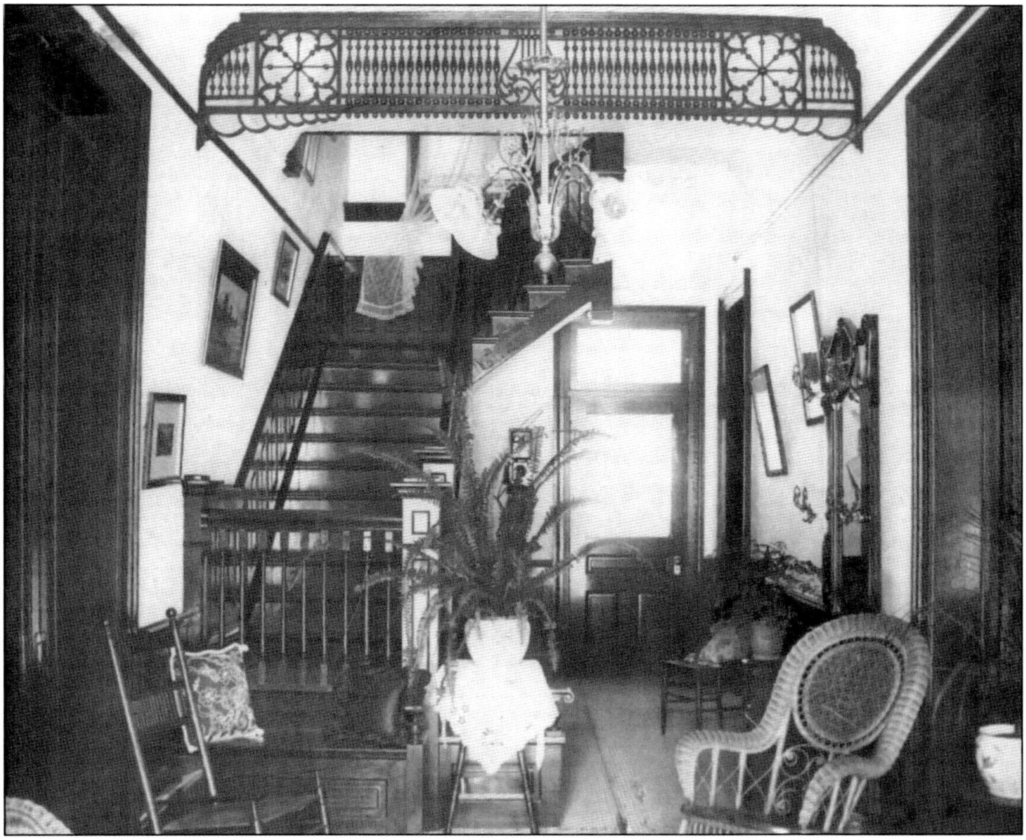

Interior of the Sartor House, c. 1895. The Sartor House was embellished with many fine Victorian architectural elements and furniture.

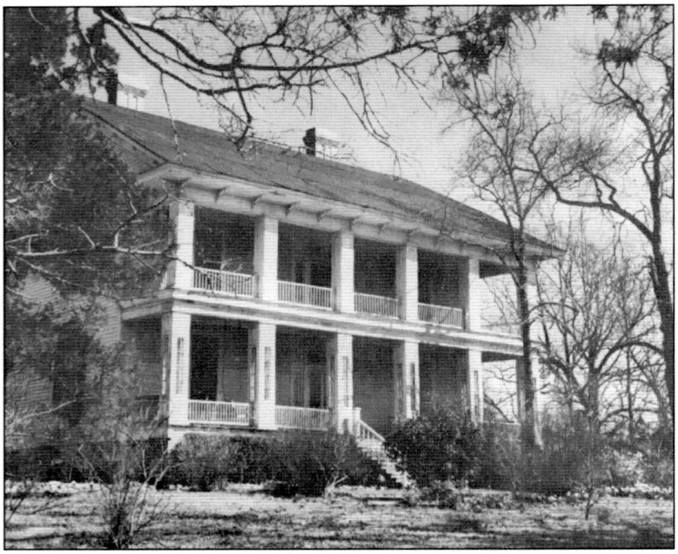

The Woodland Home. With its windowed columns that were fashioned to accommodate lanterns, the Woodland home was built in 1855. The Woodland home is also known as the Parham Jeter place.

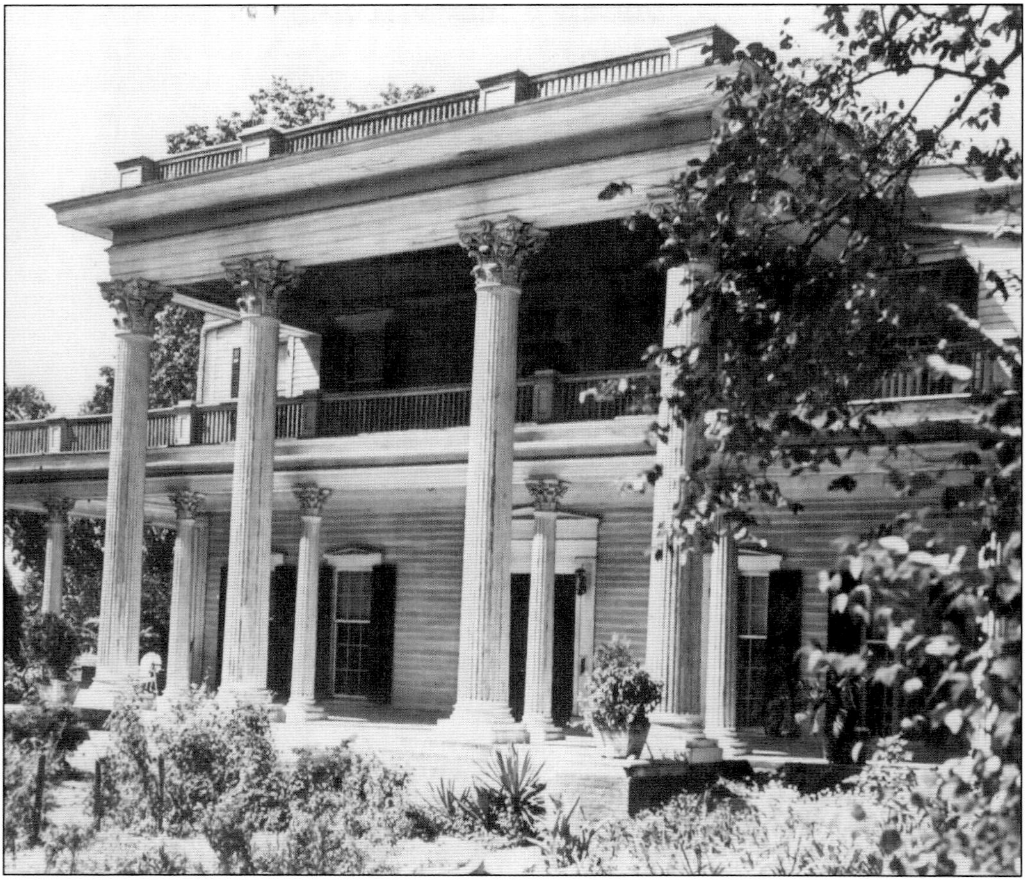

The Merridun Mansion. Including over 12,000 square feet, massive classical fluted columns, and 140-foot ceilings, the Merridun Mansion was Thomas Cary Duncan's ancestral home. William Keenan built the mansion using Doric-style elements around 1855. Duncan later embellished the home with new two-story Corinthian columns and an enlarged portico in 1911.

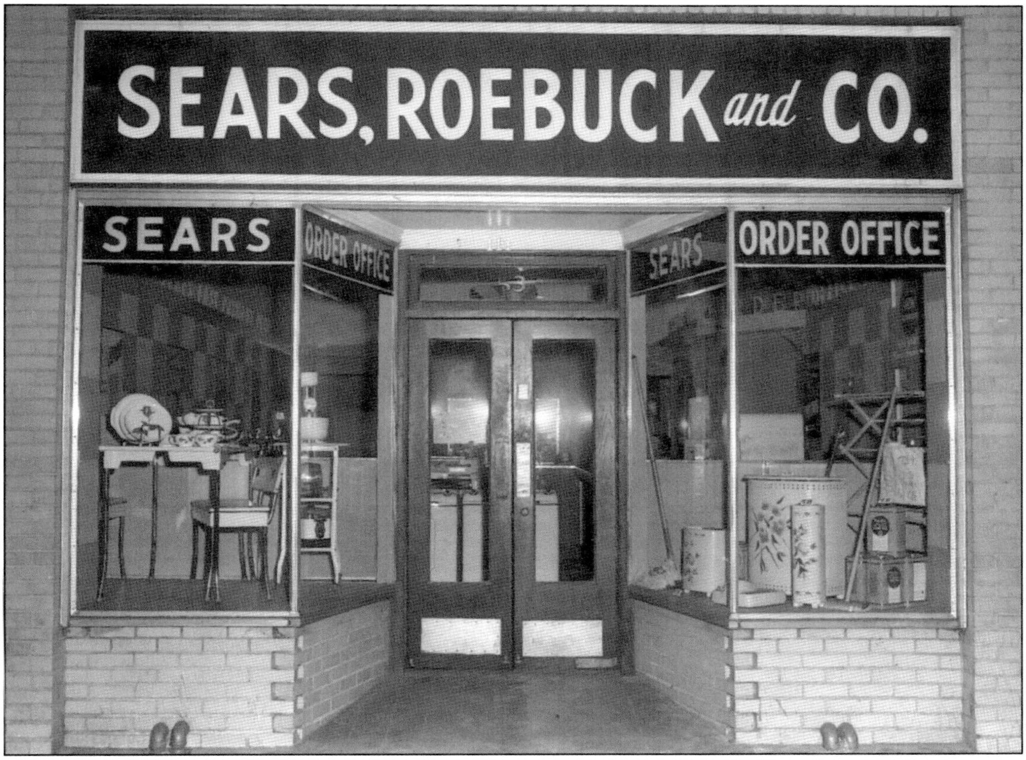

SEARS, ROEBUCK & COMPANY. Union's Main Street business district had a Sears, Belk, and Rose's five-and-dime among many numerous sole proprietary dry goods stores, hardware shops, cobblers, bottlers, and clothiers.

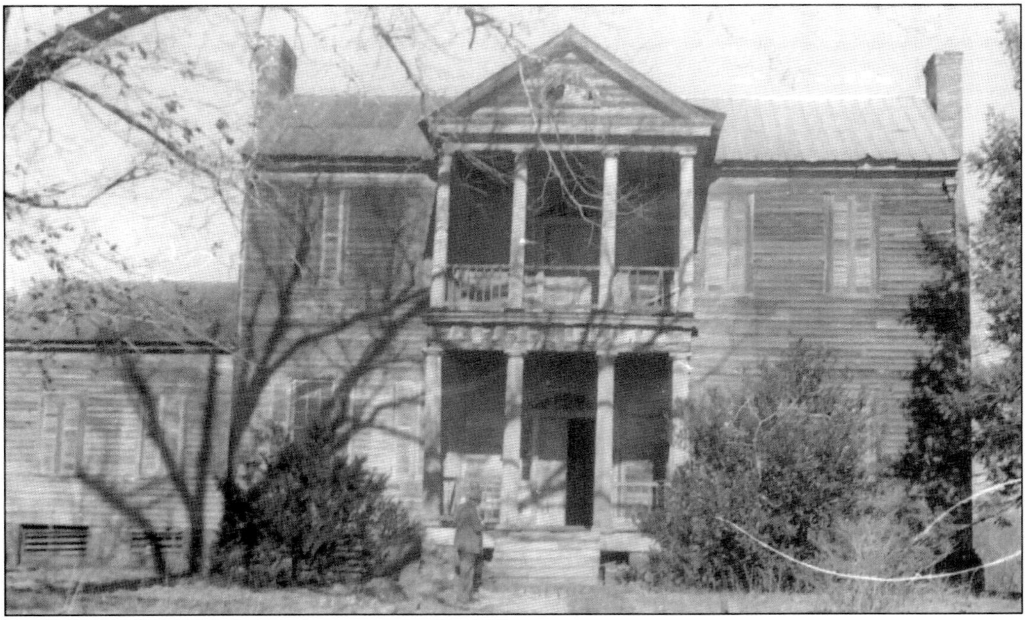

THE OAKS. The Douglas residence was built in 1839, located 16 miles south of Union on Route 35. It was the subject home of the legendary Hound of Goshen ghost story. Sadly, the home burned down in 1968.

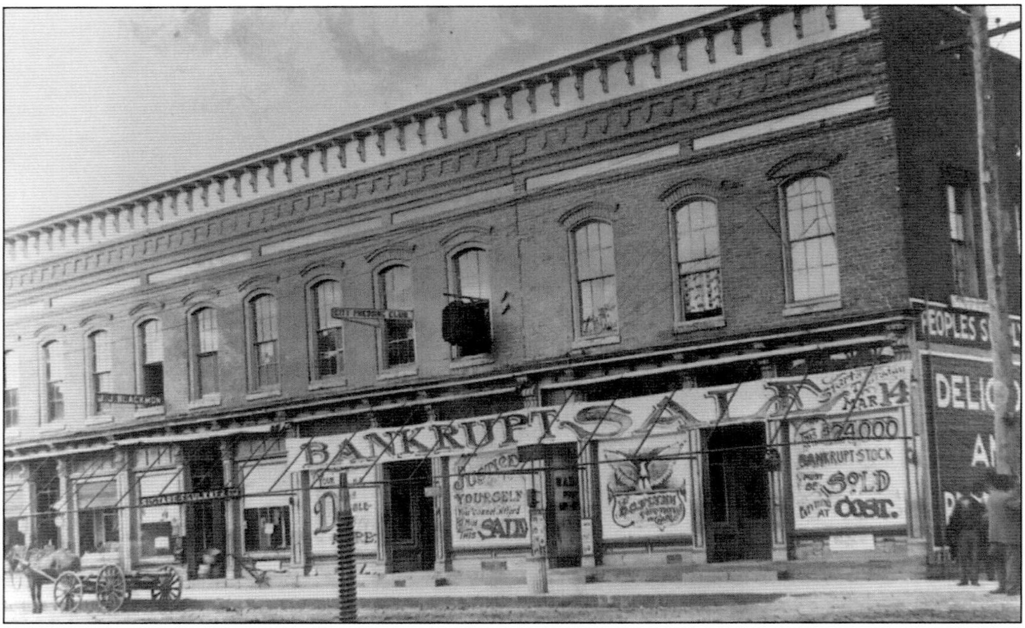

The DC Flynn Bankruptcy Sale, c. 1910. DC Flynn's store was located on north side of East Main Street near the corner of Church Street. Additionally, this stretch of brick building burned down and no longer exists.

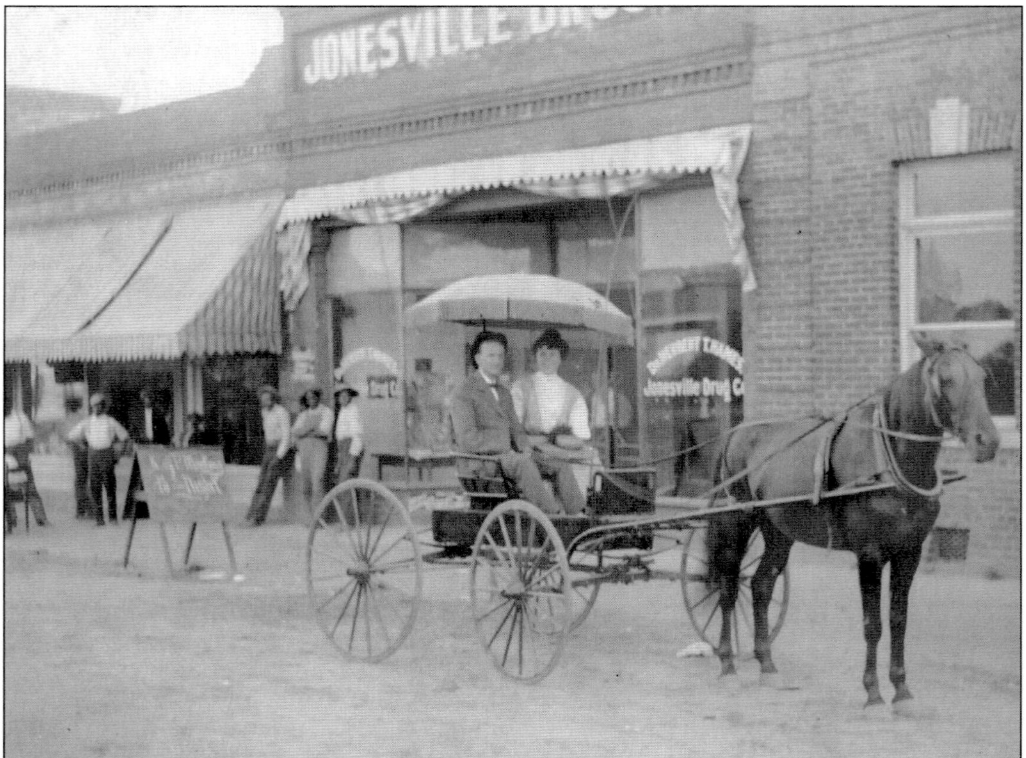

The Jonesville Drugstore. Dr. Herbert T. Hames and his wife, Ada Corkill, who originally hailed from Chester, are pictured here in front of their drugstore.

Seven

Union's Cotton and Textile Mills and Communities

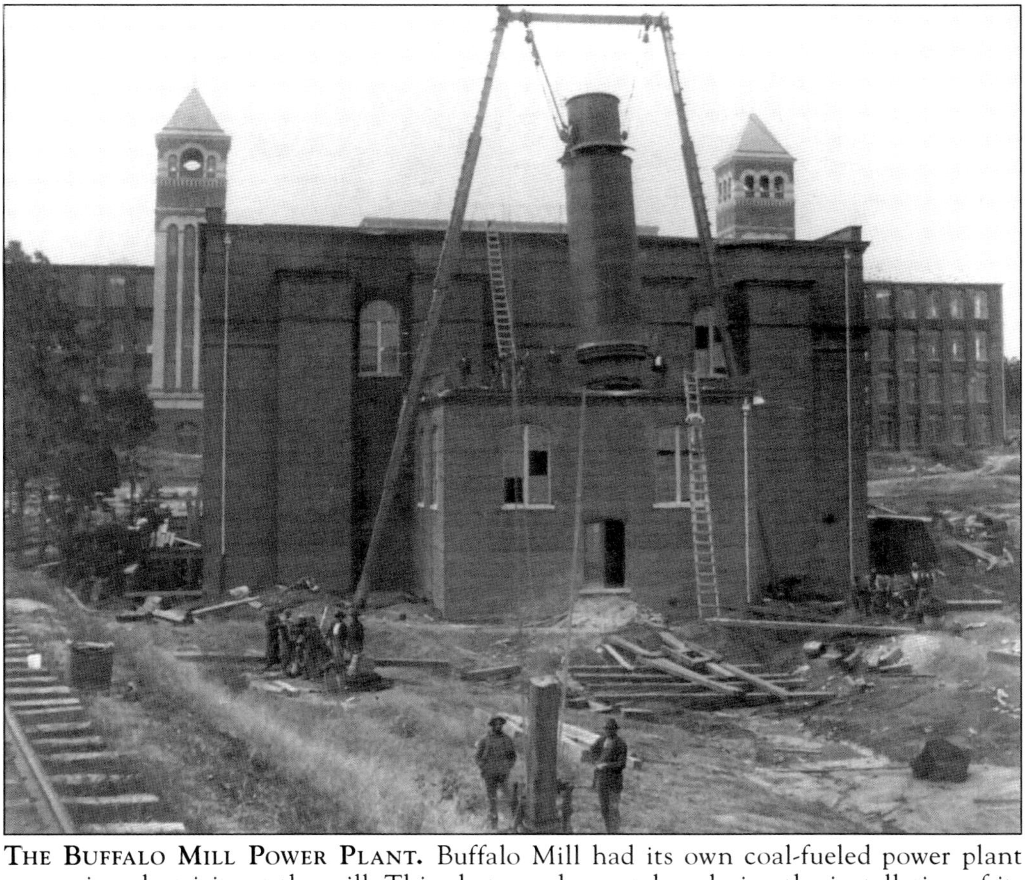

The Buffalo Mill Power Plant. Buffalo Mill had its own coal-fueled power plant generating electricity at the mill. This photograph was taken during the installation of its prefabricated smokestack.

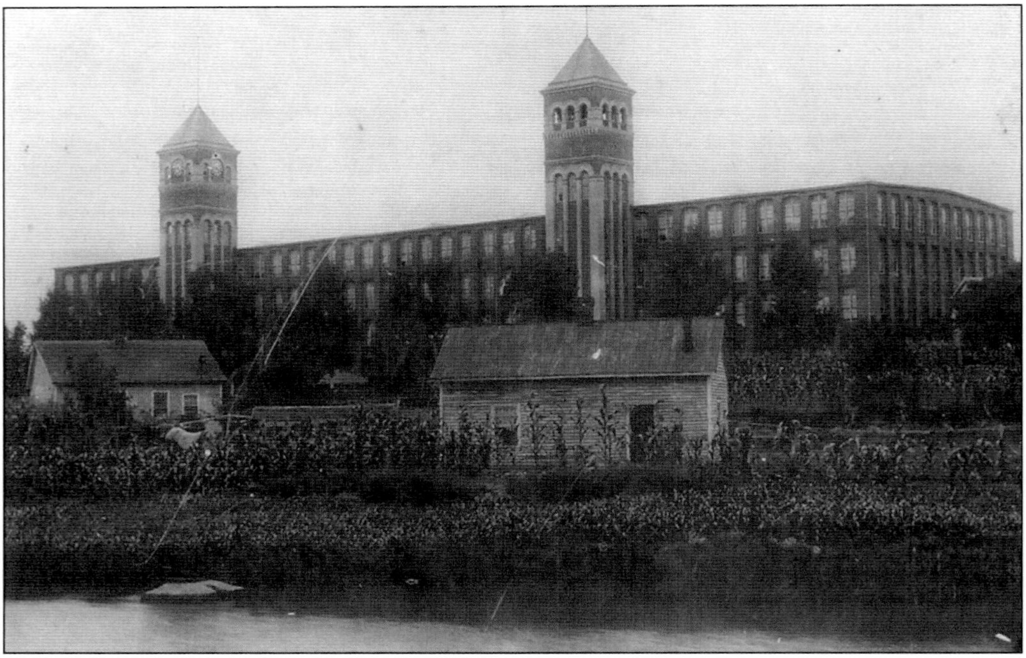

FARMING AROUND THE MILL. The Buffalo Mill is pictured here with corn crops growing in its vicinity. Prior to the Buffalo Mill being built, the acreage was part of the Rice family plantation, and it was later owned by Thomas Cary Duncan.

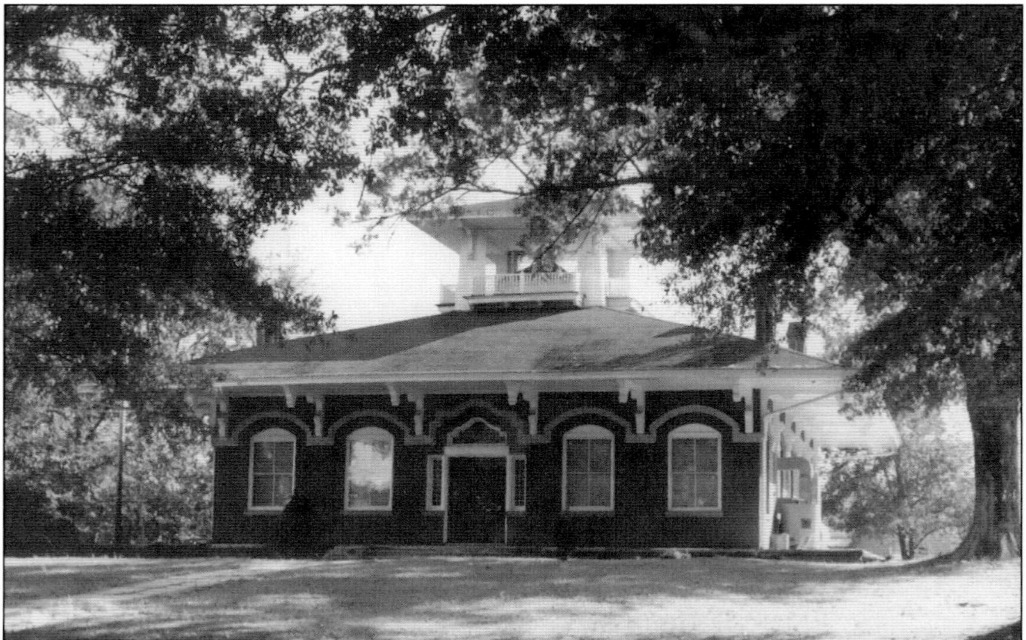

THE RED OFFICE. Buffalo Mill's "Red Office" was designed by W.B. Smith Whaley and Company about 1902. The picturesque building still exists, and it may eventually be turned into a local museum.

Red Office Interior. The elegant interior of the Buffalo Mill's Red Office remains intact to this day. The central hall of the office had a stained-glass dome and a marble fountain head in the shape of a buffalo. The town of Buffalo was named after the wild buffalo, herds of which were endemic to the area prior to modern settlements.

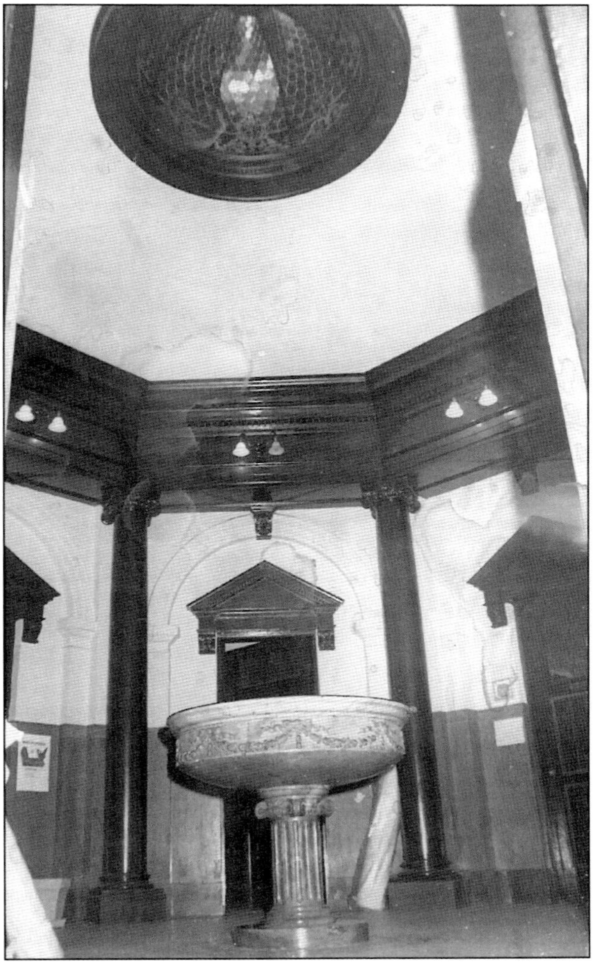

The Union Mill Baseball Team, 1921. Sports teams were an important facet of the mill community, and a few exceptional players made their way into big league sports teams.

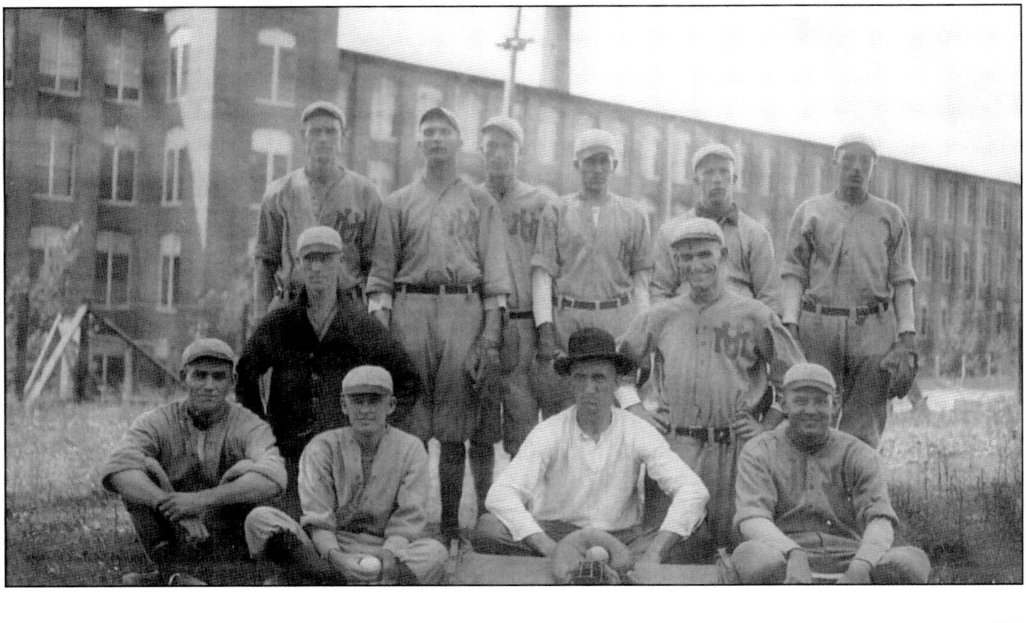

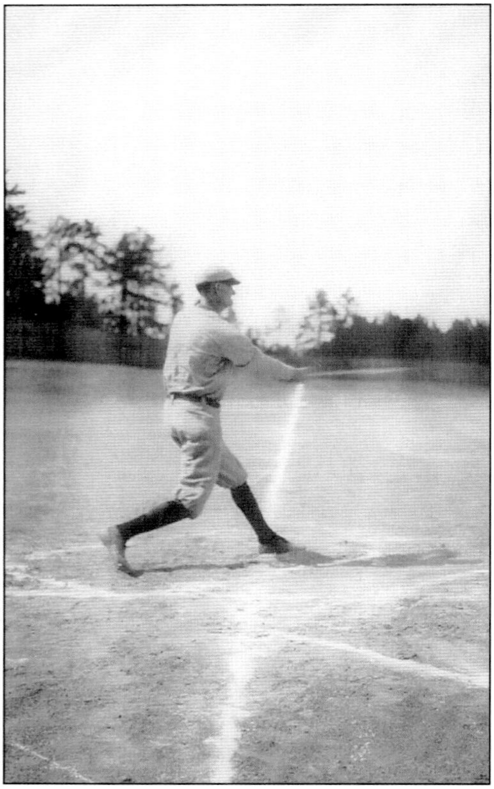

Batter Up! Preacher Thompson, a Union Mill baseball team member, hits a fly ball off home base. This field was likely located in City Park, in the vicinity of Union's hospital and Main Street.

The Immensity of the Union Mill, c. 1946. The immensity of the Union Mill is quite apparent from the air in this bird's-eye view. This photograph also encompasses part of the mill village.

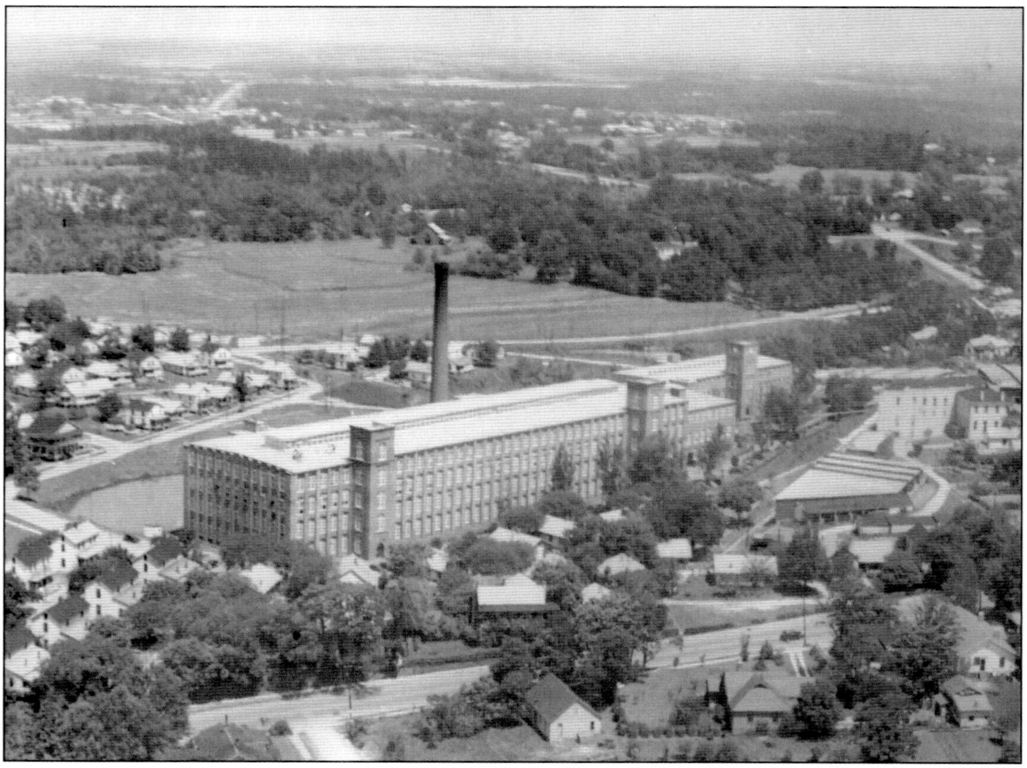

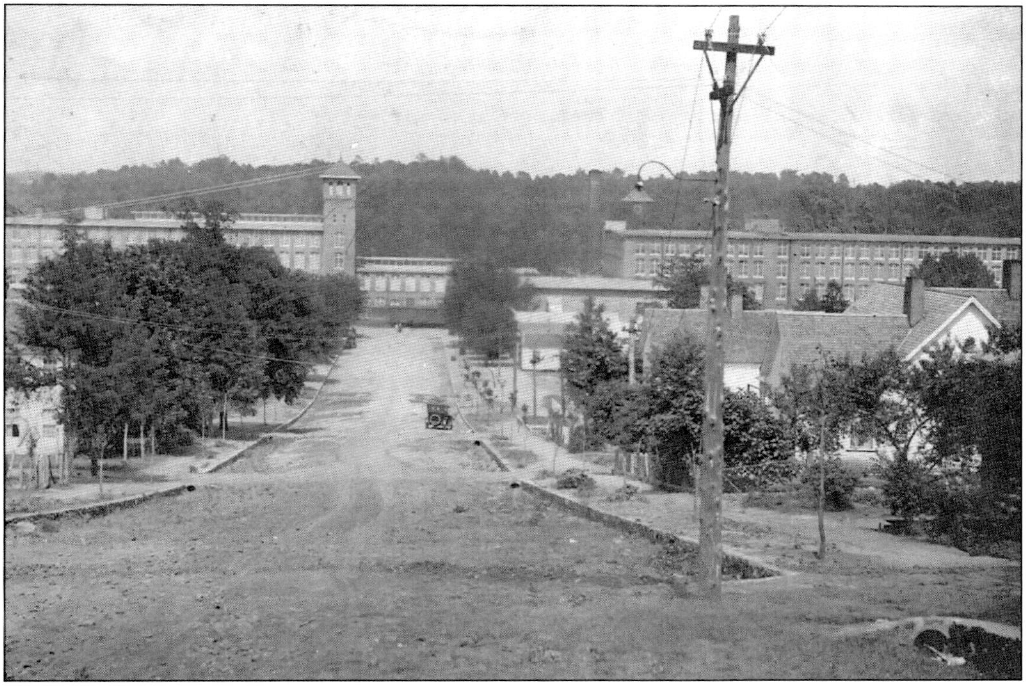

Down to the Lockhart Mill. Looking east, this photograph focuses on the dirt road towards the Lockhart Mill. The mill was built in 1895, and its business operations spurred the growth of Lockhart. The new mill town became a thriving community of approximately 2,500 people.

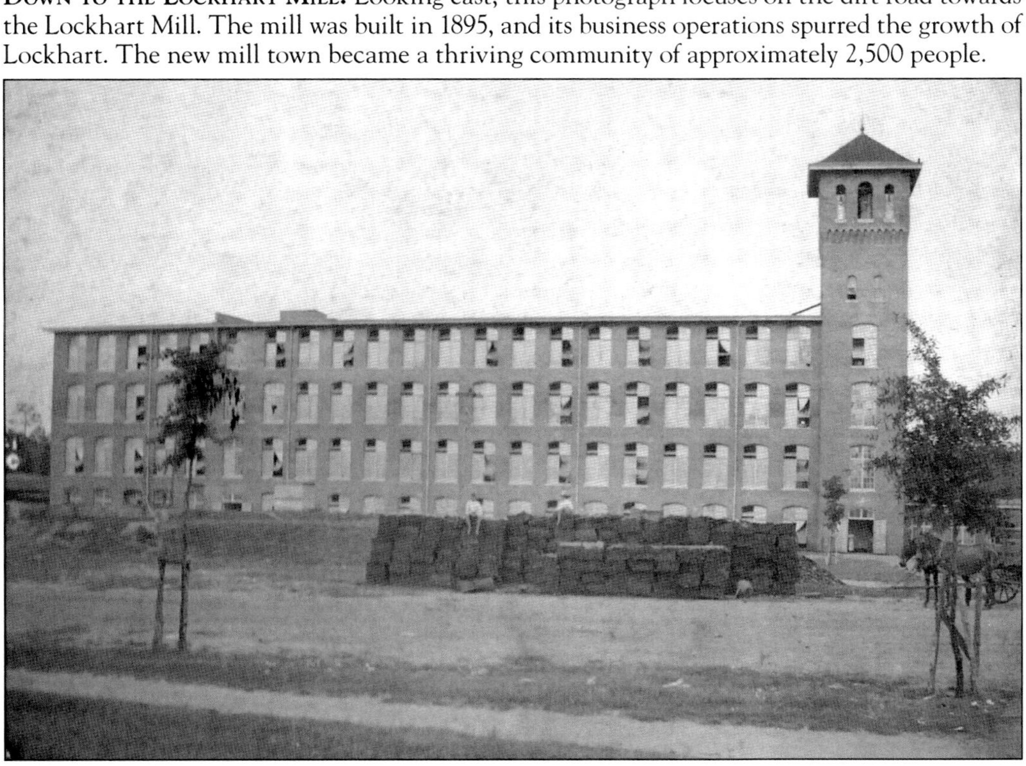

The Lockhart Mill. The first portion of the Lockhart Mill was built and used from 1895 to 1900. The bricks for the next mill addition have been delivered, and their pallets are visible in this photograph.

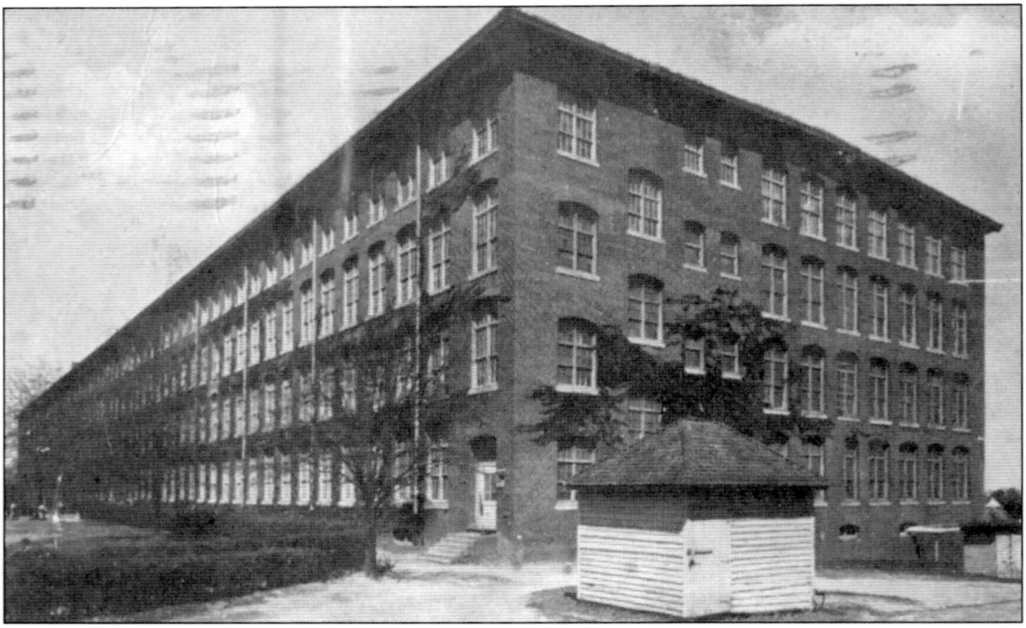

The Monarch Mill. Its founder, John A. Fant, broke ground in 1900 to initialize construction of the new $200,000 Monarch Mill. It became operational in April 1901. As of this writing, this is the only large mill building in Union that has not been salvaged and torn down.

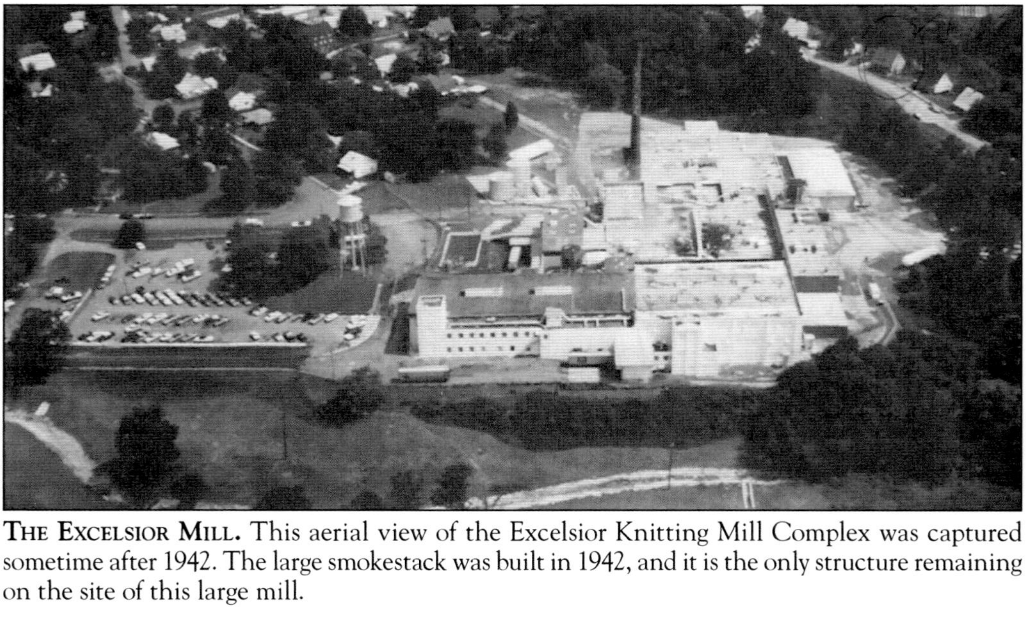

The Excelsior Mill. This aerial view of the Excelsior Knitting Mill Complex was captured sometime after 1942. The large smokestack was built in 1942, and it is the only structure remaining on the site of this large mill.

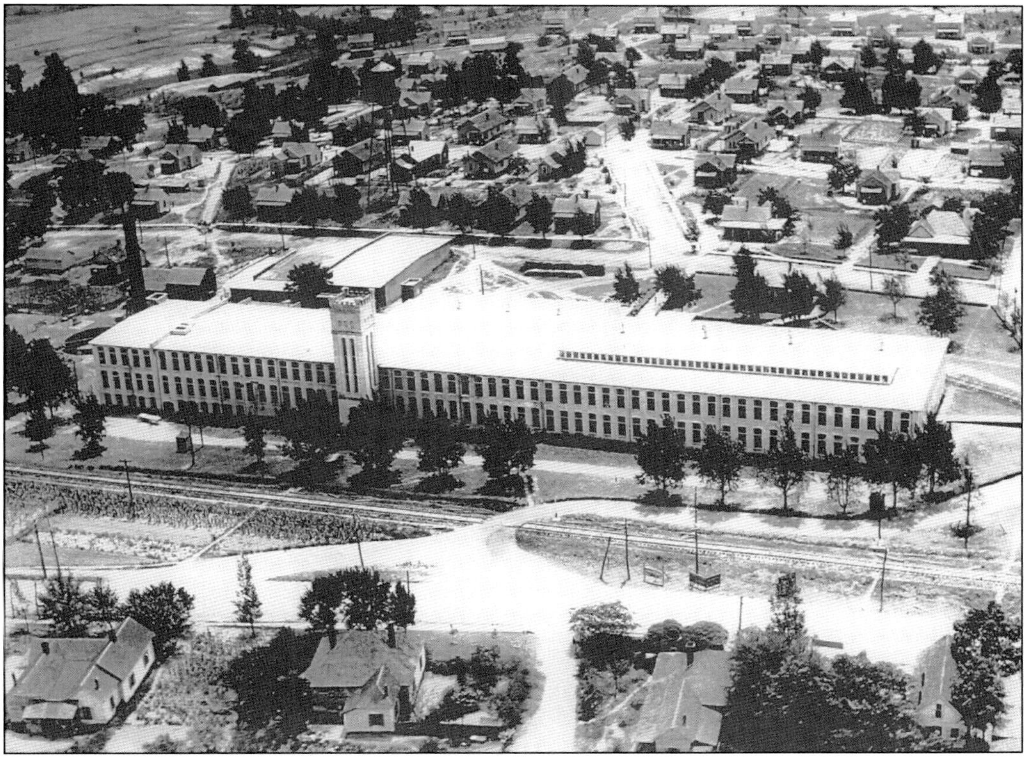

THE OTTORAY MILL. A bird's-eye view of the Ottoray Mill is pictured here along with its adjoining mill village, which was located to the rear. Initially called the Aetna Mill, ground was broken in Ottoray during the spring of April 1901. This was the same month that Monarch Mill began its operations. The Ottoray Mill officially began operations around 1904. (Courtesy of Ted Trantham.)

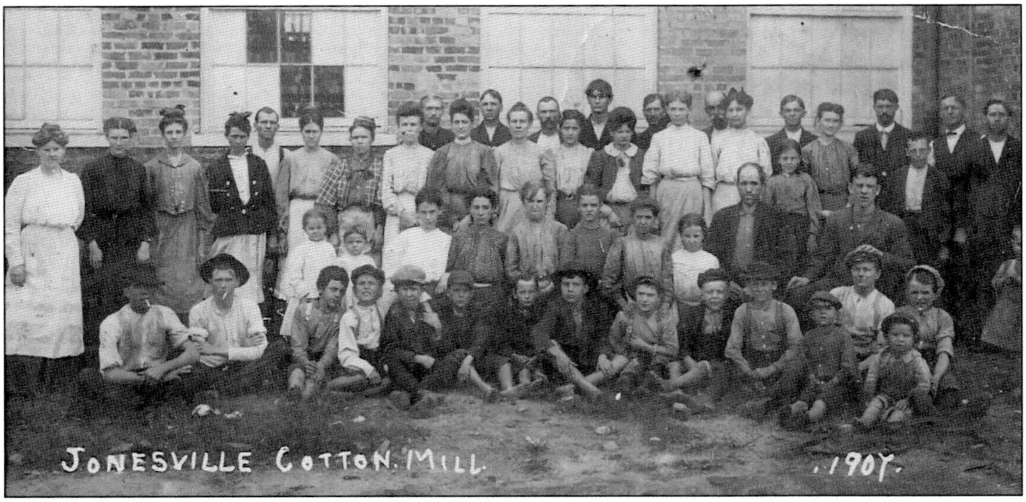

THE JONESVILLE COTTON MILL, 1907. The Jonesville Cotton Mill workers and their families pose for a photograph. Note the children present—exploited without regard to their tender years, countless youngsters were working under conditions constantly fraught with risk. However, based on the extremely young age of some of the children visible in this photograph, it is thought they may have been the offspring of parents working at the mill.

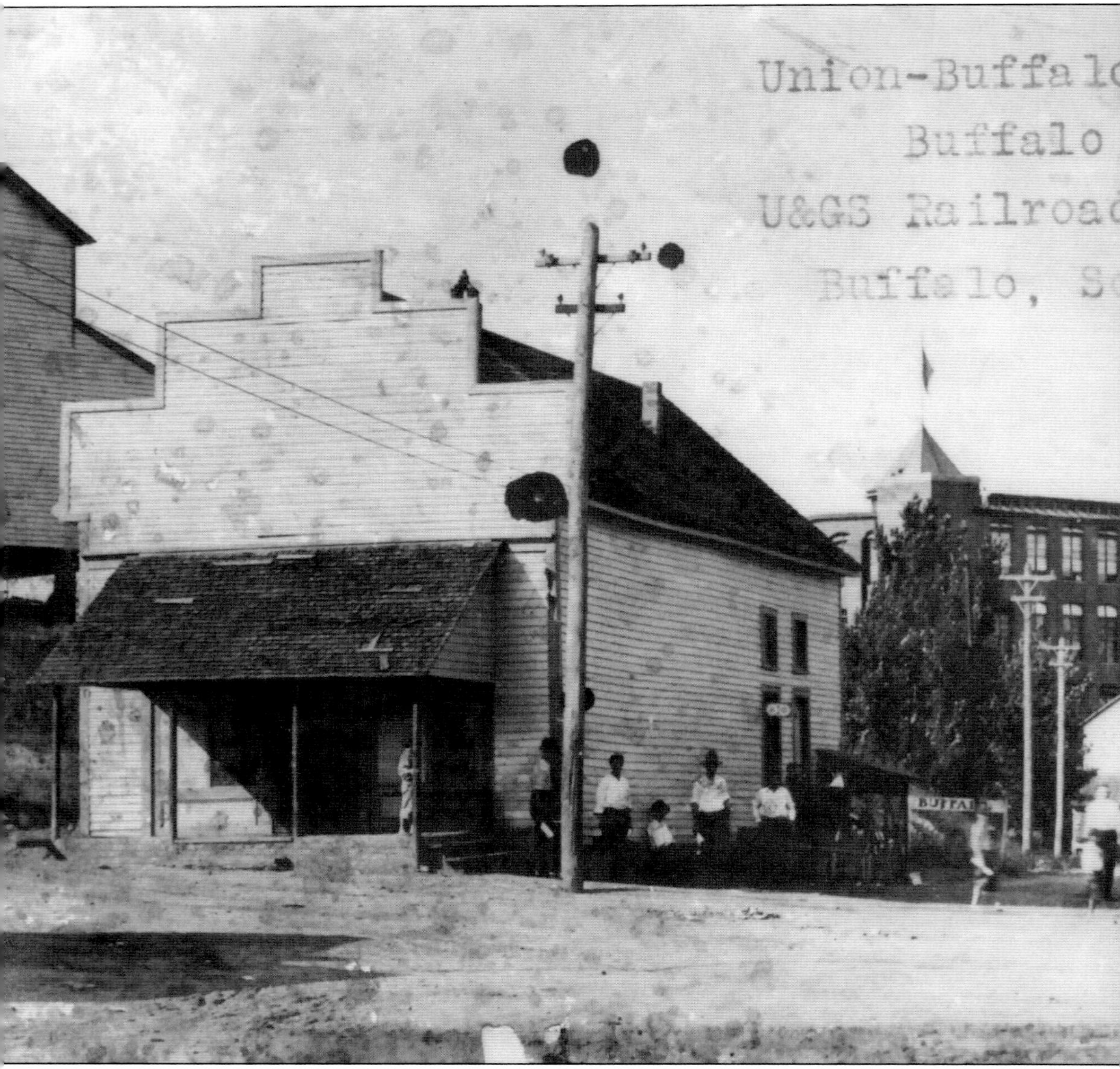

Buffalo Mill and Railroad. The Buffalo plant of the Union Buffalo Mills Company is seen in the background of this photograph. The Union & Glenn Springs train stopped at the Buffalo depot, picking up and dropping off workers. Both the mill and railroad were owned by Thomas

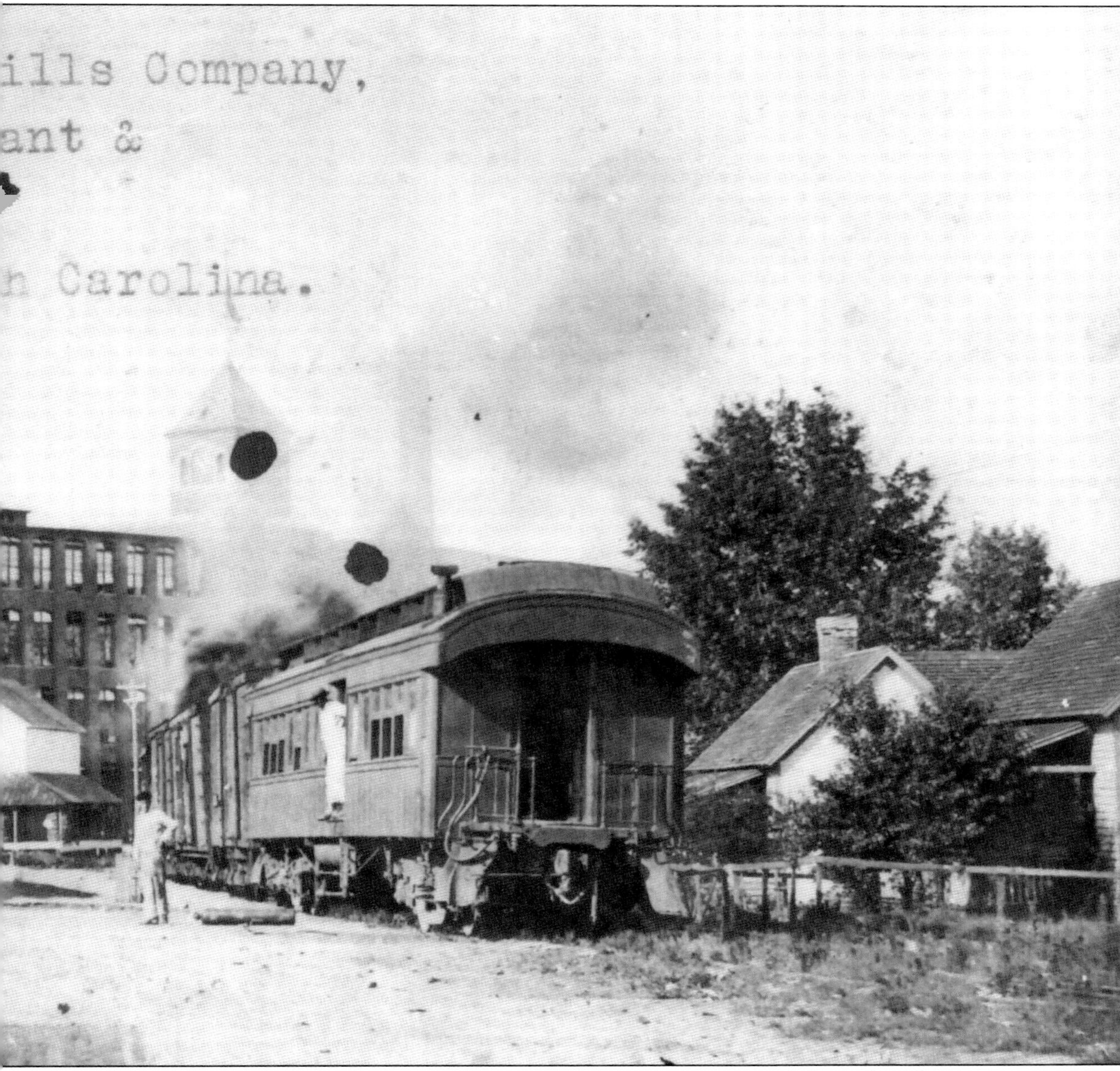

Cary Duncan, who recognized the financial benefit and necessity of the railroad in moving workers, cotton, and coal to and from his mills.

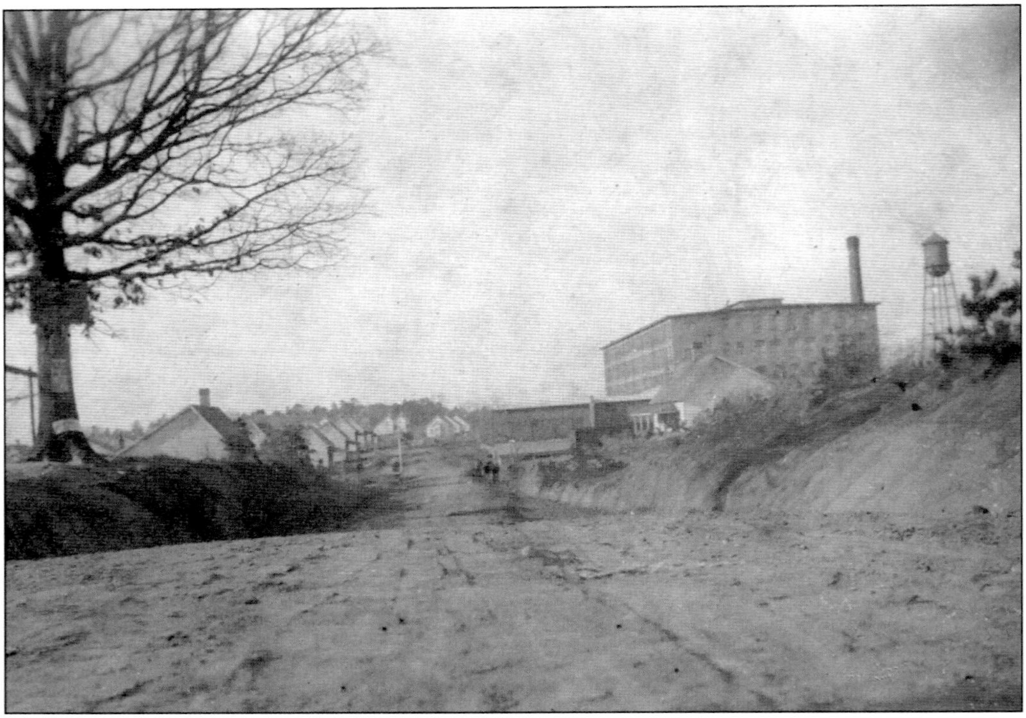

A Different View of Monarch. The Monarch Mill is captured from a rare photographic angle, looking west toward the mill from Santuc Road.

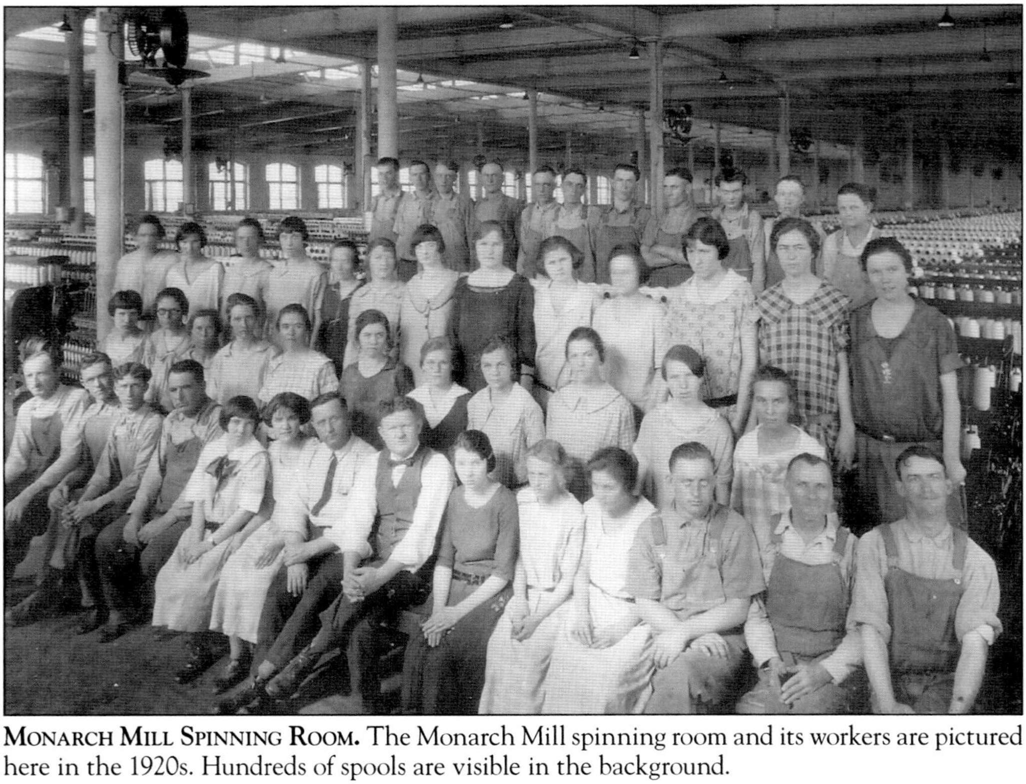

Monarch Mill Spinning Room. The Monarch Mill spinning room and its workers are pictured here in the 1920s. Hundreds of spools are visible in the background.

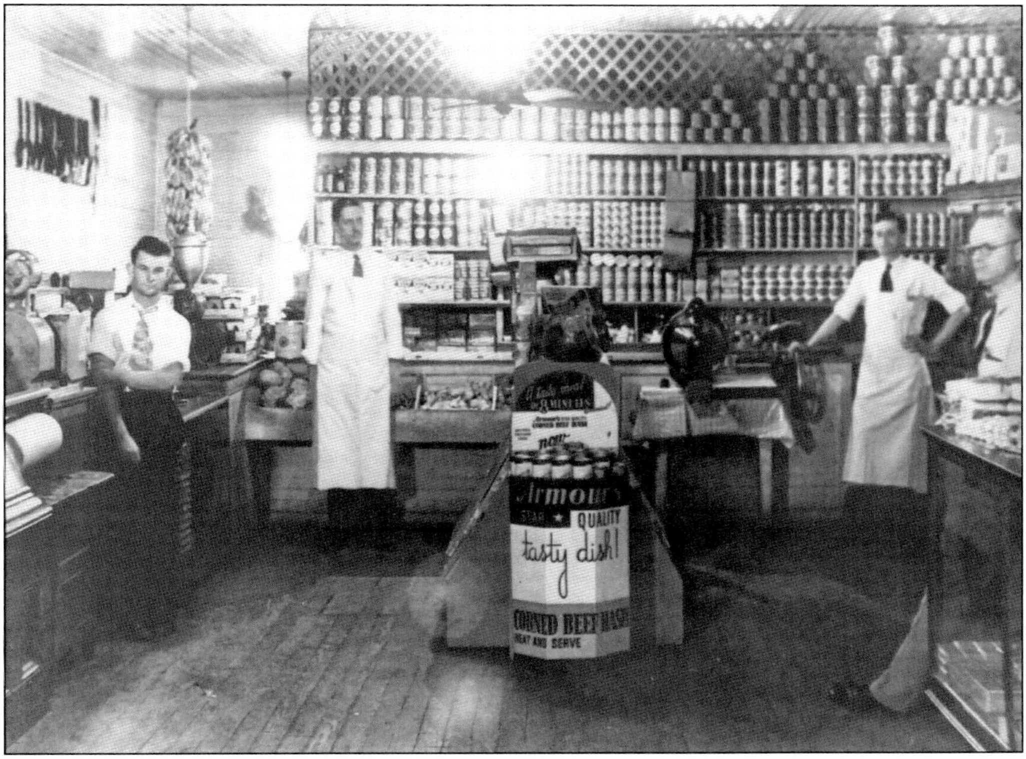

THE COMPANY STORE. Pictured here is a mill company store. As the photograph is unlabeled, it may be either the Monarch Mill's store or that of the Ottoray Mill.

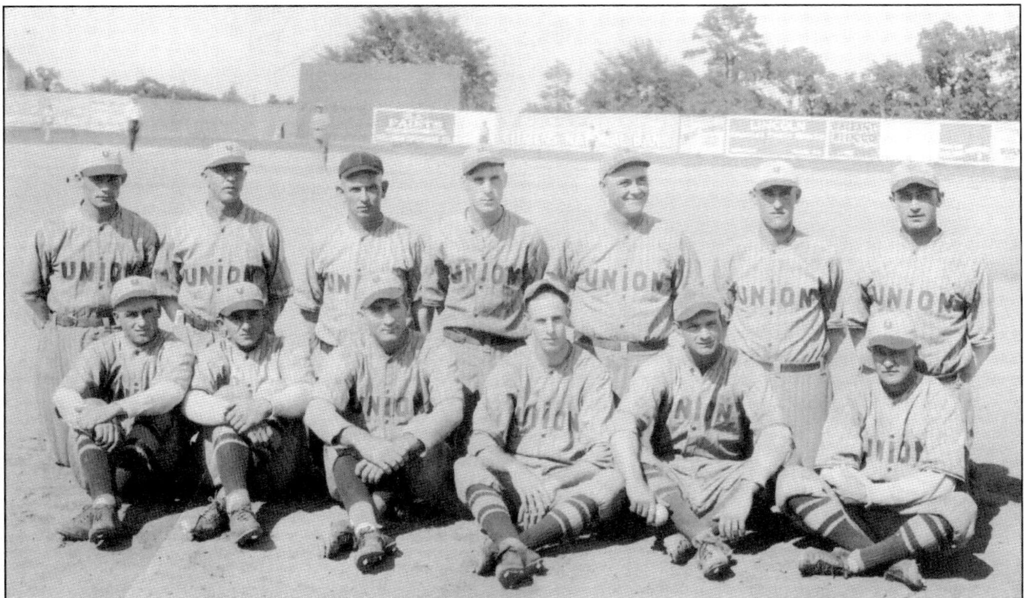

THE MILL BALL TEAM. Union's fascination with baseball dates back to the 1870s, with mill teams developing in the late 1800s. The Union Mill baseball team was a growing popular exhibition sports team for not only the mill workers, but the community as well, whose support and patronage was its backbone.

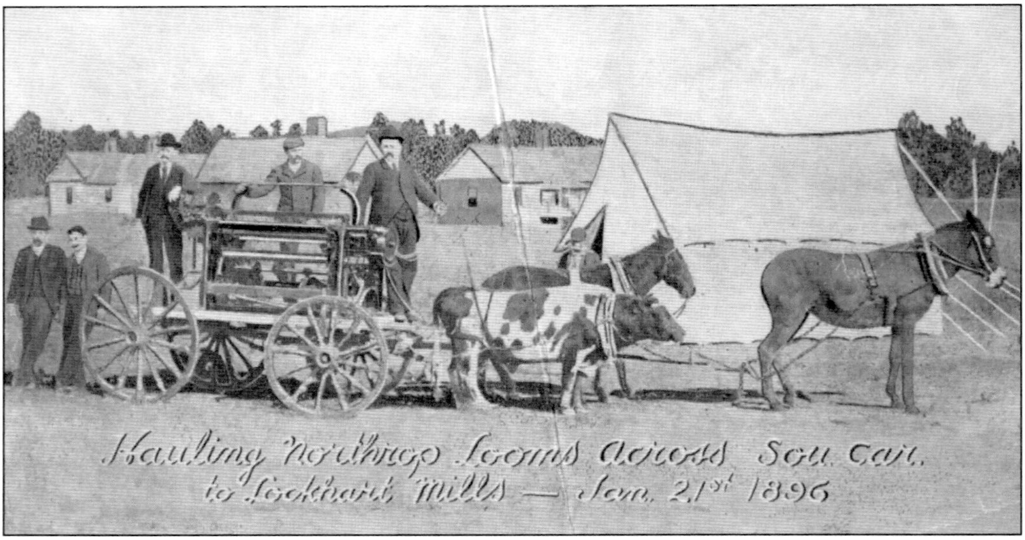

LOOM DELIVERING VIA WAGON. Pictured here is a wagon hauling looms to the Lockhart Mill. In 1896, there were no engine-powered trucks to move machinery to mills. A wagon train pulled by donkeys, horses, and cattle were used to move the new looms to their site at the Lockhart Mill.

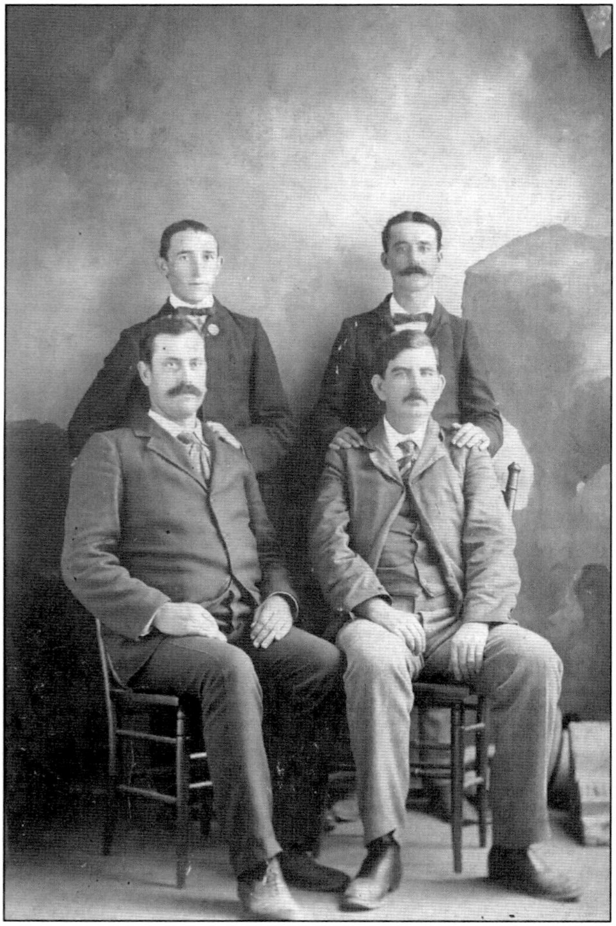

THE UNION BILLIONAIRES CLUB. Noted as the big four on the back of the postcard, the men are, from left to right, (seated) John Fant and Thomas Cary Duncan; (standing) two unidentified but one may be a Nicholson. Born in Santuc in 1857, John Fant was the founder of the Monarch Mill. Thomas Cary Duncan was a Union industrialist heavily involved in local business endeavors. He was born on July 5, 1862, and he died on July 9, 1928. He financed the first Union cotton mill in 1893. He also owned the Union and Buffalo Cotton Mills and was responsible for the construction of the BUC Railroad and the Neal Shoals hydroelectric plant. He was the mayor of Union from 1910 to 1918 and elected to the state senate for a term spanning from 1919 to 1925. Duncan lived with his family, including five children, at the Merridun Mansion. Duncan's two sons died at an early age, and his three daughters were named Medora, Louisa, and Fannie.

Eight

Music, Fire, Law, and Education

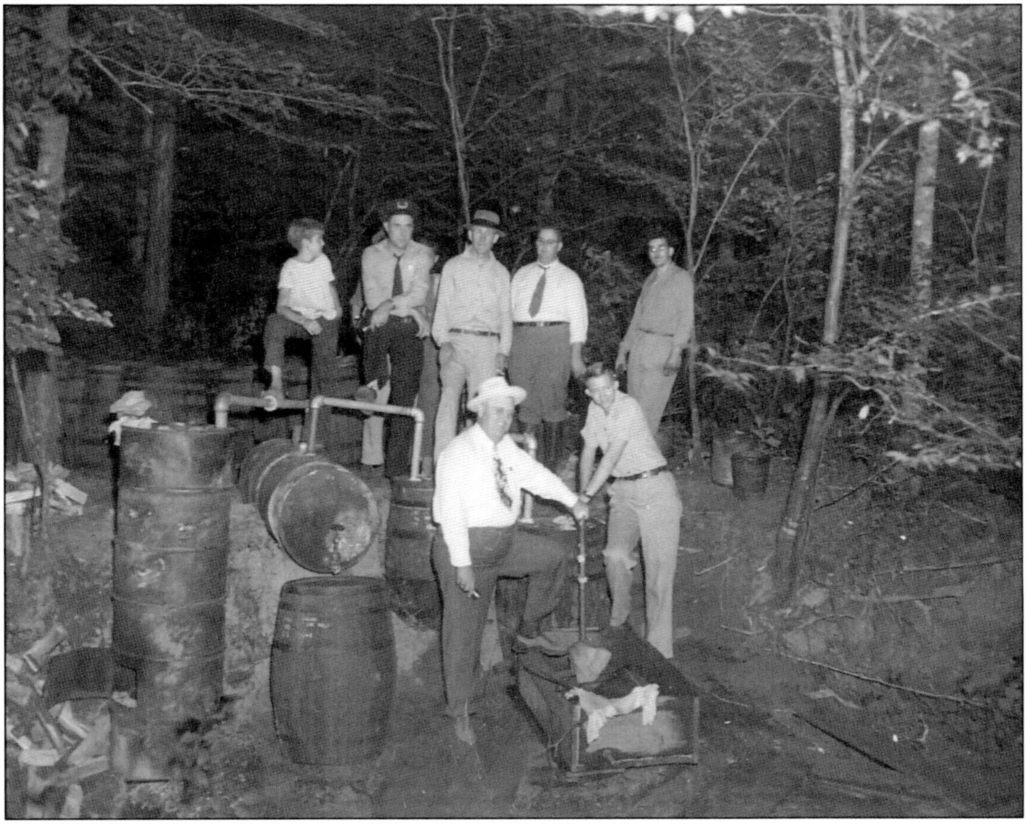

Still Busting with Sheriff Boyle. Busting down a liquor still was a simple way to guarantee the apparatus would not be used in the future. Sheriff Rochelle Boyle knew illegal steamer liquor distilleries were commonplace and hidden in the woods of Union, particularly toward the Pea Ridge section of the county. This photograph depicts a very large barrel still operation being busted up in the Hickory Nut Hollow section of Goshen in 1948. Boyle observed that although there were always more stills on Pea Ridge, the lower part of the county had the largest stills.

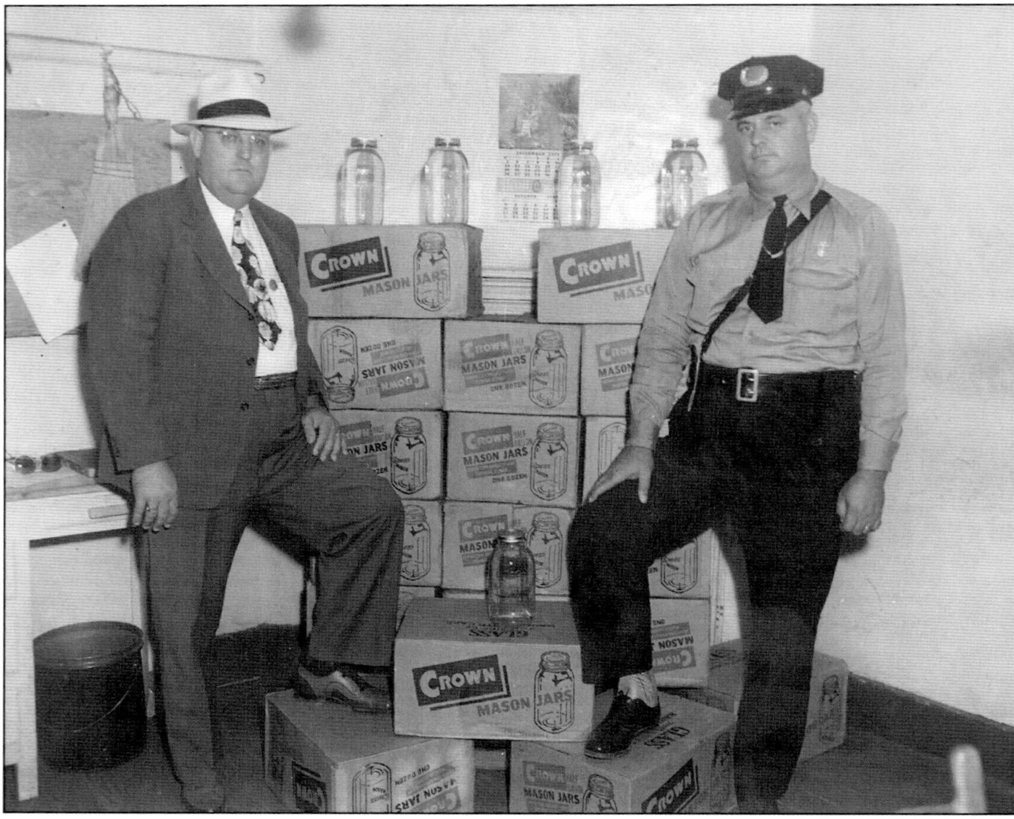

UNTAXED LIQUOR. Sheriff Boyle (left) and his deputy sheriff, Joe Porter (right), pose with their confiscated moonshine in September 1948. Rochelle Boyle was the Union sheriff from 1944 to 1948, and he was reelected to the position from 1952 to 1956. Sheriff Boyle came from a family of local potters that comprised the Robert Boyle and Family Pottery Company, which was located in a portion of Union County incorporated into Cherokee County in 1897. In regards to the family business, Boyle decided on a career in law enforcement rather than spinning stoneware.

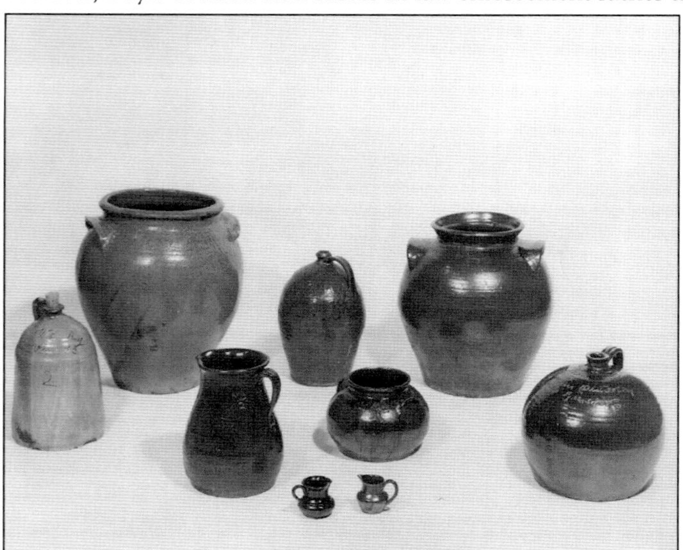

BOYLE POTTERY. Samples of Boyle family stoneware, including whiskey jugs, pitchers, and storage jars are displayed. Union had three families of potters, including the Boyles, Owensbys, and Whelchels. Union pottery business spanned over a century—from Edgefield-trained Thomas Owensby and his wife, Mary Whelchel, who initially produced stoneware in the 1820s, until the Boyle pottery works ceased operation in 1937.

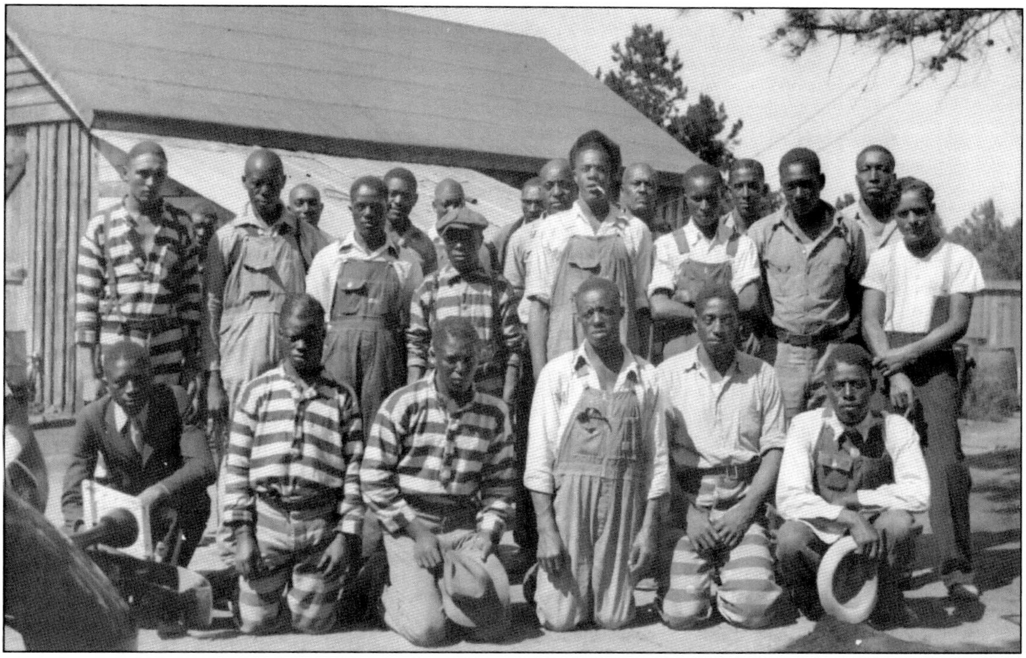

THE UNION COUNTY CHAIN GANG, 1960. The Old Union County barracks are pictured behind the Union chain gang. Responsible for performing menial or physically challenging work as a form of punishment, the chain gang assisted the county in areas such as road and park cleanup. This photograph is dated January 7, 1960.

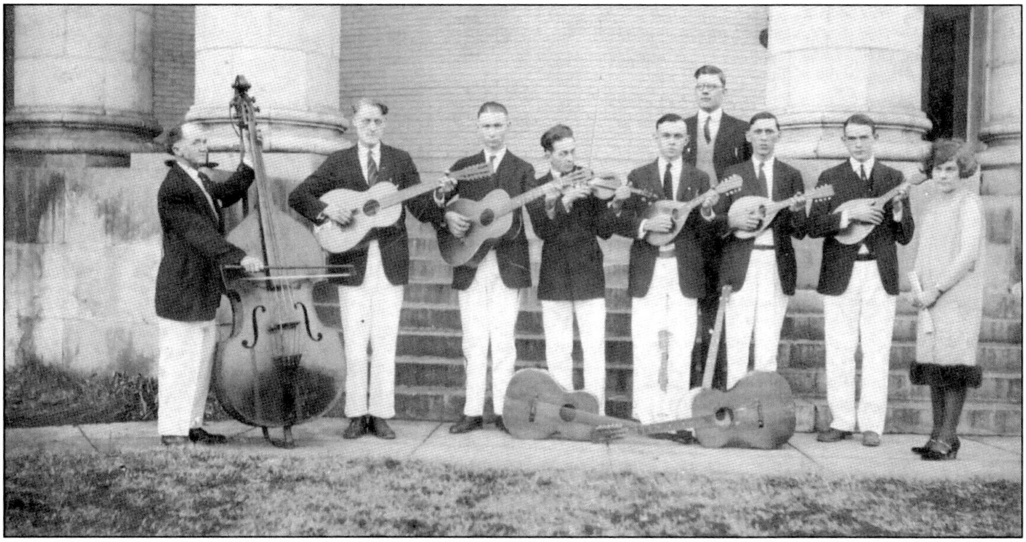

THE SHAMROCK STRING BAND. The Shamrock String Band practices in front of the courthouse. This group specialized in the latest popular music, including old Southern tunes and folk songs. Pictured here are D.U. Allman, Julius Hendrix, Herman Sprouse, Dewey Fowler, Winston M. Kindsor, John O'Shields, and J. Byrum Lawson. Band members also included Willie Hortance Blackwood (pianist, banjo musician, and mandolin player), who is pictured on the far right. Her wedding announcement to Robert Rae Cobb on June 25, 1932, indicated that she is "well known for both her charming personality and for her success in the musical world. She possesses a soprano voice of rare sweetness."

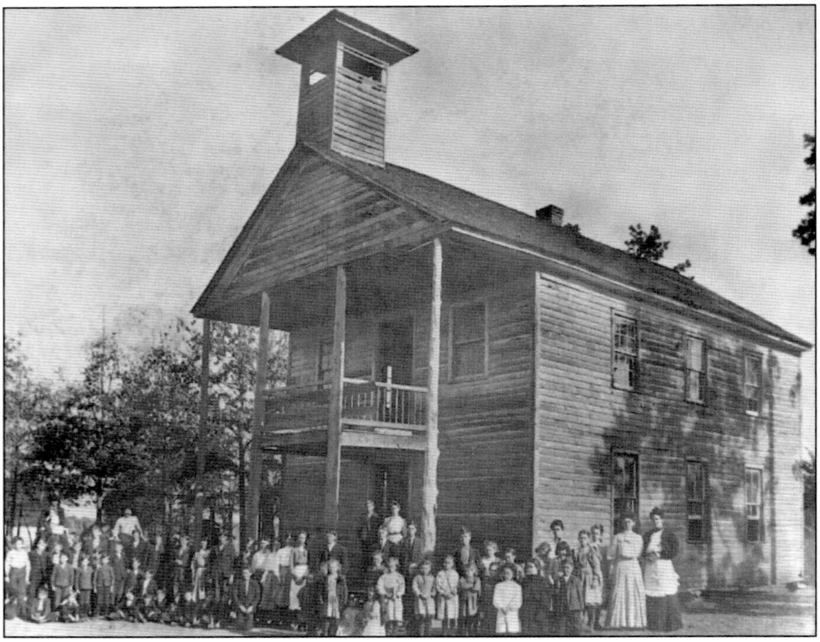

West Springs School House, 1890s. Pictured here is the West Springs School House. West Springs was noted for its early hotel and spa, and it was named after the West family, who first owned the land and mineral spring.

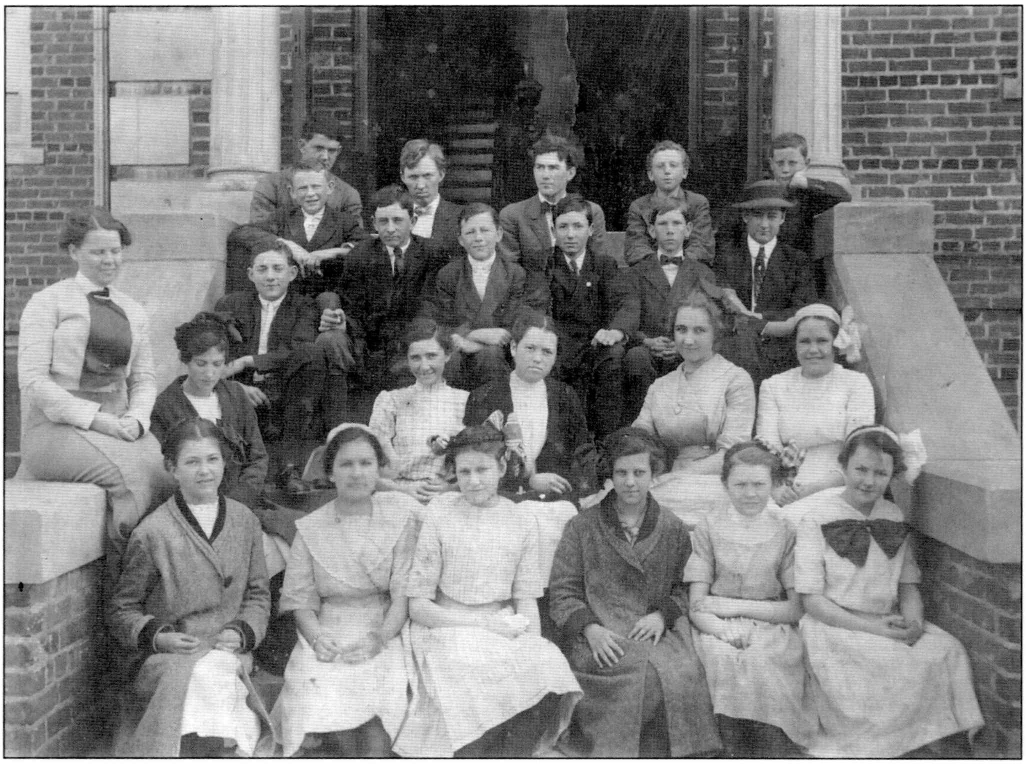

USC Graded School Class. This photograph was taken in the left-hand doorway of the new 1909 school building located on Main Street. The building was initially known as the first Union High School. The institution was later renamed the Main Street Grammar School, and it ultimately became a campus building for the University of South Carolina.

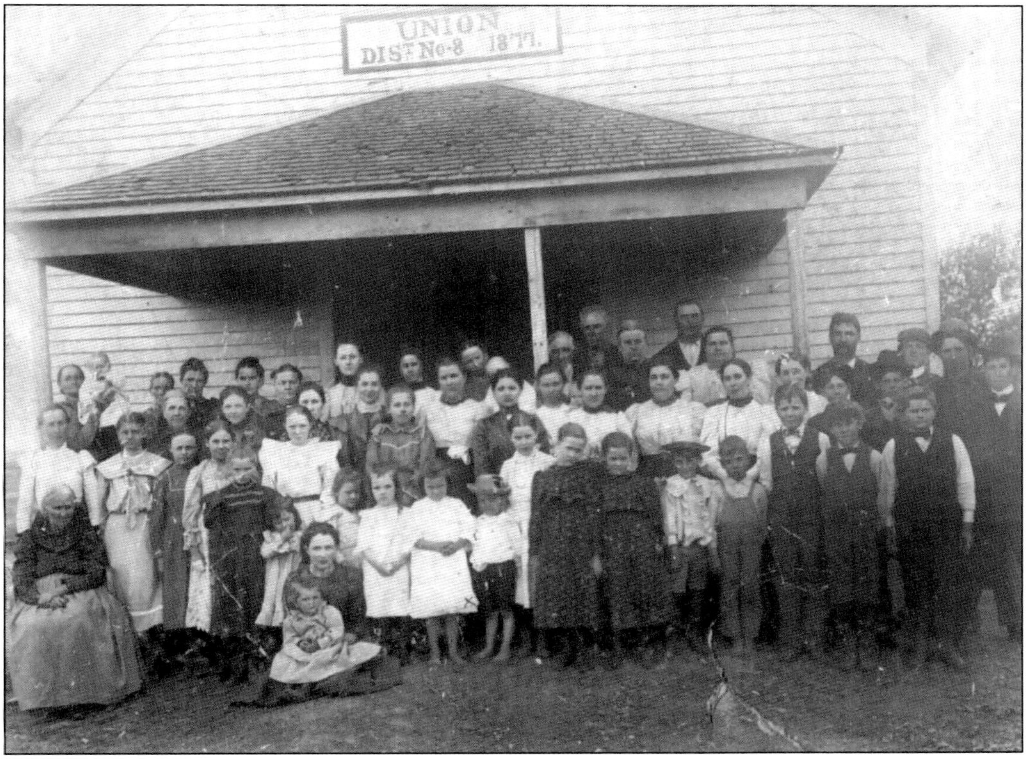

Union District No. 8 School, c. 1877. Known as one of the best postbellum rural schools in Union County, the personalities of the children are quite apparent. To dapper little gentleman in their bow ties and two sisters donning the same dress, there was a level of sophistication in these children.

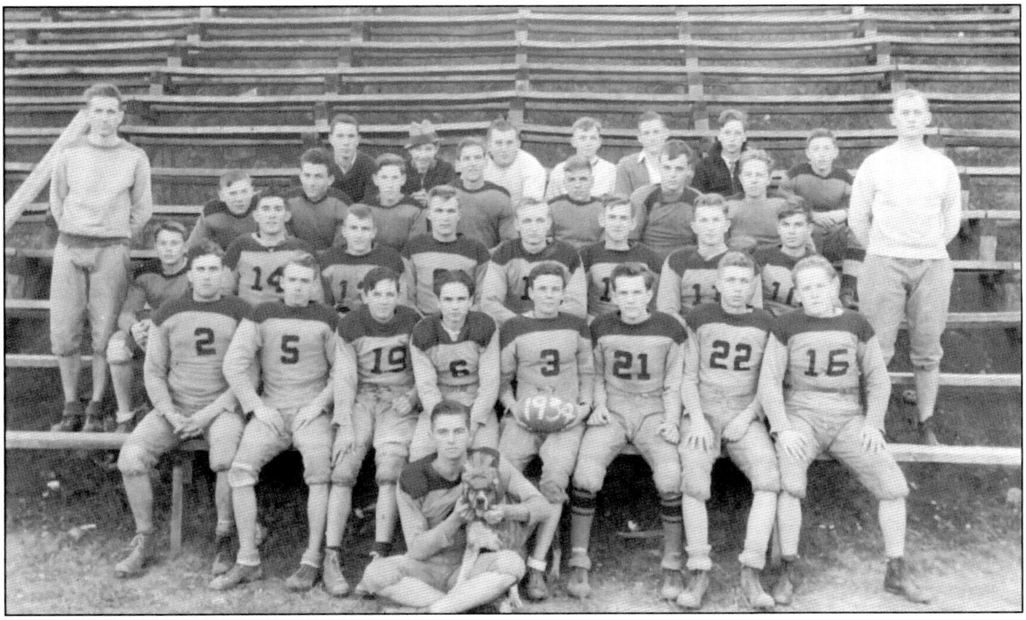

Union High School Football Team, 1934. The Union High School's football team was named the Yellow Jackets, and the team fights on to this day.

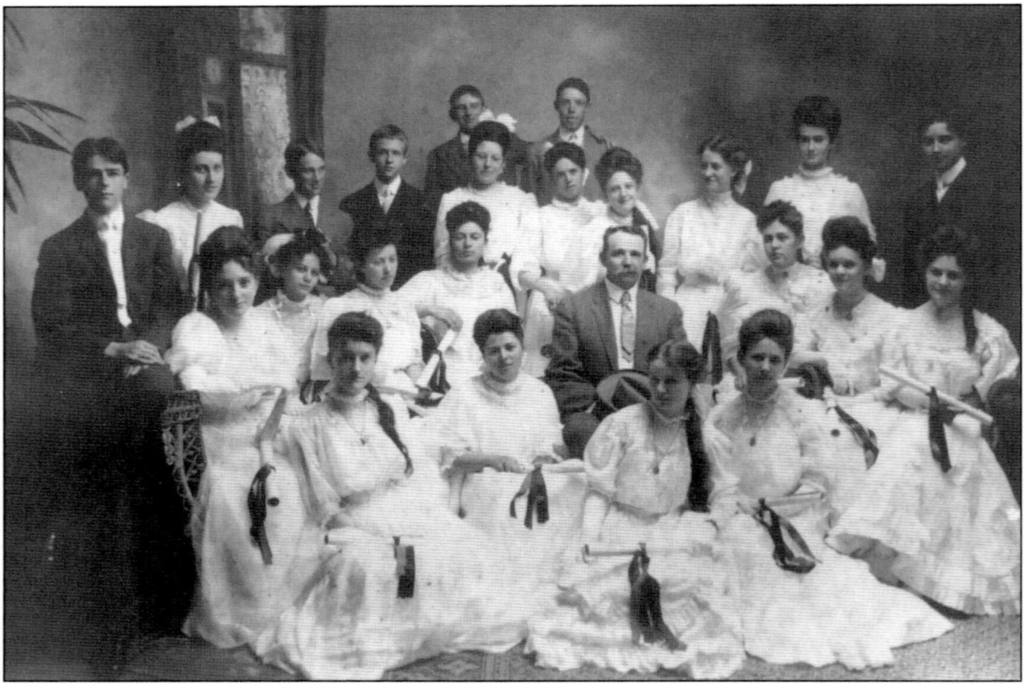

Union High Graded Class of 1906. The first graded system of grouping pupils by years in Union began around 1883. Graded schools were an advance over one-room schoolhouses, which were still ubiquitous in the Union countryside.

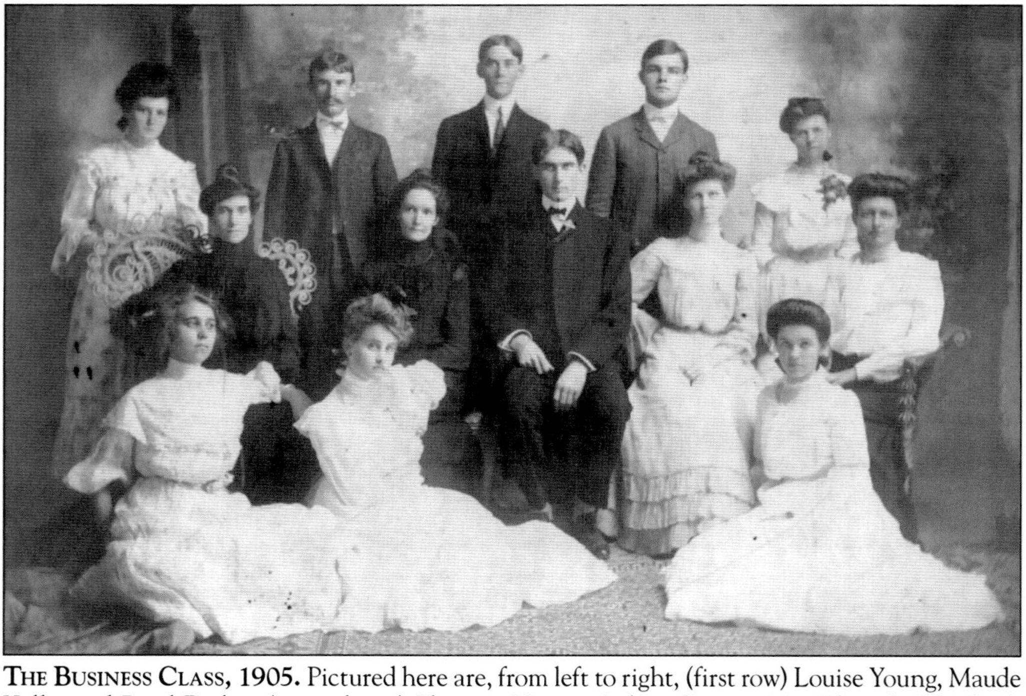

The Business Class, 1905. Pictured here are, from left to right, (first row) Louise Young, Maude Kelly, and Pearl Bailey; (second row) Phronia Harris, Aubrey Rice, a Mr. Edwards, Elizabeth McDow, and unidentified; (third row) Ruth Spears, Tom Hawkin, Wesley Greer, Poston (?), and Nina Sligh.

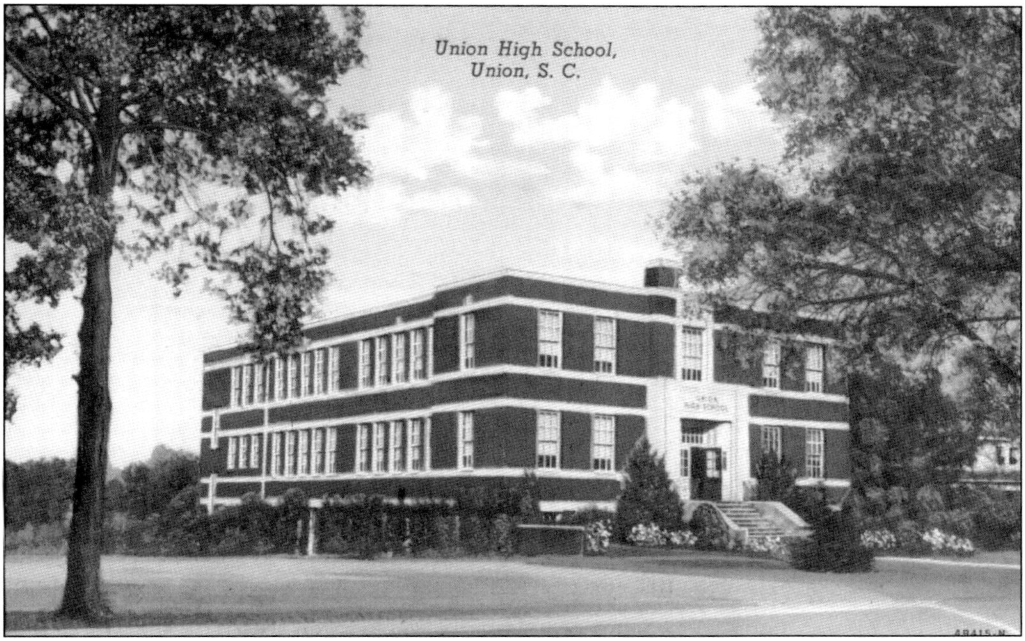

UNION HIGH SCHOOL. This 20th-century building still stands on East Main Street, and it is currently used for adult secondary education.

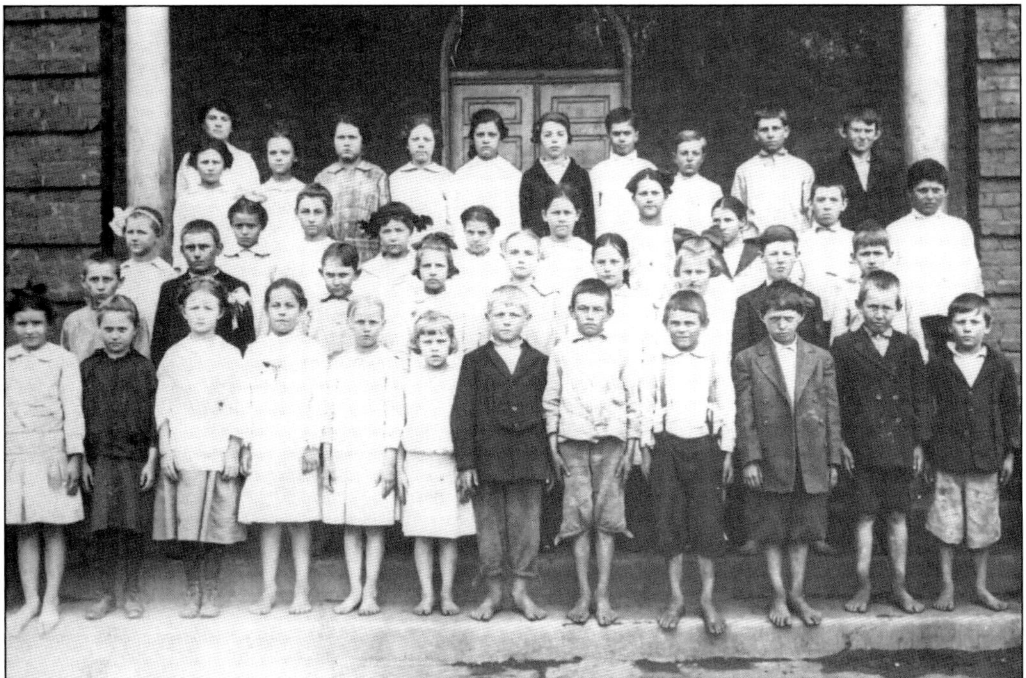

UNION SCHOOL, 1913. Giles Perry Kirby is located front and center in this photograph (first row, seventh from left). Although there were strides in the development of education standards in the early 20th century, many children still attended classes barefoot. (Courtesy of Ben Kirby.)

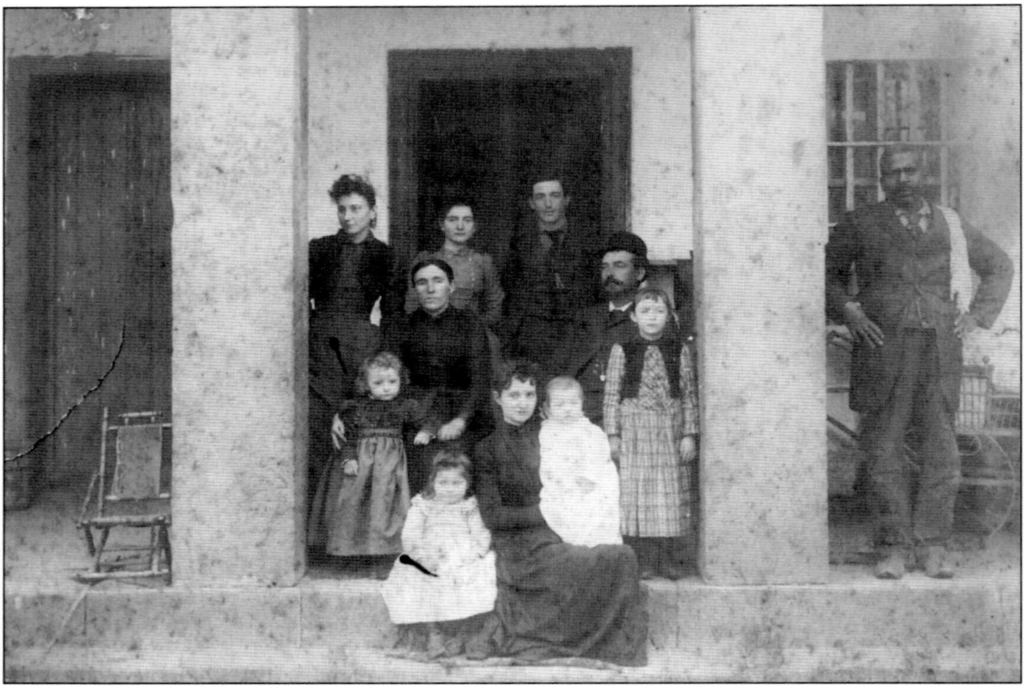

The Long Family. Sheriff Gideon Long's family poses with friend and neighbor, a Mrs. Murrah. The photograph was taken under the middle arch of the Robert Mills jailhouse. Sheriff Long's term was from 1885 to 1901 and again from 1908 to 1912.

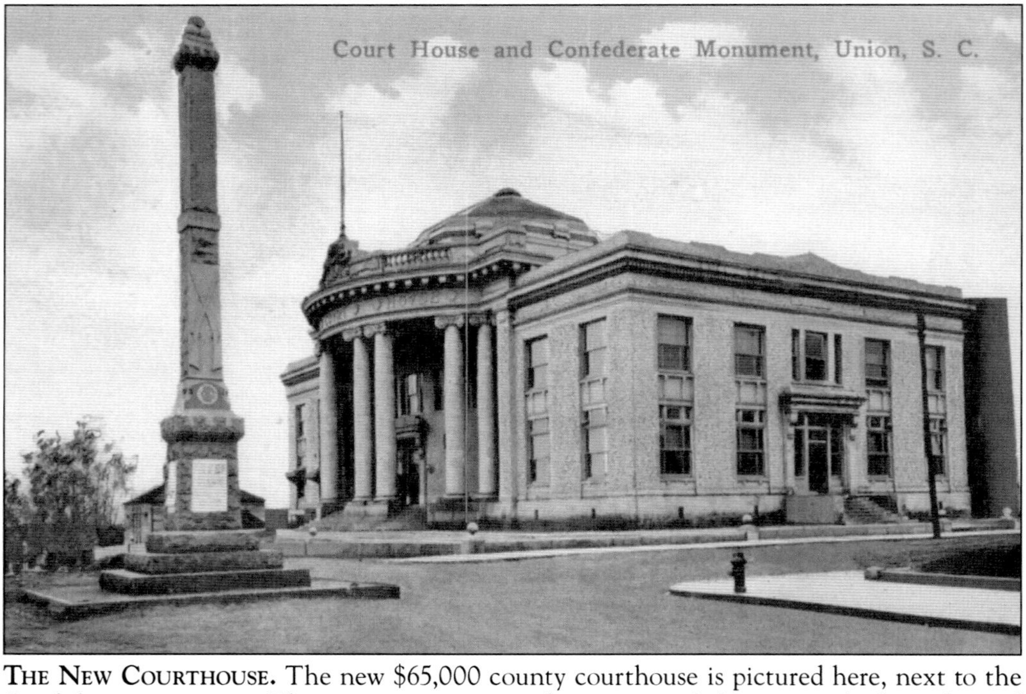

The New Courthouse. The new $65,000 county courthouse is pictured here, next to the Confederate monument. The monument is pictured in its original placement, which was located in the center of the street. The new 1912 courthouse replaced architect Robert Mills's courthouse, which was deemed too small for the growing county. Mills's courthouse was torn down in 1911.

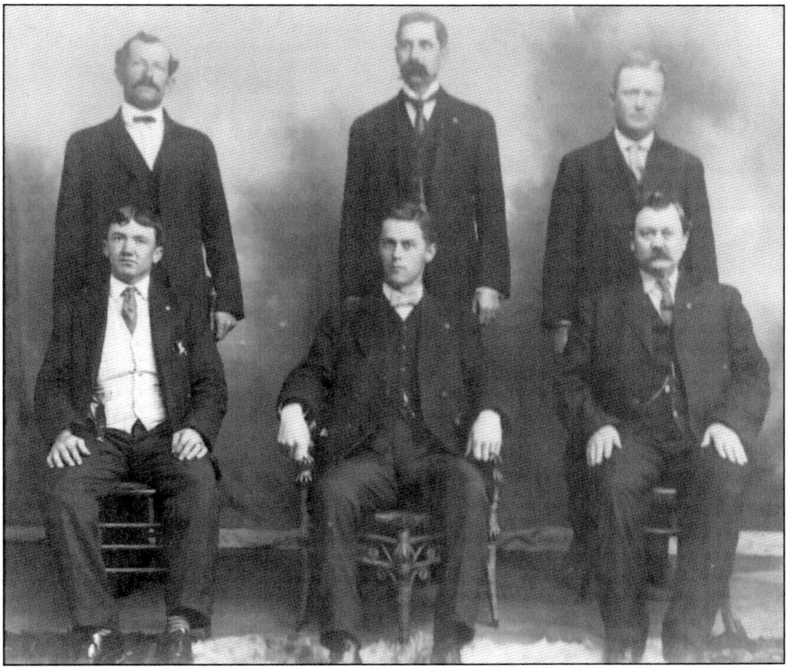

The Union City Council. The 1909–1910 Union City Council poses for a photograph. Pictured here are, from left to right, (first row) O'Shields, Wagnon, and Going; (second row) Skelton, Petty, and Kirby.

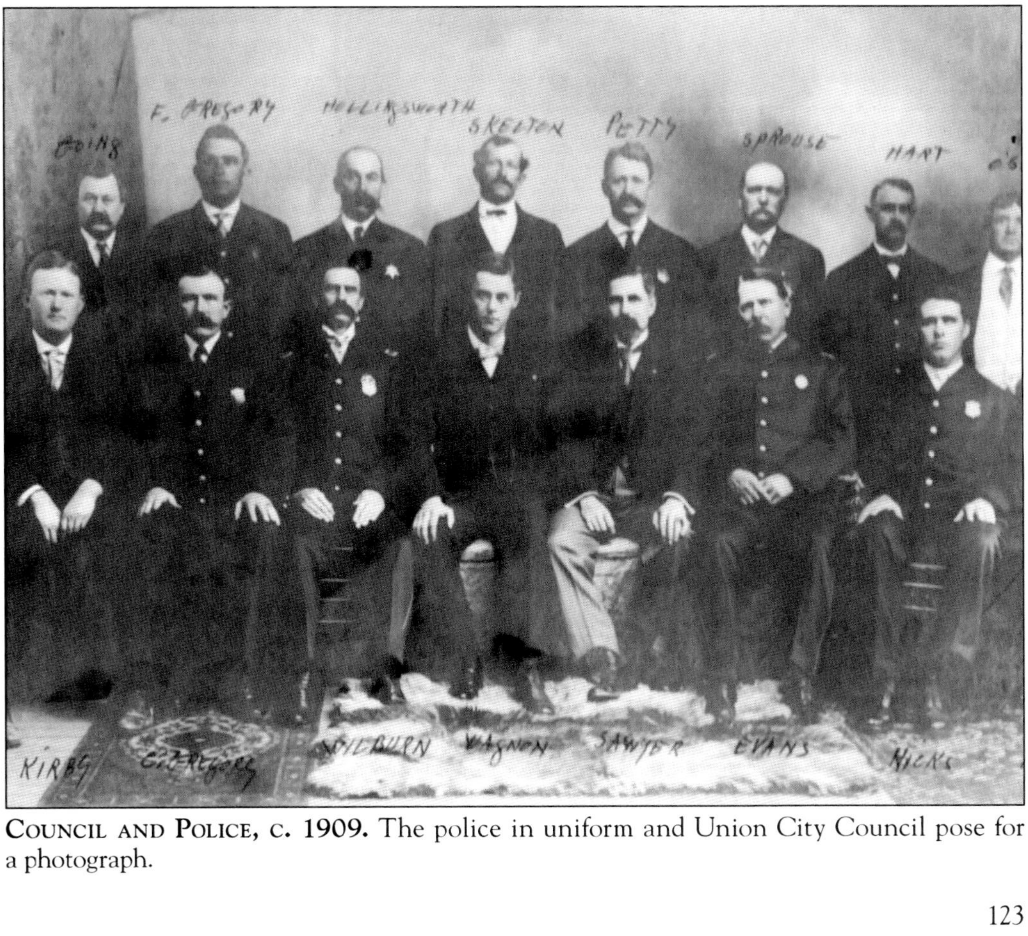

Council and Police, c. 1909. The police in uniform and Union City Council pose for a photograph.

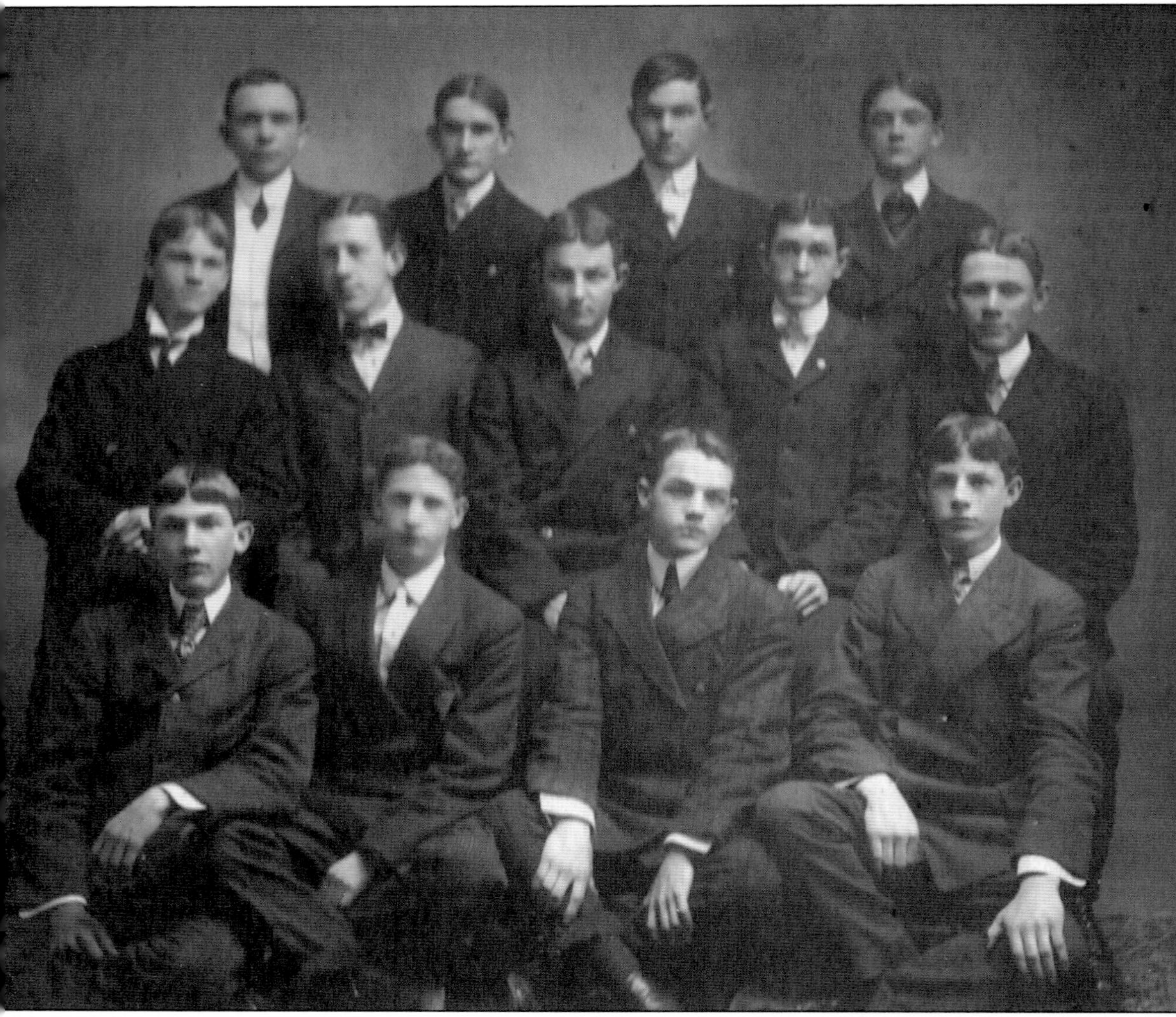

THE UNION DRAMATIC CLUB, 1905. Posing for this photograph, the dramatic club members show off their demure side. The date, February 7, 1909, is notated on the back, along with the names:. Pictured are, from left to right, (first row) Walter Counts, Jake Berlin, Claude Hicks, and Guy Wilburn; (second row) Douglas Harris, Trig Tinsley, Milam Hicks, Sims Price, and Roy Meador; (third row) Samuel Black, Charlie Hames, Louis Stoll, and Mark Sanders.

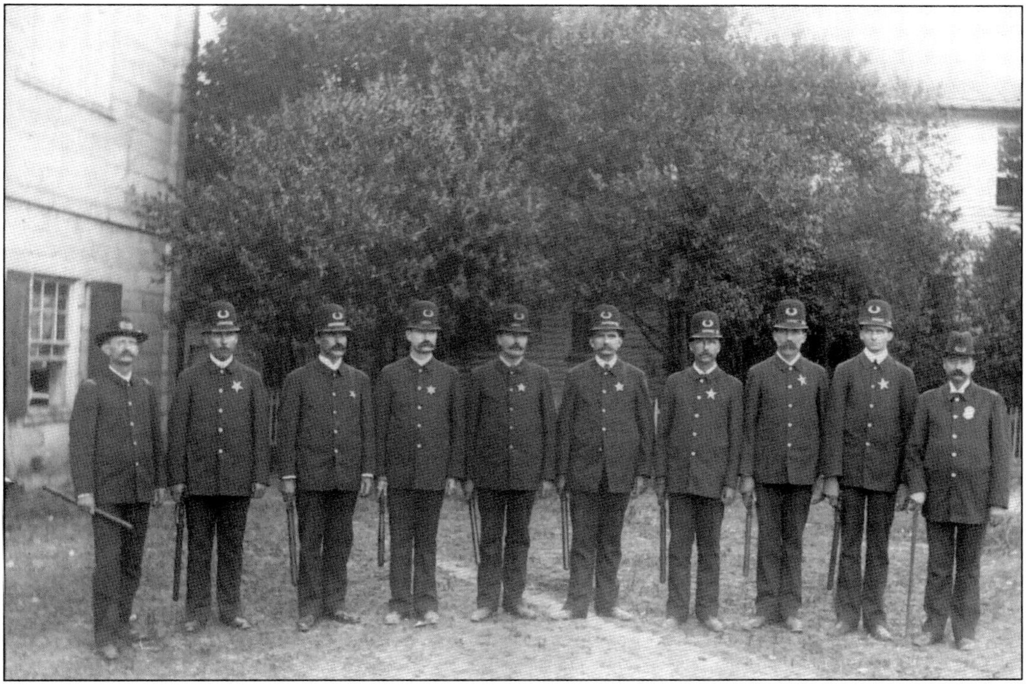

The Union Police Department, c. 1902. Union police personnel are, from left to right, Sergeant Austell, Evans, Presnell, Harris, O'Shields, Moseley, Davis, Couch, Johns, and Chief Israel. Note their derby-style police hats and billy clubs.

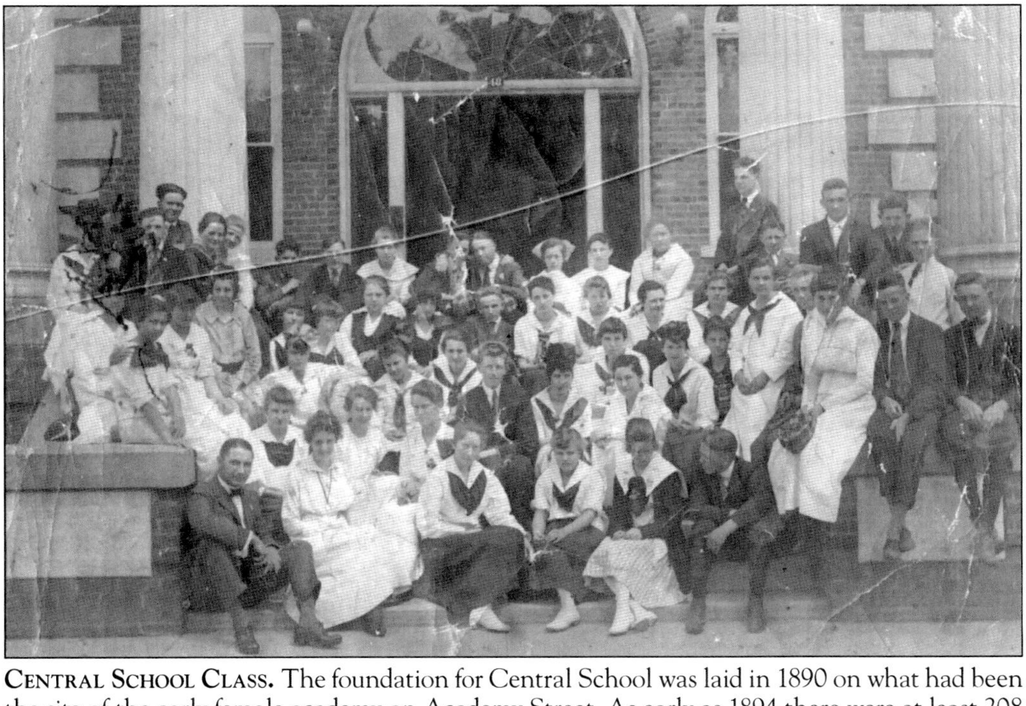

Central School Class. The foundation for Central School was laid in 1890 on what had been the site of the early female academy on Academy Street. As early as 1894 there were at least 208 students attending Central School. This building is currently a component of Union's University of South Carolina campus.

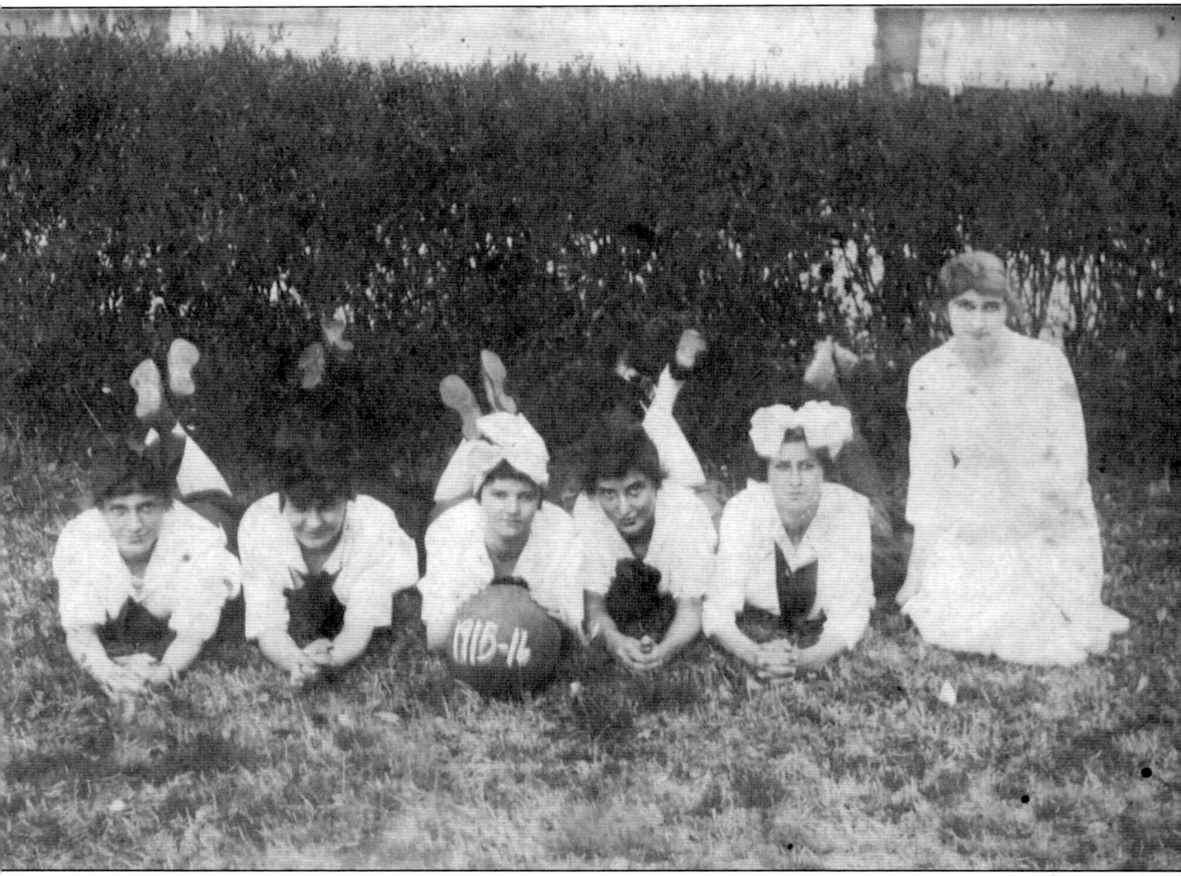

Ladies' Basketball Team, 1915–1916. The ladies' basketball team poses at the Union School. Female teams, typically smaller in membership than male teams, were nonetheless just as popular in Union.

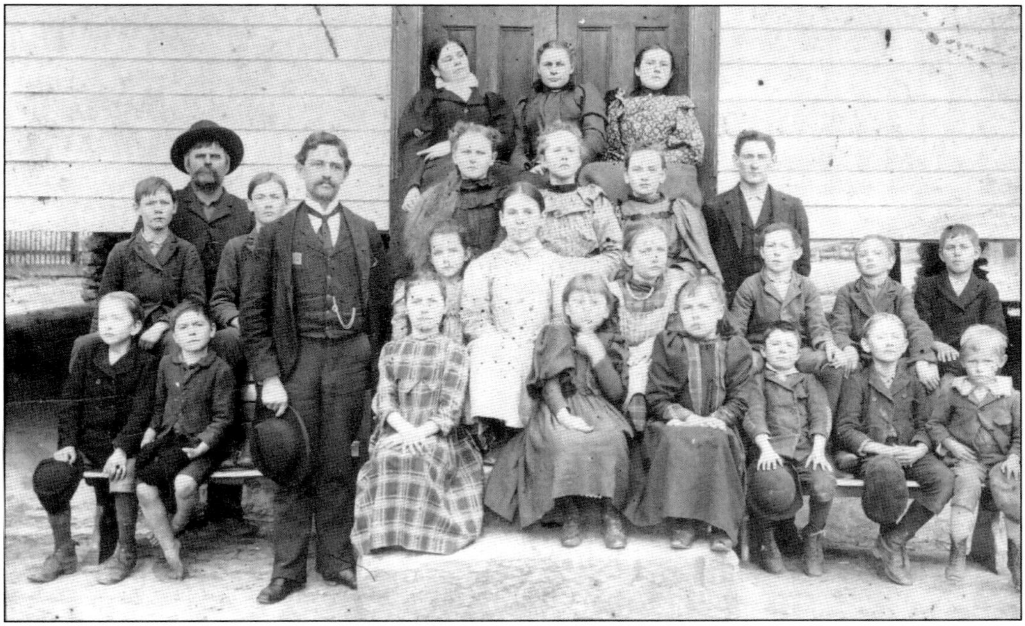

NINETEENTH-CENTURY SCHOOL. A group of pupils attending public school at Padgett's Creek Church pose for a photograph shortly before 1900. The photograph was taken at the front steps, before the church building was lowered. A few early schools held classes in church buildings, were ungraded, and catered to both male and female students of all ages. Union boasted 71 public schools by 1881, not including its private schools.

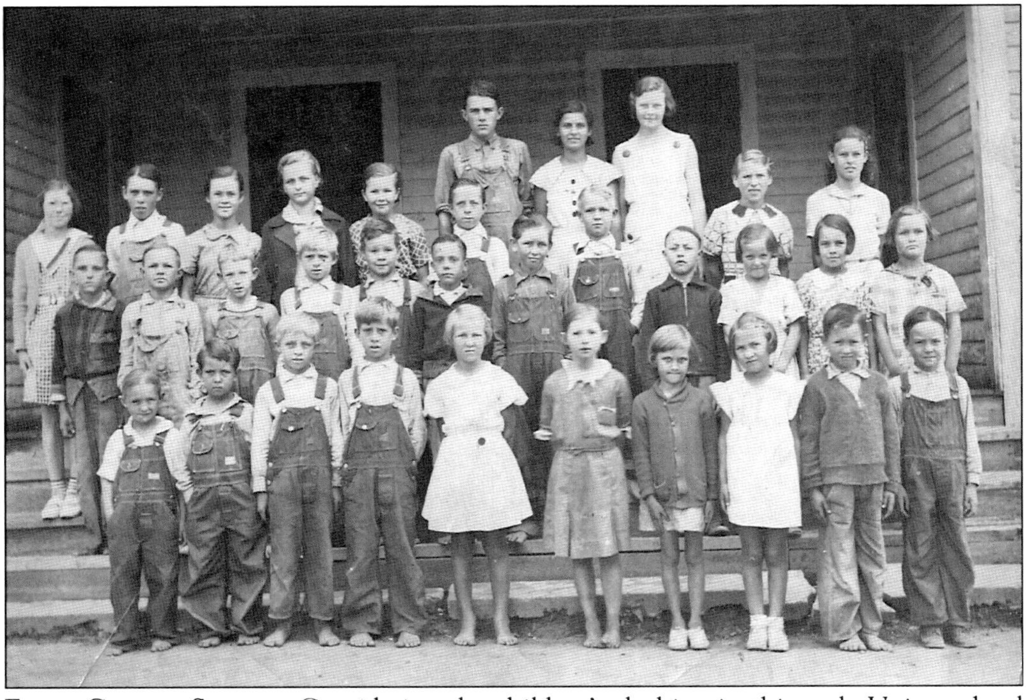

EARLY GRADED SCHOOL. Considering the children's clothing in this early Union school photograph, it is remarkable to consider many schoolchildren had no shoes to wear when they were in attendance.